ENCYCLOPAEDIA OF INDIAN WOMEN THROUGH THE AGES

ENCYCLOPAEDIA OF INDIAN WOMEN THROUGH THE AGES

Volume–2
The Middle Ages

Simmi Jain

PUBLICATIONS

KALPAZ PUBLICATIONS

DELHI–110 052

ENCYCLOPAEDIA OF INDIAN WOMEN THROUGH THE AGES
(Sociology, Women Studies)

Rs. 3600 (Set)
Rs. 900 (each volume)

ISBN: 81-7835-116-1 (Set)
ISBN: 81-7835-173-0 (Vol. 2)

Published in 2011 in India by
Kalpaz Publications
C-30, Satyawati Nagar,
Delhi-110052
E-mail: kalpaz@hotmail.com
Phone : 9212729499

Printed at: G. Print Process, Delhi

Contents

Preface

The status of women in our sub-continent passed through a most intricate and complex socio-economic terrain. The male-dominated society was indeed a glaring phenomenon and had always edged over their social and domestic environments. Being the earning member in the family, he considered himself fairly superior in terms of his status. But women could maintain their identity and emerged as useful partners and bread-earner for her household affairs. Undoubtedly she did not shirk to meet any economic challenge with dignity and respectable disposition. The volumes on *Encyclopaedia of Indian Women Through the Ages* have been diversified into four categories and cover the themes in a fairly comprehensive and analytical way which are as follows.

The volume on Ancient India deals with a detailed description on social status of women in the Vedic Period and in the Mahabharata Era. Emphasis has been laid on their marital status, numerous duties of household affairs, basic rights enjoyed by them, sexual life in practice, social status of a widow and the way of life she had to lead, ideology of motherhood, divorce and remarriage, property rights, the sati ritual, the views of Swami Vivekananda, and foreign accounts of marital arrangements.

The second volume lays emphasis on Medieval India. It includes social position of women, female slaves, women in politics, religious education and practices, observance of purdah, and divorce, *mehr* practices, nikah-marriage, valid marriage, irregular marriage, the sense of equality, women in administration, dissolution of marriage, dower, social customs like birth ceremony, naming ceremony, selection of marriage partners, women education including higher education, their academic contribution, particularly of Gulbadan Begum, Hamidah Bano Begum, Zeb-un-Nisa, Jahan Ara and others, fairs and festivals, games, mostly indoor games, playing cards or *Tash* or chess, pigeon flying, kite flying, female costumes including cotton, silken and golden clothes and a detailed study of Khanzada Begum, Ayisha-Sultan Begum, Zainab Sultan Begum, Maham Begum and Bibi Mubarika.

The third volume has deep thrust on women and freedom struggle. The role of eminent women has been a glaring phenomenon in this volume. In fact these women have become a significant part of our history. Commencing from the historic role of Begum Hazrat Mahal, Rani Lakshmi Bai of Jhansi, Rani of Ramgarh, the theme lands us comprehensively into various social Acts, viz., mobilisation of sati, 1829; Widow Remarriage Act, 1856; the role of Consent, 1891 and the prohibition of Child Marriage Act, 1929. The volume has also highlighted the role of foreign women in our freedom struggle, i.e., Sister Nivedita, The Mother, Mira Behn, and Annie Besant. Mrs. Besant was elected Congress President in 1917—during the crucial period of the first global war.

The emergence of Mahatma Gandhi on the political stage of India in 1915 generated a new spirit of sacrifice for the attainment of *swaraj.* Such women were Kasturba Gandhi, Bee Amman, Parvati Devi, Sarojini Naidu, Kamaladevi Chattopadhyaya, Durgabai Deshmukh, Margaret Cousins, Sucheta Kripalani, Hansa Mehta, Mridula Sarabhai, Usha Mehta, Rajkumari Amrit Kaur and several others. They courted arrests in the Gandhian movements along with numerous women satyagrahas. Even after the attainment of Independence, their role in several fields of development including education, medical, defence, politics and administration is quite laudable.

The last volume gives us a comprehensive analysis on historical perspective and legal review. It deals with the changing social status of women, Gandhi and his contribution for the emancipation of women in economic and political sphere, Dalit women in politics and their changing socio-economic status with new awakening, vision of Annie Besant for generating patriotic spirit among women, role of the regiment of Rani Jhansi as a significant part of the Indian National Army, women and family welfare having deep bearing on sincere initiatives shown by women rather than men to plan their families despite their law position and lesser sex ratio. Other significant aspects on women in this chapter deal with their pitiable plight as labourers in a factory, field or road work, life of working women, regional status of women, particularly in Punjab, Haryana, Madhya Pradesh, sensible findings of a survey based research on women in a slum in Mumbai. Last but not the least a chapter has been well-written on Kerala nuns and nurses in terms of their working status and social difficulties. A few significant case studies on the two categories have been well-analysed.

I feel much beholden to several eminent scholars whose writings have been used in these volumes in order to fill up necessary gaps. The consistent academic support and help of several institutions of higher learning including the members of prominent libraries deserve my respectful acknowledgement. But for sincere support from these categories of scholarly and institutional help, these volumes probably would not have seen light of the day.

With this comprehensive academic survey, it could be judged with the remark that these volumes would be certainly welcomed by eminent social scientists, researchers and students in India and abroad.

Simmi Jain

Introduction

The position of women got deteriorated from time to time in medieval India. Yet in ancient India it was generally placed at an exalted platform. The present work deals with their position in medieval India in great detail.

The position of women in the early medieval period changed gradually. The joint family system had an attitude of moral and spiritual degradation towards women. Kshemendra in particular has painted a very dull picture of women in his writings. Attempts made by the scholars to determine the position of women in urban vis-a-vis the rural areas have not been very successful. Among the middle and the lower classes their position has been found to be unsatisfactory. The literature of early medieval India contains instances of protest against the exclusion of women from equal opportunities. Examples of protests for not allowing them to participate in the religious practices, are available too. As it was felt that the competent religious practice determined the social status of a person in society, the ability of women to perform religious practices equally with men would improve their status.

During the twelfth century, tantra achieved a prominent place in the education, and several institutions of higher learning started embarking into this area of rituals and thought. Nalanda, Vikramshila, Odantapuri universities had a regular stream of teaching. Even the seats for religious propagation started participating into this new stream of learning.

Despite the recognition of the existence of *stridhan* as certain share of property for the purpose of exclusive property rights to women, the limit of the availability of this right to women is not very clearly known. The sanction and the exercise of the right of women at *stridhan* appear to be depending mainly on the strength and support of their husband. Thus explains the reason as to why the condition of widows in early medieval India was unsatisfactory. Several evidences are at hand to show that condition of widows in the medieval society, particularly those becoming widows at a young age was deplorable. The right of inheritance of the widows does not seem to be recognised. However, these general observations apply mainly to the middle as well as the lower classes. As for the condition of aged widows, we have no specific mention about their status but their condition does not seem to be as bad as compared to that of young widows. The deterioration in the condition of widows led to the eruption of the *sati* system in India. *Sati* as a custom appears to have been institutionalised in India around the seventh century.

This tradition was not very profound in the Indo-Gangetic plains. Some areas of present Madhya Pradesh also appear to be infested with this tradition. In the south it was though not so assiduously known to be followed. According to a view, the system of *sati* entered into India with the scythians. It gradually became more acceptable among the *Rajput* families in Rajasthan.

The change in the status of woman is a noticeable feature in the early medieval India. Even in the aristocratic families, the pattern of education was confined mostly to music and fine arts. There are many examples of military training in the royal families, but such training does not run to be put to any use or given on an equal basis at par with men. The theory of their economic and physical dependence on men was based on the ground of their incomplete education and incapability of understanding the complexities of life. The extinction of rational education for women and consequent rise in the illiteracy and unawareness would have produced superstitions, and witchcraft in Rajasthan.

With the advent of new social order, the role of women in politics underwent changes. By and large, the status of women in politics, but for certain regions, including Kashmir and parts of Rajasthan having stray references, had diminished. But the egalitarianism of Islam offered a more equal treatment to the women. Their retirement from the politics, which was practised rigidly, underwent a change and they started participating in the power structure.

The study of contemporary records makes it clear that prior to the advent of Islam, literacy played an important role in determining the status of women both in rural as well as urban areas. In the urban areas, education and literacy seemed to be available to women and the forms of social life offered a liberal attitude towards them. In the upper classes of the society, their position was better as compared to the lower classes and the rural areas. According to a view, Kashmir offered a greater equality to women, mainly, because of the impact of Buddhism. This tradition of women rulers in Kashmir region would have been known to the Indian rulers of North India as well and, therefore, in the aristocracy the women enjoyed a much better position. Many examples of women administrators and rulers are also found in Gujarat, Mewar and some other parts. Drawing a direct corollary from this fact, may be difficult but stating that the nomination and consequent accession of Razia to the throne of Delhi Sultanate was partly supported by these traditions would not be very far. Turkish and Iranian history also had the precedents of women enjoying the political authority.

The accession of Razia is followed by regular mentions of women in active politics including Malika-i-Jahan, Khudavandazada, Malika-i-Sultan Mahmud Sharqi, Bibi Mattu, Bibi Razi, Malika-i-Jahan, Shams Khatun, Bibi Ambha, etc.

Significant changes also appear to take place in the sartorial matters and the fashion of the time. Loose drawers, skirt and scarf were uncommon in the Indian sartorial habits. They were introduced after the advent of the new culture. The female outfits saw no marked changes during this period.

The absence of the concept of remarriage coupled with the economic dependence would have led more to slavery of females than the males. Polygamy could have absorbed some of them but majority would have been seeking rehabilitation by being sold as slaves or concubines. It is difficult on the basis of available sources to make an estimate of the male-female ratio, but a closer study of the accounts makes us conclude definitely that females were more in number and thus cheaper in the slave market than their male counterparts. It would be incorrect to say that majority of destitute women adopted prostitution—a recognised and highly protected profession.

Al-Umari has stated that 'The prostitutes are found in every town of India. They belong to particular families and sections. . . . If some non-prostitute decides to become a prostitute, her relations severe off all ties with her family and turn her out of the house . . . Only those prostitutes can be witness in the court whose mothers or grandmothers also happened to be prostitutes. They are heard and believed . . . and are always reliable. Nevertheless these inequalities of treatment such as wages, adult suffrage and opportunities remained long after the early middle ages.

1

Status-General

The status of women in Indian society underwent many changes as a result of the social changes in the country. The honoured position which the women enjoyed before the advent of Muslims in India gradually deteriorated during the Turkish rule. While the older tradition of high respect for them continued in a section of society,[1] there were some people who looked down upon them and denounced them as the root cause of the ruin of men.[2] A girl in a Hindu house was taught to respect the members of the family, especially the elders, from her very childhood. She was supposed to worship her husband like God and obey his commands.[3] She was expected to be true to her husband and serve him even in the time of adversity.[4] She was to follow her *pativrata dharma* (complete loyalty and devotion to husband) and lead a very chaste life.[5]

Domestic sphere was the most important field of a woman's activities. She had to do all the household work.[6] In the early morning she used to grind the corn. Then she prepared food and served it herself.[7] She went to fetch water from the well.[8] She would mud-plaster the floor and sweep the house. In leisure she would spin for making garments.[9] Thus, her whole day was occupied with the domestic affairs which formed the usual routine.

Social Ills

Dowry. The marriage of the girls was sometimes a difficult problem because of the custom of dowry (*Dahej*). It was given at the time of the marriage of the girl by her parents. It consisted of presents like jewels, ornaments, furniture, elephants, horses, maids and other articles of luxury. It was an old custom and gradually it became rigorous. This system was prevalent more among the rich than among the commoners. It also appears that it was absent among the Brahmins.[10] The nature of dowry differed with the economic standards of the parents. The foreign travellers also took notice of the system of dowry prevalent in India.[11]

Usually it was the bridegroom's side which received the dowry. But the reverse cannot be ruled out and in some cases the parents or guardians of the bride also received the dowry. This custom was prevalent mostly among the lower classes in the region comprising today of the states of Uttar Pradesh and Bihar. It was particularly followed in cases of aged and moneyed grooms who wanted to marry young girls. In this connection references to the practice of purchasing brides are also found.[12] It appears that the evils of dowry system prevailed with greater rigour in Bengal.[13] There was also a curious custom of giving away a younger sister of the bride to the bridegroom as a part of dowry.[14]

Child Marriage. Child marriage had become a popular feature of the social life in the Mughal period. Girls were generally married before they reached the age of nine or ten years.[15] Both the Hindus and the Muslims had fallen prey to this evil practices. Among the Hindus sometimes daughters were married even before they had learnt to talk.[16] Among the Muslims, daughters were generally married at a very young age.[17]

Child Birth. Another noteworthy thing which is observed by the foreign travellers too was that childbirth was taken by the common Indian women very easily. After the birth of the child the very next day the mothers would be found moving about and doing work. If they gave birth to a child on their journey, the next day they would ride on horseback carrying along their child.[18] But this was true only in the case of the poor women of labour class.

Sati. The greatest tragedy in the life of a Hindu woman was the death of her husband. Unlike the Muslims, widow-remarriage was not permitted among the Hindus in the Mughal period except among some lower classes.[19] A widow had to burn herself with the dead body of her husband or had to lead a life of suffering and misery and was treated with contempt by the other members of the family.[20] Society looked down upon the widows who did not perform *Sati*[21]. They were not allowed to grow their hair long or to put on ornaments and good dresses.[22] Widowhood was considered a punishment of the sins of previous lives.[23] The practice of performing *Sati* voluntarily was an ancient custom,[24] but gradually emphasis was laid on becoming *Sati* after the death of her husband even against her wishes.[25] It was mostly performed by the ladies of the Brahmin, Kshtriya and Bania community. Almost all the foreign travellers who visited India during the Mughal period mention that women used to burn themselves with the dead body of their husbands.[26] Still there were many ladies who refused to perform it.[27]

Just like *Sati, Jauhar* was also performed by ladies particularly in Rajputana. When a Rajput Chief and his soldiers became sure of their defeat in battle, they either killed their women and children or locked them and set them to fire; thereafter they went to battle-field and gallantly died fighting.[28]

Some of the Mughal Emperors tried to ban this practice. Akbar is said to have issued an order that a woman should not be forced to be a *Sati.*[29] Jahangir is also said to have prohibited *Sati.* It could not be performed without the permission of the King especially in case of young widows.[30] In the year 1663 A.D. Aurangzeb issued an order banning the *Sati* system.[31] Still those widows who did not have children were allowed to perform *Sati* while those who had, were not.[32] In spite of all these efforts *Sati* could not be altogether suppressed under the Mughals.

Parda. *Parda* was observed mainly by the Muslim ladies and was not so rigid with the Hindu ladies.[33] The practice of strict veiling was common among the Mohammedans. With the advent of Turks in India it was also adopted by the Hindu women as a protective measure to save their honour at the hands of the foreign invaders. It appears that the tendency to imitate the ruling class also gave impetus to the *parda* system. Abundant references of the observance of *parda* are found in the accounts of contemporary foreign travellers.[34] *Parda* was mainly confined to the rich and well-to-do classes.[35] Poor women, especially in villages, worked in fields and could not afford to observe *Parda.*[36]

Property Rights

Some of the ladies held *Zamindaris* (villages), *Milkiyat*-rights, and lands. They had the liberty of inheriting, selling and disposing of their properties.[37] A lady named Sabhanu, who was the sister of one Mahan Singh sold her village Debidaspur in about 1681 A.D.[38] Another lady named Bhikan was the owner (proprietress) of two villages, Baidaura and Baidauri in the year 1672 A.D.[39] Other similar references are also found in various contemporary records.[40]

Many *farmans* issued during this period confirm the possession of lands, gardens and *sarais* by women. Inayatullah Vakil, on behalf of his wife Bibi Rakhi, sold a plot of land to Mir Ghulam Haider.[41] Bibi Sukhi sold a plot of land outside the *Qila* in Kol for two hundred rupees. The transcription on her behalf was done by Abdur Razzaqq.[42] Sheikh Sadullah, on behalf of his mother Bibi Saba sold a garden of five *biswa* for rupees one hundred and one of Sheikh Mohammad Yusuf of Kol.[43] Abdul Razzaq, on behalf of his mother Sakhi, sold a *sarai* for two hundred rupees.[44]

Some women also received grants of lands in form of *Madad-i-Maash.*[45] Seventy *bighas* of land was measured by *Ilahi* yard in pargana Kol and was given to Khatoon as *Madad-i-Maash* in the forty-first regnal year of Aurangzeb.[46] Again forty-five *biswas* of land was conferred on Maham in the same pargana.[47] Achhi Bibi possessed eighteen *bighas* of *Pukhta* land as *Madad-i-Maash* (1739 A.D.).[48] During the reign of Farrukhsiyar eighty-five *bighas* of land in pargana Kol was confirmed as *Madad-i-Maash* to a lady named Aisha.[49] Two *bighas* of land in pargana Jalali was confirmed as *Madad-i-Maash* on another lady named Shah Bibi.[50] Many such references are found in the Mughal farmans which bear out that women used to hold land in form of *Madad-i-Maash.*[51]

Religion

Religion was predominant in the lives of the ladies whether they were Hindus or Muslims. A Hindu lady kept various fasts, visited temples, and read religious books, while a Muslim woman similarly read Quran, offered prayers called *Namaz* and also kept fasts. Both celebrated their religious festivals with great enthusiasm.

There were some women who devoted themselves wholly to religion and became saints or mystics. Bibi Fatima Saiman, the sister of Sheikh Fariduddin, and Bibi Zulekha, the mother of Nizamuddin Aulia, were among them.[52] Another lady named Bibi Nauni, who used to sell tobacco, later on attained the highest degree of mysticism.[53] Mata Sundari, a lady in the harem of Guru Govind Singh, established a monastery of her own and many Sikhs came to join her monastery.[54]

Thus, it appears that women also took to asceticism and

sometimes became *Joginis* (lady ascetics).[55]

Education

As regards the education of common women, girls belonging to middle-class family did not receive much education. Some of them visited schools, run in private houses by some elderly ladies.[56] Sometimes the father of the girl also acted as her teacher.[57] Girls of the poor family were almost left illiterate except a few who were collected and sometimes given instructions by the Mullas of the mosque[58] or by some Pandits in *Pathshalas.*[59] The subject of studies were mainly domestic-science such as needle work, embroidery, cooking and household work.[60]

On the whole, the education of common women was not widespread. There were no regular and separate schools for them. Boys and girls in the early years studied together, but even that seems doubtful due to the strict *parda* system prevalent in those days.[61] Moreover, their studies were hampered due to the practice of early marriages.[62]

Literary Activities

During the Mughal period though the education of the common women was ignored, yet there were many ladies who took keen interest in literary activities. They were not only the inspiration of the poets of that period but they also enriched the contemporary literature by their own works.

A close examination of the contemporary Hindi literature reveals that the contribution of ladies is fairly rich, qualitatively as well as quantitatively. For the sake of convenience the women writers of the Mughal period can be divided into three major groups—those who were influenced by *Bhakti* Movement and composed verses devoted to Rama or Krishna; those who were influenced by the contemporary *Reeti kavya* devoted to rhetorics and prosody and the physical beauty of women; and finally those who composed verses on various diverse subjects. However, most of them derived their inspiration from religion and composed verses devoted to their favourite form of God.

Saint Poetesses

The *Nirgun* aspect of *Bhakti* (devotion) also influenced a number of poetesses. The subjects which they usually dealt with were the importance of teacher *(Guru),* praises of renowned saints, importance of knowledge, etc. They excelled in expressing their emotions and feelings, but usually wrote didactic poetry.

Among the saint poetesses, the earliest reference is found of Indra Mati, the wife of Pran Nath who flourished in the sixteenth century and composed some *Dohas* in 1549 A.D.[63]

During the reign of Akbar a number of saint poetesses flourished. Ganga and Jamuna, the two disciples of Hit ji, belong to this period. Others of the same school were Kalmashi Devi, Rani Rar Dhari and Navla Devi[64] but the details about them are not available.

The tradition continued even afterwards and some of them flourished in the eighteenth century. Among them, mention may be made of Daya Bai, the disciple of Charan Das. She composed her poems about the middle of the eighteenth century. Two of her works which are available today are 'Daya Bodh' and 'Vinaya Malika."[65] A contemporary of Daya Bai was Sahjo Bai who was also a disciple of Charan Das. One of her works, known as 'Sahaj Prakash', is available, in which she has written about the importance of a good teacher and the qualities of a saint.[66]

Poetesses of Krishnait School

Sagun Bhakti had two streams—the Krishnait School and the Ramait School. Lord Krishna attracted a number of female devotees, some of whom composed exquisite verses in praise of their Lord. Mira Bai, who flourished in early sixteenth century, is the most prominent among them. She was married to Kumbha, the ruler of Udaipur.[67] Mira was a great devotee of Lord Krishna and composed many poems in His praise. Various works of Mira such as 'Narsi Ji Ka Mahra', 'Gita Govinda Ki Tika', 'Rag Govinda', 'Garva Geet', 'Sphuta Pad' and 'Meera Ke Pad' are found even today.[68] Her verses are plain, simple and often set to music. They are composed in Rajasthani, Braj and Gujrati languages.

Another poetess of this school was Bavri Saheb, who was a contemporary of Akbar. She was the disciple of Bhayanand and due to her excessive love for God, she was known as Bavri (meaning mad). She wrote many *padas* and had a good command of Hindi and Urdu.[69]

A third poetess of Krishnait School was Ganga Bai. She lived in Mahavan (near Mathura) and was disciple of Vitthal Das.[70] Not much is known about her life. She worshipped the child form of

Krishna. She wrote an independent work known as 'Ganga Bai ke pad'. Some of her *padas* are also found in the collection of the works of *Pushtimarg* saints.

Son Kumari who flourished in the latter half of sixteenth century also belongs to this group. She was a princess of Amber family. She composed a work known as 'Swarn Beli Ki Kavita.'[71]

One of the most famous poetesses of this period was Taj who wrote in seventeenth century. Details of her life are not available. She lived in village Karoli.[72] Though she was a Muhammedan, yet she worshipped Krishna. She wrote many verses in Braj *bhasha.* From the point of view of art she stands next to Meera Bai.[73]

Thus in Krishnait School a good number of poetesses flourished. The main theme of their works was devotion to Lord Krishna in various forms. From the point of view of art, they were quite successful and some of them such as Meera Bai and Taj achieved high distinction.

Poetesses of Ramait School

In the Ramait School of poetry, ıeference to only one poetess is found. It appears that this school was not so popular as the Krishnait School in which there was full freedom for the expression of feelings. Rama was idolized (as *Maryada Purushottam*) and so there was to be maintained some restraint in expression.

The only poetess of this school whose reference is available is Madhur Ali who wrote in the latter half of the sixteenth century. She lived in Orchha at a time when the Kingdom was ruled by Madhukar Shah.[74] It is quite surprising that in an atmosphere of feudal grandeur Madhur Ali preferred devotion to *Shringar.* Amongst her works are *Ram Charit* and *Ganesh Dev Leela,* but none of them are available.

During the sixteenth century, in Bengal also flourished a poetess named Chandravati. She was the daughter of famous poet Bamsidas. She composed a Ramayan which is noted for its originality and poetic beauty.[75]

Poetesses of Reeti Kavya

During the Mughal period there developed in Hindi poetry a tendency to emphasize the technique of poetry and to describe in vivid detail the physical beauty of women; the followers of this school were known the *Reeti* poets. Some ladies also were attracted to it—particularly to the second aspect of it which is known as *Shringar* poetry—and those worth mentioning are Praveen Rai Patur, Rup Mati, Teen Tarang and Rangarejin. They all flourished in the latter half of sixteenth and the first half of seventeenth centuries.

Praveen Rai Patur was a singer and dancer by profession. She developed her art in the court of Raja Indrajeet, the king of Orchha, who was her patron and was himself an expert in music.[76] It is said that Rai Praveen used to sing her own compositions. The complete collection of her verses are not available but whatever scattered verses are available, they are sufficient to prove her genius and her originality of expression.[77]

Another poetess of this school was Rup Mati who was the daughter of a prostitute of Sarangpur near Ujjain. No detailed information is available about her.[78]

A third poetess, named Teen Tarang also belonged to this group. She carried on her devotion to the art of poetry under the patronage of Raja Madhukar Shah of Orchha.[79]

The last of them was Sheikh Rangrejin. She was born in a Muslim family and was a dyer by caste.[80] She used to earn her livelihood by dyeing clothes. It appears that she had free access to the Mughal Court and often visited the court of Prince Muazzam.[81] She was, later on, married to Alam, and both, husband and wife, composed verses. Their verses are mostly in Braj *bhasha* with an admixture of Arabic and Persian words.[82] Her poems are compiled in a book known as *Alam Keli* which is a good example of *Shringar Ras.*[83]

Poetesses of Diverse Subjects

Besides this, there was another group of poetesses who composed verses on diverse subjects such as morals, duty of women, devotion to husband, etc. The first amongst them is Ratnavali, the wife of famous saint-poet Tulsi Das. She composed many couplets.[84]

Another poetess was Khaganiya who flourished in seventeenth century. She was born in a village near Unnao. She composed many riddles called *Pahelis* which are very popular.[85]

A third poetess, about whom scanty information is available, was the daughter-in-law of Keshava Das, the famous Hindi poet of the seventeenth century. She is said to have composed some verses in a meter known *Savaiyya.*[86]

Finally one more lady who also composed some verses was Kavi Rani Chaube, the wife of Lok Nath Chaube, who was in the court of Budh Singh, the King of Bundi. The period of her compositions is towards the close of the seventeenth century.[87]

In addition to above there were some ladies in Rajasthan who composed verses in *Dingal.* The poetesses of *Dingal* resided in the palaces where they served the queens and entertained them.[88] One among them was Champa De Rani. She was married to Prithviraj, the brother of the King of Bikaner, who also used to compose verses. She assisted her husband in composing verses. Her works are not available.[89] Her period of composition is towards the close of the sixteenth century.

Another poetess of *Dingal* was Padma Charini[90] who also flourished during the same period. She was the daughter of Charan Mal Ji Sahu and the wife of Bharat Shankar. She served in the palace of Bikaner to earn her livelihood.[91]

A third poetess named Kak Rechi Ji also belonged to this group. She flourished during the reign of Shahjahan. She was the daughter of Thakur Baghela Aggra Ji and was married to Nahar Narhar Das of Marwar. Her husband died in a war during the reign of Shahjahan.[92]

A poetess named Nathi, who was a devotee of Lord Vishnu, also composed some good verses. She flourished in the reign of Aurangzeb.[93]

All these poetesses of *Dingal* composed verses, devotional *padas* and *dohas*. *Shringar Ras* predominates their verses. From the literary point of view their poems cannot be rated very highly.[94]

On the whole, the attempt made by the ladies in the sphere of Hindi literature is praiseworthy. In those circumstances it is fairly creditable that they tried their best to touch every branch of literature except the *Prem Margi* school in which no poetess contributed anything. Not only from the point of view of subject matter, but also in matter of art, some of them like Sahjo Bai, Daya Bai, Ganga Bai, Sheikh Rangrejin and Praveen Rai are remarkable and their contributions in this field can hardly be ignored.

Women and Sanskrit Learning

The interest of ladies was gradually declining in Sanskrit. It seems that the education of Sanskrit was limited to certain classes and women were not especially encouraged to it. Consequently, they did not attain much proficiency in it. Even then, in Southern India the tradition of women taking to Sanskrit learning continued to some extent. There seems to be certain reasons for it. First, there was the rise of regional languages which was welcomed by the ladies. They had facilities for learning them and found it convenient and easier to express themselves through these languages rather than through Sanskrit. Secondly, there was the lack of proper Sanskrit education without which the ladies could not excel in this sphere. Finally, it was the impact of Persian language (which was also the court language during this period) that Sanskrit was not given so much importance. Naturally, the ladies could not attain much proficiency in it.

Reference is found of one Sanskrit poetess who flourished during this period. She was Priyamvada, the daughter of Shiva Ram, and the wife of Raghunath. She lived in Faridpur (in 1600 A.D.) in East Bengal. She wrote the famous poem 'Shyama Rahasya' and her earliest verse is written in praise of Krishna.[95]

Dress

The dress of common women among the Muslims consisted of a shirt and a trouser.[96] The shape of their trousers varied. Some wore *Shalwar* (breaches) and others *Ghagra* (loose skirt).[97] Some ladies of rich families used Kashmiri shawls and *Qabas.*[98] While going out, the ladies covered their head with veil.[99] The dress of Muslim ladies is often described by foreign travellers.[100]

Hindu women generally wore *Choli* which was a small jacket worn round the chest.[101] Below it they wore *Sari.*[102]

Reference of *Sari* frequently occurs in Hindi literature.[103] Hindu women were mostly fond of red colour.[104] Manucci, while describing the dress of Hindu girls, writes that upto the age of nine or ten the Hindu girls wear the same clothes as the boys. "After that time they wear a piece of white or red cotton cloth that they bind on the petticoat. Sometimes the pane (*Punjam*)[105]—for so they call this cloth—is striped in two colours. One half of the said pane *(Punjam)* is thrown over the shoulders or the head when speaking to a person of any position, but when they go to the well or a spring to fetch water, and when at work in their houses, they keep the whole pane *(Punjam)* bound round the waist, and hence upwards are naked."[106]

The costumes of Bengali women was of a bit different pattern.

They used *Saris* made of fine fabric.[107] Saris were of varied patterns—for example *Mayur pankhi, Magh damber, Pater Bhuni, Nilambari, Ganga-jali,* etc. They also wore *Kanchuki* (blouse).[108] The *Kanchukis* were of two types—one used to be short, covering only the breast and the other used to be long, reaching down to the waist. It was fastened at the back with ribbons. The *Kanchuk* was decorated with fine and artistic embroidery. They also used an underwear resembling a petticoat. In aristocratic families *Ghaghra* was used.[109]

The popular dress of Rajput ladies was *Lahanga* and *Choli. Lahanga* was a long and loose skirt and *Choli* or *Angiya* (blouse) was worn on the upper portion. A *Dupatta* or long scarf was thrown over to cover the head and upper part of the body.[110]

As regards their dress, the Sikh women wore trousers called *Suthan.*[111] It was made of *Susi,* a type of coloured cotton cloth. Many women wore a *kurta* and waistcoat.[112] A *chadar* was worn over the head and shoulder. It used to be either coloured (in case of young women) or uncoloured. It was made of *Garha* (coarse cloth) or *Dhotar* which used to be thick in winter and thin in summer. Sometimes it was a dyed cloth and often it was worked with silk flowers, (*phulkari sitari).*[113] Sometimes they also wore *Ghagra, Choli* and *Saris.*[114] The clothes for daily use were made from the home-spun material which, though rough, was strong and durable.[115] The ordinary dyes were indigo for blue and saffron flower for red and yellow.

About the dress of Gujrati women, Durate Barbosa, who visited India in the first quarter of the sixteenth century, says "Their dress is as long as that of their husbands. They wear silken bodices with tight sleeves, cut low at the back and other long garments called Chandes *(chadar)* which they throw over themselves like cloaks when they go out."[116]

The women of Kashmir wore an effiminate gown[117] or long tunic coming down to the feet. They did not use drawers. Waist-band was used by both the sexes. The Hindu ladies wore dresses of dark maroon or blue colour and fastened a girdle of white cloth round their waist.[118] The Muslim women in Kashmir wore no girdle and their tunic was richly embroidered.[119] Besides this, the women had a fillet on the forehead and above it was a mantilla (long gown) which fell from the head over the shoulders to the legs.[120] The head-dress of Muslims women was called *Qasaba* and of Hindu women called *Tarange* which was tied to a hanging bonnet falling to the heels from behind.[121]

Ornaments

The names of the ornaments used by the common women among the Hindus and the Muslims were the same as worn by the ladies of the Mughal aristocracy. The main difference between their ornaments was that of material and sometimes of pattern or name.[122] The common women instead of gold, silver and precious jewels, used copper, tin, glass and ivory.[123]

References

1. *The Laws of Manu,* Tr. by Buhler, p. 85 (Shlokas, 55-59).
2. Kabir Das, *Bijak,* p. 189 writes
   'नारी सवल पुरुषहि खायी, ताते रही अकेला' ।
   He also says, *Kabir Vachanamrita,* pp. 71-73.
   'नारी कुंड नरक का', 'जोरू जूठणि जगत की'
   Dadu Dayal, *Dadu Dayal Ki Bani,* Part I, pp. 131-32) says
   "नारी बैरणि पुरुष की, पुरिषा बैरी नारि ।
   अंति कालि दून्यूं सुए, कछु न आया हाथ" ।।
   Sur Das, *Sur Sagar,* Part II, p. 1187, writes
   "भामिनी और भुजंगिनी करी, इनके विषहिं डरैये ।
   राचेहुँ विरचे सुख नाही, भूलित कवहुँ पत्यैये ।।
   इनके वस मन परै मनोहर, बहुत जतन करि पैये ।
   कामी होई काम आतुर, तिहिं कैसे के समुझैये ।।"
   Tulsi Das, *Ram Charitmanas,* p. 778, writes
   'डोल गंवार शूद्र पशु नारी, ये सब ताड़न के अधिकारी' ।
3. Keshav, *Ram Chandrika,* Part I, p. 134, writes
   "नित पति पंथहि चलिये, दुख सुख का दलु दलिये ।
   तन मन सेवहु पति को, तब लहिये सुभ गति को" ।।
   'धर्म कर्म सब निरफल देवा, हीह एक फल के पति सेवा' ।
   Tulsi Das, *Ram Charitmanas,* pp. 631-32, writes
   "एकै धर्म एक व्रत नेमा, काय वचन मन पति पद प्रेमा' ।
4. Keshav, *Ram Chandrika,* Part I, p. 135, writes
   'नारि तजे न अपना सपनेहू भरतार,
   पंगु गुंग गौरा बधिर अंध अनाथ अपार' ।
5. Dadu Dayal, *Dadu Dayal Ki Bani,* p. 95, writes
   'पतिव्रता गृह आपने करे खसम की सेब,
   ज्यों राखे त्योंहि रहे आज्ञाकारी टेव' ।

6. *Hindu Manners, Customs and Ceremonies* by Dubois, p. 346; *Travels in the Seventeenth Century* by Roe and Fryer, pp. 117-18.
7. Reference to her domestic activities are found in folk-lore. For example 'ननदी भउजिया गोंहू पीसे मोरे राम'
   Bhojpuri Gram Geet by K.D. Upadhyaya, p. 132, also pp. 163, 166 and 170. 'रोटी पोवे महलों में राम के रसोइया' p. 216, Bihari, *Bihari Satsai,* Doha 641, p. 255 also writes
   "टटकी धोई धोवती, चटकीली मुख ज्योति ।
   फिरती रसोई के बगर, जगर मगर दुति होति" ।।
   Ghagh and Bhadri, p. 30.
8. Fitch, *Early Travels,* p. 19; *Maithili Lok Geet* by R. Singh, p. 59.
9. *Bhojpuri Gram Geet* by K.D. Upadhyaya, p. 150; *Rajasthani Lok Geet* by S. Pareek, p. 75; *Kannauji Lok Geet* by S. Anil, p. 212.
10. *Ain,* Vol. III, p. 339.
11. Manucci, Vol. III, p. 61; Careri, p. 248; *Bhojpuri Gram Geet Me Karun Ras* by D.P. Singh, p. 368.
12. Manucci says that it is not uncommon for a husband to buy his wife. In case after the ceremony the groom refused to marry the girl, he lost the money; and if the girl refused, her parents had to return double the amount. Manucci, Vol. III, p. 55.
13. *Aspects of Bengali Society* by T.C. Das Gupta, p. 4; *History of Bengali Subah* by K. Dutta, p. 71.
14. *Aspects of Bengali Society* by T.C. Das Gupta, p. 3.
15. *Ain.,* Vol. I, p. 277. Abul Fazl writes: "(Akbar) abhors marriages which take place between men and women before the age of puberty". Fitch, *Early Travels,* pp. 16, 19. Withington, *Early Travels,* p. 221. Pelsaert writes: "The Hindus join their children in marriage at the age of only four or five years", Pelsaert, p. 84; *Bhojpuri Gram Geet Me Karun Ras* by D.P. Singh, p. 404; *Maithili Lok Geet,* p. 58.
16. Manucci, Vol. III, p. 54-59. He also writes that the normal age for the marriage of the daughter of the Brahmins was four or five years, and in some cases, the marriage could be postponed upto ten years of age but never beyond that.
17. Careri particularly refers to Muslims, saying, "The Mohamedan Indians marry very young but the idolators at all ages", Careri, p. 248.
18. Terry, *Early Travels,* p. 309; Purchas, Vol. I, p. 31; Marshal, p. 328; Thevenot, pp. 66, 118: Careri, p. 248.
19. Badauni, Vol. II (Lowe), p. 367; Thevenot, p. 119; Careri, pp. 256-57. Careri says that the low class Hindus like milkmen,

gardeners, washermen, fishermen, etc. allowed their widows to remarry.

20. Manucci, Vol. III, p. 60; Thevenot, p. 84.
21. Bernier, p. 314; Thevenot, p. 84; Stavorinus, Vol. I, pp. 440-41.
22. Withington, *Early Travels,* p. 219; Manucci, Vol. III, p. 61.
23. Pietra Della Valle, p. 435; Bernier, p. 314.
24. Careri, p. 250.
25. Bernier describes that a young widow of twelve was forcibly asked to perform *Sati.* Bernier, pp. 313-14.
26. William Fitch (1583-91) refers to *Sati;* "When the husband dies, his wife, if she be alive, is buried with him, if she will not, her hair is shaven and then is never any account made of her after." Early *Travels,* pp. 20, 22) Withington referring to the *Sati* system cites the instance of a girl widow not more than ten years old. *Early Travels,* p. 219. Hawkins, *Early Travels,* p. 119; Purchas, Vol. III, pp. 49-50. De Laet says: "When her husband dies, the widow, of her own free will, leaps upon his pyre and is burnt up together with his corpse, as is a well known fact.", pp. 87-88. Pelsaert observes, "When a Rajput dies, his wives allow themselves to be burnt alive, as is the practice among the Banias and Kshatriya, and in Agra this commonly occurs two or three times a week.", pp. 78-79. Pietra Della Valle, Vol. I, p. 84, Vol. II, pp. 273-74. Tavernier, Vol. II, pp. 78-79. Pietra Della Valle, Vol. 1, p. 84, pp. 24-36; Manucci, Vol. II, p. 97. He also writes that once in the company of his young American friend, he rescued a widow from being burnt and his friend baptised and married her. Vol. III, p. 60; Bernier, pp. 306-15; Thevenot, pp. 72, 119-120; Careri, pp. 249-50, 255.
27. Pelsaert says, "There are hundreds and even thousands who do not do it." p. 80. Bernier says, "The accounts given of it have been certainly exaggerated, and the number of victims is less now than formerly, the Mahometans by whom the country is governed doing all in their power to suppress the barbarous custom . . ." p. 306.
28. Abul Fazl refers to this fatal custom performed by the Rajputs of Chittor on its fall, "For it is an Indian custom that when such a calamity has occurred a pile is made of sandalwood, aloes etc., as large as possible and to add to this dry firewood and oil. Then they leave hard-hearted confidants incharge of their women. As soon as it is certain that there has been a defeat and that the men have been killed these stubborn onces reduce the innocent women to ashes." *A.N.* (Bev.), Vol. II, p. 472; *Annals and Antiquities of Rajasthan* by Tod, Vol. I, pp. 363, 381, Vol. II, pp. 744-46.

29. Badauni says, "If a Hindu woman wished to be burnt with her husband, they should not prevent her, but she should not be forced against her will." Badauni, Vol. II, p. 388.
30. Withington, *Early Travels,* p. 219; but this order was not always carried and Jahangir could not succeed in preventing *Sati* at Agra. Hawkins. *Early Travels,* p. 119.
31. Manucci says, "Aurangzeb) issued an order that in all lands under the Mughal control never again should the officials allow a woman to be burnt." Manucci, Vol. II, p. 97; Thevenot, p. 120; Careri, p. 250.
32. Manucci says that the principal wife of a Rajput Raja who had sons, was not allowed to perform *sati* in order to maintain the family line. Manucci, Vol. III, p. 156; Careri, p. 255; Tavernier, Vol. II, pp. 210-16.
33. De Laet, p. 81; Manucci, Vol. I, p. 62; Fryer, p. 181.
34. De Laet writes, "The Mohammedan women do not come out into public unless they are poor or immodest; they veil their heads . . ." p. 80; Pietra Della Valle says, "For these (Muslim ladies) unless they be dishonest or poor never come abroad." Vol. I, pp. 44-45. He further says that the Mohammedans would not allow their wives to talk even to their relatives, except in their presence. p. 430; Also see Tavernier, p. 181. Manucci writes, "Among the Mohammedans it was a great dishonour for a family when a wife is compelled to uncover herself." Vol. II, p. 175, also Vol. I, p. 62. Thevenot writes, "If these Indian women be idolators they go bare-faced and if Mohamedans, they are veiled." p. 53. Careri observes, "The Mohamedan women do not appear in public except only the vulgar sort and lewd ones. They cover their heads . . ." p. 248. Hamilton writes, "The Mohammedan women always go veiled when they appear abroad". Vol. I, p. 163; Fryer, Vol. II, pp. 117-18. Barbosa says that every Mohammedan has three or four wives. They keep them carefully shut up. Barbosa, Vol. II, p. 147. Bowry wrote that the Bengalis did not allow their wives and concubines to go abroad but kept them under eunuchs' care. Bowry, p. 207; *Bengal Under Akbar and Jahangir* by T. Raychaudhuri, p. 206. Even Badauni refers to it, "And if a young woman were found running about the lanes and bazars of the town and while so doing either did not veil herself or allowed herself to be in veil . . . she was to go to the quarters of the prostitutes and take up the profession." Badauni, Vol. II, p. 405.
35. Bernier, p. 413; Pietra Della Valle, p. 461; *Society and Culture in Mughal Age* by P.N. Chopra, p. 104.
36. De Laet, p. 81.
37. *Agrarian System in Mughal India* by Dr. Irfan Habib, p. 155.

38. U.P. Records Office, Allahabad, Accession Register of the U.P. Records Inquiry Committee Records. Nos. 1215 and 1216, as quoted in *Agrarian System in Mughal India,* by Dr. Irfan Habib, p. 155.
39. *Ibid.,* p. 155.
40. *Ibid.*
41. *Farman* No. 2 (1737 A.D.) in the Azad Library, Aligarh Muslim University. It is a Sale Deed.
42. *Farman* No. 22, in the Azad Library, Aligarh Muslim University.
43. *Farman* Nos. 49, 57 in the Azad Library, Aligarh Muslim University.
44. *Ibid.,* No. 15.
45. *Madad-i-Maash* was an act of charity. They were given to the learned, religious or destitute persons who had no capacity to work, and also to persons of noble lineage. Women also received it. *Ain,* Vol. I, pp. 198-99. Abul Fazl says Turani and Irani women held grants. A special sister of Jahangir's father was in charge of grants to women *Tuzuk* (R. & B.), Vol. 1, p. 46. *Mazhar-i-Shahjahan,* 158, refers to two categories of lands, held by women, called (Chakhai-Musammati) and held by men, Muzakkarati as quoted in *Agrarian System in Mughal India* by Dr. Irfan Habib, p. 707.
46. *Farman* No. 212 in the Azad Library, Aligarh Muslim University.
47. *Ibid.,* Nos. 213 and 220.
48. *Ibid.,* No. 176 (1739 A.D.).
49. *Farman* No. 195 in the Azad Library, Aligarh Muslim University.
50. *Ibid.,* No. 196.
51. *Ibid.,* Nos. 198, 201, 205, 207, 209, 216-221, 223-225, 238, 246 and 255.
52. *Chahar Gulshan* by Chattarman Kayatha, f. 28a.
53. Once Shah Naga, a saint, passed in front of her shop. She gave him some tobacco. When he left the shop Bibi Nauni felt a peculiar sensation. She followed the Sufi and reached his monastery. The Sufi got very angry and asked her to go away, but she did not leave the place and, after some days, she obtained mystic light and attained highest degree of mysticism, *Chahar Gulshan* by Chattarman Kayatha, ff. 36b, 37a.
54. *Ibid.,* f. 150a.
55. There is a painting which shows a Yogini in the company of the Court ladies. *The Art and Architecture of Bikaner State* by Herman Goetz, p. 172. Another painting depicts a woman ascetic, sitting with her companion, and a lady is offering something to her with folded hands. The woman ascetic is wearing a *pagri* and is sitting on a loin-cloth with a rosary in her hands. Stchoukine, Plate no. 1x.

56. *The Educational System in Medieval India* by Yusuf Husain (Islamic Culture Vol. XXX, 1956) p. 122; *Glimpses of Medieval Indian Culture* by Yusuf Husain, p. 93; Jafar, p. 8.
57. Sarkar, *Studies,* pp. 301-02.
58. *Ibid.,* Jafar, p. 8.
59. *Some Aspects of Northern Indian Social Life* by P.N. Ojha, p. 110.
60. Manucci, Vol. III, p. 55; *Annals and Antiquities of Rajasthan* by Tod, Vol. II, p. 712.
61. Law, p. 200.
62. Sarkar, *Studies,* p. 301.
63. Sinha, p. 83.
64. *Sahitya Prakash* by Rasal, p. 109.
65. Sinha, p. 67.
66. *Ibid.,* pp. 51-52.
67. *Ibid.,* p. 105.
68. *Ibid.,* pp. 131-32.
69. *Hindi Sahitya* by Dwivedi, p. 140.
70. Sinha, p. 158.
71. *Ibid.,* p. 163.
72. *Ibid.,* p. 186.
73. Sinha, p. 192.
74. *Ibid.,* p. 222.
75. *Aspects of Bengali Society* by T.C. Das Gupta, p. 201.
76. Sinha, pp. 239-40.
77. *Ibid.,* pp. 240-41.
78. *Ibid.,* p. 248.
79. *Kok Shashtra Granth* is said to have been written by her. See Sinha, p. 252.
80. *Ibid.*
81. Sinha, p. 254.
82. *Ibid.,* p. 268.
83. *Ibid.,* p. 254.
84. *Ibid.,* p. 280.
85. *Ibid.,* p. 287.
86. Sinha, p. 288.
87. *Ibid.,* p. 289.
88. *Ibid.,* p. 28.
89. *Ibid.,* pp. 36-37.
90. Sinha, pp. 30-31.
91. It is said that once while Amar Singh, the King of Bikaner, was asleep, Akbar invaded his palace. No one dared to wake him up and (finally) Padma woke him up by her songs. Sinha, p. 31.
92. Sinha, p. 35. It is said that her father-in-law, husband and sons served under Shahjahan.

93. Sinha, p. 34, it is suggested that she was the daughter of Bhoj Raj. No definite information about her life is found.
94. *Ibid.*, p. 28.
95. *History of Classical Sanskrit Literature* by M. Krishnamachari, p. 394.
96. Pietra Della Valle, p. 411.
97. Shalwar and *Ghagra* were worn below the shirt. The former was tight and plated from above while the latter though plated from above was loose at the end.
98. Manucci, Vol. II, p. 341.
99. De Laet, p. 81; Terry, *Early Travels,* p. 309; Pietra Della Valle, Vol. I, pp. 44-45; Thevenot, p. 53; Hamilton, Vol. I, p. 163; Fryer, Vol. II, pp. 117-18.
100. Hamilton, who visited India from 1688 to 1723, writes about the garments of women "Their garments differ but little from the man's. Their coats which also serve both sexes for shirts are close-bodied. The man's are gathered in pleats below the navel and the women's are gathered a pretty way above to make their waist seem short. They both wear breaches to the ankles. "Hamilton, Vol. I, p. 163; *Book of Costume,* p. 415; Forbes, Vol. I, p. 94.
101. *Ain.,* Vol. III, p. 343.
102. Babar described *Sari* "as cloth one end of which goes round the waist the other is thrown over the head". *B.N.* (Bev.), Vol. I, p. 519.

Tavernier writes, "The dress of women is simple cloth making five or six turns like petticoat from the waist downward as if they had three or four rounds above the other." *Tavernier,* Vol. II, p. 42.

Thevenot, p. 37; Forbes, Vol. I, p. 74; Stavorinus, Vol. I, p. 415; *Indian Costumes* by G.S. Ghurye, pp. 140-41; *Catalogue of Indian Collection,* Plate li, *Book of Costume,* pp. 414-15.
103. *Padmavat* of Jayasi, p. 176; *Sursagar,* Part I, p. 265; *Raskhan Granthavali,* p. 62; *Bihari Satsai* p. 43, Doha 121, p. 46, Doha 127 (blue *Sari*), p. 57, Doha 131, p. 48, Doha 132 (white *Sari*), *Mati Ram Satsai,* pp. 452-493.
104. Manucci, Vol. II, p. 341; Pietra Della Valle, Vol. I, p. 45. Printed cloth was also used by them.
105. In Northern India it is called *Sari* Manucci, Vol. II, p. 40 (Footnote).
106. Manucci, Vol. II, p. 40.
107. *Aspects of Bengali Society* by T.C. Das Gupta, Introduction, p. xxvii and pp. 46, 228, 270.
108. *Ibid.,* pp. xxvii, and 42, 288-89; Stavorinus writes "They support their breast and press them towards by a piece of linen which

passes under the arms and made fast on the back." Vol. I, p. 415.

109. *Aspects of Bengali Society by* T.C. Das Gupta, p. xxvii.
110. *Ain.*, Vol. III, p. 342. *History of Rajputana* by J.S. Gahlot, Vol. I, p. 105; *History of Rajputana* by Ojha, Vol. I, p. 19.
111. *History of the Sikhs* by H.R. Gupta, p. 291; *The Punjab Being a Brief Account* by Col. Steinbach, p. 112.
112. *Ibid.*, p. 112.
113. *History of the Sikhs* by H.R. Gupta, p. 291.
114. *Ibid.*, p. 291; *Punjab Under the Mughals* by Muhammad Akbar, p. 258.
115. *History of the Sikhs* by H.R. Gupta, p. 291.
116. *Book of Durate Barbosa* by Mansel Longworth Dames, Vol. I, pp. 113-14; *Indian Costume* by Ghurye, pp. 143-44.
117. *The Valley of Kashmir* by W.R. Lawrence, p. 251.
118. *Ibid.*, p. 252; *Kashmir from Shahmir to Shahjahan* by Dr. R.K. Parmu (Thesis), p. 323.
119. *The Valley of Kashmir* by W.R. Lawrence, p. 252.
120. *Kashmir Under the Sultans* by Mohibul Hasan, p. 229.
121. *Ibid.*, p. 229; *The Valley of Kashmir* by W.R. Lawrence, p. 251.
122. In Bengal the names of these ornaments were different. The head ornaments was known there as *Sinthi* and that of nose was called *Besar* or *Nakh Chhabi.* The names of ornaments worn in the ear was *Kundal, Kanbala, Hiraman-Salkadi, Madan Kadi;* in neck were *Sateswari, Gribapatra;* in arms *Tad, Angada, Ananta, Keyur, Maduli, Ratanchud* and in toes *Unchchat* and *Ujjhatika. Aspects of Bengali Society by* T.C. Das Gupta, pp. 51-56; *Bengal in the sixteenth Century* by J.N. Das Gupta, p. 184.
123. Fitch, *Early Travels,* p. 13; Ralph Fitch, *England's Pioneer to India and Burma,* Vol. I, p. 128, Part II, p. 107.

2

Social Customs

Life begins with birth and birth of a child was a great joyful occasion in the life of a married couple in medieval times and to celebrate their ecstasy. Both the parents had their assemblies according to their means. On this occasion, a number of customs were observed in a Muslim family. Truly, the *Quran* has no special injunctions regarding observance at the birth of a child, but the subject is frequently referred to in traditions and in Muhammadan books on Ethics. In he Mughal period, the Muslims had so largely incorporated the Hindu customs especially those observed at the birth of children, that it, sometimes, appears difficult to distinguish those which are special characteristics of Islam. Most ceremonies and traditions regarding a child's birth, are not based on religion and their observance in the Mughal period was a matter of customs only. They originated in the Indian environment where Hindusim had its impact over islam and therefore, were peculiar to the Indian Muslims.

Though Islam gives an honourable place to girls, yet in the Mughal period their place does not appear so exalted. The Muslims experienced problems in setting their daughters suitably after marriage and cared to giving high dowries. Similar practice prevailed among the Hindus. Besides, a girl's inevitable departure to her conjugal house one day or the other also was important cause of displeasure in her birth, as they were generally referred to as 'birds who will fly away at any time. So, under these circumstances, the birth of a girl always created subdued atmosphere and annoyance. Though the desires for the boy did not influence the Muslims to the same extent as it did the Hindus, but the fact cannot be denied that a son was always preferred to a daugher, and craving for a boy was so deep[1] that people approached holymen and tombs to ask for sons.[2] Even Mughal Emperors like Akbar[3] and Shahjahan[4] could not escape and rushed to the tomb of the great saint, Muinuddin Chishti, and earnestly prayed for the birth of a son.

During middle ages, generally, the birth of a girl produced a temporary gloom in the whole family. Even in the royal family, in case, of princess' birth, the ladies of the royal *harem* only celebrated her birth, whereas in a prince's birth, the whole empire took intense interest and part in the celebration.[5] The news of the birth of a male child was followed by gifts to the new born[6], from not only the relatives but also truly from the nobles. Sometimes, the mother of a prince was also honoured with money and valuable gifts.[7]

Therefore, in these circumstances, naturally the mother blessed with a son, was almost the idol of the family and that mother naturally got a soft corner in her husband's heart and remained without a rival throughout her life which was because of nothing but polygamy. While on the other hand, a woman giving birth to a daughter, was bound to be lower in status as compared to her sisters blessed with sons and was, therefore, ill-treated throughout. Hence, they were often tortured by their mothers-in-law and husbands.[8]

This ranking of a Muslim woman's status was the outcome of various socio-cultural and biological factors. However at a child's birth a number of ceremonies were celebrated everywhere in India. Following were the main birth ceremonies observed by the Muslims during the Mughal age.

Birth Ceremonies

In anticipation of a child's birth, Muslim women were greatly interested in taking out omens and got themselves satisfied by knowing the sex of the child,[9] and while doing so they made merry and amused each other. After the birth, the child was cleaned and bathed by the mid-wife in compliance with the Muslim customs and swathed in swaddling bands.[10] Now, the child could be carried to the male assembly. Following this custom, Jahan Ara, on her birth, was brought to Jahangir in the male apartment.[11]

After the birth of a child,[12] the custom of reciting *Azaan* and *Iqamat* was observed without fail, as has been imposed by Islam, and the Prophet Mohammad himself is said to have done so at the birth of his own grandson, Hassan.[13] In this ceremony, *Azaan* (the call to prayer) was read by any pious person in the infant's right ear first and then with the addition the *Iqamat*, leading to the meaning 'We are standing up for the prayer' in the left ear of the child. The idea behind this custom was to instil the holy words relating to God Himself into the ears of the child when it first opened its eyes and saw the light of the early world for the first time after birth. This was followed by distribution of 'pan' and '*batasha*' among friends and relatives.[14]

Then a little dry fruit chewed by a venerable man was inserted into the infant's mouth,[15] a custom also based upon the example of Prophet Mohammad.[16] This was observed before the infant was put to the breast, so that the wisdom of that holy person might be transmitted to the child.[17]

On the first day of its birth, the child was made to suck honey water[18], with the help of a piece of clean soft cloth rolled up like a tapper. On the second day, the infant was given Gutti (a special preparation of food for babies) and from the third day milk was supplied to the infant.

With regards to the first robe of the child it was customary to make it out of any used garments deserving special reference. For this, worn dress of some ancient worthy[19] man was greatly admirable. Following this, Akbar's first garments were fashioned from Saint Sayyed Ali Shirazi's clothes.[20] It was believed hereby that good qualities of that pious person might be transferred to the infant instantly.

After the birth of a child, the breasts of the child were pressed medically, like today, so that the milkdrops could come out effectively. As in the Mughals, in case of a female child, the brother of the infant was asked to suckle that milk, so that the milk could produce prolonged motherly attachment in his sister's heart from the brother. Considering it justified, Jahangir was directed to suckle that type of milk of his step sister Shakrun Nisa Begum, the daughter of Bibi Shad.[21]

After observing the aforesaid customs, parents and relatives wished for the good health and prosperity of the child. For this, '*Nisaar*' was offered and then the custom—'*Pa Andaz*' was followed[22], and alms (*Nazr*)[23] were offered to the poor and the needy according to the family status.

The head of the family circulated the joyful news to friends and relatives and offered them sweets. They paid congratulatory compliments[24] and presented gifts.[25] For cheers and soothing, ladies chanted with musical rhythm also on such occasions.

The birth of a prince was not only witnessed as the ecstatic event by the ladies of the royal *harem* but also by the Emperor and his courtiers. The person who had the credit to bring the news first to the Emperor, was also rewarded handsomely.[26] At this moment, the Emperor after paying thanks to God, ordered to make rejoicings. On getting the news, the ladies of the *harem* expressed their joy and good wishes, and sang and danced[27] unitedly. Taking advantages, ingenious men also composed congratulatory odes,[28] and received handsome gifts in from the Emperor. In a royal family, at the time of departure of visitors, it was customary to distribute small artificial fruits like pistachios, almonds and walnuts made of gold and silver to all the guests. These artificial fruits were prepared beforehand in anticipation of the child's birth.[29]

It was a special feature during the Mughal age that amongst the rich people the mothers hardly nourished their infants and a nurse, having a well balanced temperament and good qualities, was employed for this purpose and she was styled as Dai Dudh Pilai, Anna or Anaga.[30] This custom was also prevalent in Islam, and Prophet Mohammad himself was nourished and reared by Bibi Halima. As the maintenance of a wet nurse is inclined by Islam to the infant's father's duty,[31] generally she was kept in the child's home where she retained alongwith her own family till the end of her life. There she gained full respect as a member of that family. Indeed, she was only second in estimation of the parents to the child reared and nourished by her, and with the child she had more privileges than his natural parents. Akbar always showed great honour to Maham Anaga. In view of this, Nurjahan also showed a favour and posted her wet nurse, Dil-Aram, as the head of her charity department.[32]

Those families having heavy income could keep wet nurses, but the poor ladies having little income either from land or labour, trade or service were bound to feed their infants by themselves.

There was no fixed age limit for the period of nourishing during the Mughal age. Islam directs that children can be nursed till two and half years,[33] but practically, the Muslim women nursed their children till the expectation of the next issue. But in case of a big gap, the child was restricted to suck on attaining the age of 3–4 years[34].

Naming Ceremony

It was a very important ceremony among the Muslims of India. Generally the infant was named on the day of births,[35] as directed by Islam,[36] but in case where *'Aqiqa'* could not be performed, the naming ceremony was done on the seventh day. Abul Fazl opines in this connection that on the second day, after passing the date of impurity the child was assigned a name. The grand-father[37] of the new born generally fixed a name in an auspicious hour.[38] But there was no objection in fixing the name of the child by his parents and relatives.[39] At the time of naming certain factors were highly considered. They first avoided the names used by idolators.[40] Names consisting of more than four letters were treated as inausticious. It was not customary to offer their own names to their children. Some families also avoided the name of a forefather within two or three generations.[41] However, it was prevalent among the Mughals to give the child the name of a relation or a member of the family,[42] which was unusually avoided by other Muslim communities. In order to perpetuate the faminine name in the family of Prophet Mohammad, the Muslims adopted such names as Amna (Mother of Prophet Mohammad), Fatima (his daughter), Khadija (his first wife), Zainab (his daughter), Ayisha (his most favourite and youngest wife) etc. assuming that these names were very dear to him and that such religious names would imprint special repercussions on the girls themselves. On the one hand, beautiful names were given to their girls by the Mughals,[43] while on the other, approbrious names, implying degradation, frustration, impurity etc. were often preferred by the lower class Muslims for baffling the evil eye or the peril from the exaggerated appreciations.[44] It was customary to make rejoicings after naming the child.[45] In royal families, courtlers and other members of the family received expensive gifts on such occasion.[46]

Chhatthi

Both the Hindus[47] and the Muslims of India celebrated *Chhatti* on the sixth day of a child's birth,[48] with deep interest. It was commonly celebrated on the sixth day, but often on the seventh or ninth day after the child's birth.[49] Where any death had taken place in a house, *Chhatthi* was performed on the third day, as a change the infant's lot.[50]

For celebration of *Chhatthi,* the Muslim ladies cleaned and decorated the house carefully where the child was born to remove the impurity completely. They also made all preparations for festivities themselves. As per the prevalent custom the grand-father of the child had to spend handsome amount in birth festivities. That's why the birth of every grand-child Shah Jahan spent two lakh rupees for birth celebration.[51] On the fixed day, both the mother and the child were bathed and dressed in new costly outfits.[52] Friends and relatives were invited, and singing and dancing parties were organised. Rich dishes were also cooked and all guests were entertained. '*Nisaar*' was made for the health of the infant and handsome gifts were offered to friends, relatives and family members.[53] Arrangements were also made for illumination, especially on the night of *Chhatthi* in case of prince's birth.[54]

On this occasion, special gifts for the new born and his/her parents must come from the former's mother's parental house alongwith their close relatives including infant's clothes like *Kurta, Topi,* jewels like *Tauq, Hansli, Kara,* Toys, sweetmeats besides several other things.

The Indian child, entered the world amid a cloud of strange blind-faiths and various superstitious views followed, as if directed by religion. Some of the superstitious rites mentioned by the Muslim ladies during the Mughal period are described as follows:

Tare Dikhana (Showing Stars)

'Tare Dikhana' means to show the stars. This rite was very common among the Mughals.[55] At the very night of *Chhatthi'*, therefore, the mother of the new born child accompanied by her friends used to carry the infant in the open courtyard. The child remained under her arms holding the '*Quran*' on her head and keeping her eyes shut for a few moments till she reached in the open air and had a glance of the stars with the naked eyes which was repeated seven times one after the other.[56]

Mirg Marna

When the child's mother was in the courtyard, another rite at the same time was performed by the father of the child also, known as *Mirg Marna*. At this moment he remained standing on the vacant bed of his wife, and saying "*Bismillah*" he would shoot an arrow towards the roof of the room. For this, the father received gifts from his mother-in-law. Bahadur Shah Zafar is said to have observed this rite on his son's birth.[57]

The Muslim ladies during the Mughal age, generally believed that on the night of *'Chatthi'* the infant's destiny was written by the angel whose duty was to write people's fate.[58] Thus, the night passed in singing, dancing, illuminations, fire-work display and merry making.[59]

Bageer Bachcha[60]

On this occasion one more Turkish ceremony was observed by the Muslim ladies, known as "Bageer Bachcha". The Child had to cross from under the legs of seven *Suhagan* ladies (whose husbands were alive). While doing so one asked from other *'Bageer Bachcha'* and she replied *'Allah Nigahban Bachcha'* for surrendering the child under God's protection.

Chillah

The fortieth day after the child's birth was called *'chillah'*. It was celebrated with great rejoicings, being the day of purification[61] for the infant's mother. From that day onwards she was free to go about as usual. Before *chillah* she was not permitted to dress, food, including meat.[62] For the day of *chillah,* the whole house was cleaned by the ladies, and the infant and her mother were bathed and dressed in new clothes. Lady friends and relatives were invited and they presented clothes to the child. The mother also received clothes from both her parental and mother's-in-law houses. The child was gifted a golden or silver amulet, on which verses from the *Quran* were engraved.[63] From that day the child could place in *'Gahwarah'* or swinging cradle.[64] On this occasion, friends, relatives and poor peoples were feasted. On that day the mother of the child could visit her parental home (if she was in her husband's house during the delivery period), for the first time after delivery, with her child.

Aqiqa Ceremony

'Aqiqa' has been religious ceremony. It originated in the age of Prophet Musa (Mosses), much before the birth of Prophet Mohammad. Prophet Mohammad laid stress on its performance only for those who could afford it. As he himself observed it when a son, Ibrahim, was born to him;[65] (died in infancy) so Muslims liked to follow his foot prints. They usually performed it on the seventh day of the child's birth, as instructed by the religion.[66]

Some people also performed it on the day of *Chhatthi, chillah* or any other convenient day,[67] which was allowed by Islam. On the fixed *Aqiqa* day, relatives and friends were invited and the hair of the child was shaved by silver mounted razor and silver cup first time after birth.[68] After shaving, the child's head was rubbed with saffron, as instructed by Prophet Mohammad. Then the amount of gold or silver (according to one's means) was distributed as alms, equal to the weight of the hair.[69] This hair was, then, either buried or floated in streams.[70]

In this ceremony animal was sacrificed for removing the child's impurities and protecting him against all calamities.[71] For a male child, two 'he goats' were sacrificed and for a girl only one was required.[72] Now the meat was divided into three equal parts, the one distributed in charity, other to friends and the rest was fed to relatives.[73] In some families unlike Islamic law, the parents and grand parents of the child were forbidden to eat this meat. If the child was not already named before, it was done on the day of *Aqiqa.* The child was presented heavy gifts and child's aunts, barber, matrons, wet nurses and singing and dancing girls also received presents.[74] In lieu of *Aqiqa* some Indian Muslims adopted '*Mundan*'—a purely Hindu ceremony. In this ceremony the child's hair (*chotis* or *tufts*) was shaved at the '*dargah*', i.e., shrine of that particular saint or wali,[75] by whose blessings, the child was born. For this, in the name of that particular saint, people left child's *chotis* or *tufts* unshaved for one, four or five years.[76] Sometimes, for good fortune, people shaved child's head at a shrine. Akbar's head was also shaved at the shrine of Baba Hasan Abdal.[77]

During this period, in a Muslim family, in every step of the child's development, they observed some sort of rites. It was either his fisting for the first time or his first tooth appearance there was a festivity. Not only that, when child began to walk, people rejoiced. In Turks, for protecting the child from the evil eye, when he began to walk, his father or grandfather or whoever represented the family, striked the child with his turban, so that the child might fall down,[78] because it was treated to be auspicious. When Akbar was about one year and three months, Maham Anaga represented Mirza Askari to observe this custom and so did he.[79]

Salgirah

During the Mughal age *'Sal-girah'* of a Muslim girl was celebrated only in well-to-do families and in the royal *harem*. The lower and poor classes of the Muslim Society did not observe this custom.

In fact, birthday ceremony was a Christian custom, but in India, the Muslims adopted it from the Hindus as this ceremony was not at all celebrated in any Islamic country. The Hindus[80] called this ceremony *'Varsh Ganth',* and so the muslims started call it *'Sal-girah',* on the same purport and those who terms meant same as that of the 'year knot'. *'Sal-girah'* was of course, a day of annual rejoicings performed through the entire house. It was celebrated when a year had passed from the day of the child's birth. Relatives and friends were invited. The child was bathed and dressed in costly dress and scents were sprinkled on her dress. For birthday celebration the mother of the child or any old lady made a very long cord of yellow or red silken.[81] At the end of that cord she made a knot just to record the first year of the child and after this, in due sequence at the end of each twelve months another knot was made, which was actually year knot or *'Sal-girah'*. This was continued till the end of life.[82] The child's mother kept this string and produced it at each of her child's birthday.

In case of a girl, on the contrary, her years were numbered by a silver loop being added annually to her silver neck ring.[83] Then sweet meats were consecrated in the name of Prophet Mohammad and Prophet Nuh, to make the child attain the great age of the Patriarch.

In royal household *'Sal-girah'* was celebrated with special rejoicings.[84] At the moment, music, dancing, illuminations, display of fire works and whatever amusement suited their age and taste, were liberally conferred on to celebrate their happiness. For the birth day ceremony of a princess,[85] all ladies of the royal *harem* made preparations since months before. On her birth day she dressed in her most beautiful and expensive and heavily perfumed outfit.[86] Lady guests of the nobles' family and other relatives were invited. Thus the chief ladies of the Court were obliged to attend the palace and to make their comments to the Queen and the princess.[87] They all presented presents, according to their status, to the princess. This birthday ceremony was concluded with a great banquet[88] in which poor were also not neglected. All the lady guests received, at this happy occasion, costly gifts of jewels and *sarapas* (robes) alongwith other articles.[89] Before departure, the queen and the princesses happily showered gold and silver coins, with pearls and precious stones, on the friends, relatives and poor, singing and dancing women.[90]

In case of the Emperor's birthday, it was customary to pay visit to his queen mother, if alive. There he received her felicitations and offered her gifts.[91] Hawkins informed that Jahangir, on his birthday, 'goes to the mother's house with all better kind of his nobles, where every man gifted a jewel to his mother according to his estate'.[92]

Goshwarah or the Ceremony of Piercing the Ears

This was a ceremony when the lobes of a small girl's ears were pierced. In this ceremony, on a fixed date, the girl was made to sit in the assembly of the lady guests, wearing her new clothes. Then either a gold smith or a barber would pierce her ears' lobes[93] to enable her to wear ear rings. Hereafter were distributed among all who assembled there. Sweets, coconut, and *Misri* (sugar candy) were sent to the child's grand parents' house. The man piercing her ears, was presented suitable gifts. This ceremony was also known as '*Kanchhedan* ceremony' and was borrowed from the Hindus.

Bal Gunthan Ceremony

Among the wealthier section of the Muslim society the plaiting of the hair ceremony was celebrated. The little girl's hair was plainted for the first time, generally on the day of *'Bismillah'*[94] (rite of initiation), the girl in her best clothes brought to the ladies assembly. Her hair was plaited with black silk ribbon. Following this, sweets were distributed to all,[95] and thus concluded the function/ceremony.

Marriage

Marriage one of the prime requirements of man, is an institution 'as old as Adam'. In Islam, marriage is a civil contract between two opposite sexes for the protection and development of society, and as a shield against sexual weakness, fouliness and unchastity. Prophet Mohammad openly announced, "Marriage is a sacred duty and whoever dislikes this way of life is disbeliever of

Islam'. Marriage, hence, has been considered as the most stormy event in the life of a Muslim woman as it confers some rights, duties and privileges accompanied by additional responsibilities upon the bride which she is expected to observe faithfully, on reaching her conjugal-house, for a happy and prosperous marital life.

During the Mughal age, the father of a girl believing 'Nikah' a sacred duty would be searching a suitable partner for his daughter, before she attained puberty. It was so, because, Islam greatly emphasised on the performance of a girl's marriage by saying, "When they (girls) reach the marriageable age, no time should be lost in marrying them to proper mates".[96]

The Muslims of India generally celebrated observing a number of ceremonies and customs. During the early and middle ages of Islam, in Arabia as well as in other Muslim countries, very few ceremonies were celebrated. Only *'Nikah'* and *'Walima'* feasts were thought important. So it is clear that the various customs and ceremonies involved in a Muslim marriage in India, had evolved from the Indian atmosphere. In fact because of the existing political, social, economic, cultural, moral and ecological conditions, the Muslims in India borrowed many customs and rites from their Hindu contemporaries.

During the period, two types of marriages were prevalent among the Muslims, *'Sharayee'* and *'Urfi'*. The more strict and educated persons followed the former, while the rich and common people, the latter.

The *Sharayee* Marriage

Sharayee marriages involved no ceremonies. This was performed in a simple way, according to the principle of Islam, as Prophet Mohammad observed in the marriage of his own daughter, Bibi Fatima Zohra. There might or might not be many persons at the time of *Nikah.* A remarkable feature of such marriage was the small amount of 'Mehr' (Dower) preferably paid at the time of *Nikah*[97] itself as compared to '*Urfi*' marriage. The '*Sharayee*' marriage was not observed only by the middle and the lower class Muslims but by the royal families[98] too. The nuptial ceremony of Gulrukh Bano, daughter of Shuja, with Aurangzeb's eldest son *Sultan* Mohammad was celebrated according to the strict injunctions of the *Shariya.*[99] (Practical actions and observations witnessed by Mohammad himself and followed accordingly by his disciples, and others afterwards.

The *'Urfi'* Marriage

The *'Urfi'* marriage was much prevalent among the richer sections of the Muslim community. The *'Mehr'* was always fixed before the marriage. In rich and imperial families it was mostly determined at lakhs and *crores* of rupees, while in middle and lower orders in several thousand rupees. Usually the heavy sum of *'Mehr'* was impossible for a bridegroom to pay it off, during his life time and therefore Akbar disapproved of it completely.[100]

The 'Urfi' marriage was performed with elaborate ceremonies. Many people, therefore, had to accompany the marriage party in compliance with the rites and customs on both—the bride and the groom sides.

Selection of Marriage Partners

In every age selection of suitable matches for sons and daughters, has been worrying all the Muslim families since children's earliest years upto the period of its accomplishment.

During the Mughal age, marriage partners were particularly chosen by parents, guardians and relatives. Sometimes mother played an important role.[101] Marriage with one's own choice was also not unknow among the Muslims,[102] but it was rare.

Marriage was generally organised on the basis of established reports, interests or respect[103] held by the family. The selection of a marriage partner depended on social and economic considerations, including the status of the family, their stands and relationship. However birth, position and eligibility were considered seriously Besides the family status included income, health, behaviour, temperament, inclination, social and economic conditions, relations and field of influence.

As regards the merits of the bride according to 'the *Quran*' a Muslim male must enter into marriage preferably with a girl having good moral behaviour,[104] but during the Mughal age, people preferred a beautiful girl having good character and conduct, and also possessing mental and physical health.[105] Her training in domestic management and accomplishments such as cooking, needle work, embroidery etc. were also considered.

Widowed girls were generally avoided for the first marriage by the boy's party.[106]

All cases followed these considerations but the chief factor was every one's desire to settle marriage within his own trade or occupation, division or tribe and even in the same school of religious thought, and not beyond it.[107] Thus, inter-caste marriage was strictly forbidden. But even then, in some cases, marriages between Turks and Indians[108] and *Shias* and *Sunnis* were celebrated. Babur, who was a *Sunni* married *Mehr* Begum, a *Shia.* His son Humayun also married, Hamida Bano begum a *Shia.* Besides, Jahangir's wife Nur Jahan and Aurangzeb's wife, Dilras Bano were also *Shia*s.

During the Mughal age, sometimes, political enmities were terminated due to fresh settlement of marriage between two kings or parties. Babur married Mubarika Bibi, promising not to attack on Yusuf Zai tribe to which she belonged.[109] Afterwards Babur married his sister Khanzada Begum to Shahi Beg Khan Shaibani, when he seized Samarqand from Babur, to bring peace and a lasting alliance between Babur and Shaibani.[110]

Though beyond a few special degrees of prohibition, as consanguinity,[111] affinity,[112] fosterage[113] and in some other special cases, the *Quran* gives perfect freedom in the selection of life partner, but it forbids inter religious marriages.[114] In India at Rajaur, Jahangir observed inter religious marriages.[115] In royal household also similar marriage was in vogue. Out of political considerations and as a mark of distinction, few Mughal emperors perferred Rajput brides. Akbar himself married Bihari Mal's daughter.[116] His son Jahangir married the daughters of Jagat Singh,[117] Raja Bhagwan Das[118] and Raja Uday Singh.[119] Dara's son Sulaiman Shukhoh married the daughter of Rao Amar Singh Rathor.[120]

Contrarily, the Mughal emperors never married their sisters and daughters to any one outside the religion and the imperial family. Hence, during the reign of Shahjahan and Aurangzeb, the princesses either remained unmarried or got married within the royal household. In imperial family such strict regard was not followed and such marriages were also not considered important from the political point of view.[121] To maintain their pomp and splendour, the Mughal emperors usually negotiated for their family members into families whose members not only possessed very high ranks but had also the reputation of a long aristocratic lineage. In addition, in a Muslim societty men of mercenary minds also preferred manying their girls to noble men or men of wealth, in a designed way uniting them with a life-partner of their own status with whom the girl would most likely to live without a rival.

During this age, among the Muslims, marriage meant a

ceremony involving extravagant expenditures, which hampered men throughout life. Therefore, it was sometimes difficult for indigent parents to secure a suitable partner for their daughters and offer them a decent dowry. In such cases some of the Mughal princesses regarded it liberally as a charitable act to provide dowry to poor Muslim girls to save them from calamities. Nurjahan,[122] throughout her life had the credit to get performed approximately five hundred marriages of poor girls. Similarly, Mumtaz Mahal[123] organised several indigent girls' marriages.

Like many other communities of the world, 'The Muslims of the Mughal period, too, gave preference to certain of their kin while settling marriages'. On account of some socio-cultural factors, 'cousins' had an important place in the matrimonial alliances, and hence they evolved 'cross cousin' and 'parallel cousin' marriages, still popular and continuing in Muslim society. During this period, such marriages were quite common, Babur's wives Ayishah Sultan Begum, Bega Begum Bayqra and Zainab Sultan Begum Miran Shahi were his cousins.[124] Humayun also married his cousin Bega (Haji) Begum.[125] Mirza Hakim's sister Sakina Banu Begum was married to her cousin Shah Ghazi Khan.[126] Dara also married his cousin Nadira Banu Begum, the daughter of Sultan Parwez.[127] Dara also married his daughter Jahan Zeb Banu to Aurangzeb's son Mohammad Azam.[128] Aurangzeb's two daughters Zubdatun Nisa Begum and Mehrun Nisa Begum were married to Siphr Shukoh (son of Dara) and Ezad Bakhsh (son of Murad[129]). Shuja's daughter Gulrukh Banu was married to Aurangzeb's son Mohammad Sultan.[130]

Such matrimonial alliances were established perhaps due to pride of lineage and concept for maintaining purity of blood, family solidarity and the prospect of the dowry offered to the daughter at the time of marriage remaining in the same family. But it was Akbar who, for the first time, forbade marriages between cousins.[131]

Marriageable Age

During this period, among the Muslims no fixed age limit existed for the marriage. But, as, it was an age of early marriage, generally girls were married at the age of seven, eight and nine.[132] Young girls were considered a burden and parents remained worried to get their daughters married as early as possible.[133] But they were not adamant about their sons' early marriage.[134] In a Muslim family girls of sixteen and seventeen years were considered to have crossed their prime. For girls marriage by the age of thirteen or fourteen, and for boys, eighteen was generally preferred.[135]

In imperial families, the marriage of boys and girls were arranged after the age of fifteen.[136] Arjumand Bano Begum was married to Shah Jahan when she was of 19 years 7 months and 25 days.[137] One or two years' seniority of bridegroom from his bride was considered perfect, but disparity in age was also in vogue. Sometimes the husband was ten, sixteen or even nineteen years older than his wife.[138]

It appears that sometimes young men married old wealthy ladies for their wealth. This evil practice spread so much that Akbar issued orders proclaiming such marriages illegal, and annulled when the bride was 12 years older than her husband.[139] With a few exceptions, generally elder children were married before their younger.[140]

Initiation of Marriage Proposal

The initiation of marriage proposal, as such, has been a very important item, for it provides the way to negotiation and settlement. Like today, in the Mughal period also, the main initiation started, obviously, with the parents or guardians concerned, but other people were also connected with it as relatives, friends and intermediaries. In case of a royal family persons related to court and *harem* were sent[141] for the discussion. There was also a class of people known as 'match makers' or match brokers'[142] whose business was to negotiate marriages. In addition, *Qawal*s and eunuchs were also sent for negotiations.[143] But it was regarded a matter of great respect to be asked for the hand of one's daughter, by any lady of the youth's family.[144]

Amongst the Hindus negotiation started from the side of the girl herself but amongst the Muslims it was always started from the boy's side. The right to initiate a marriage by the mates themselves has been approved by Islam, but during that period it was a social custom that usually the boys and girls did not initiate the proposal on their own cases.

Islam prescribes no party to initiate the proposal first though usually the guardian of the boy initiated in this respect,[145] and the guardian of the girl was free to accept or reject the proposal. A marriage proposal from the girl's side was considered to be humiliating or indecent and, with few exceptions,[146] it was always avoided. But now a days this custom has changed because of the socio-cultural influence of the Hindu society and circumstances.

Parties and Procedure in Negotiation

After initiation, negotiations were either started through intermediaries, friends or relatives, and when concurrence was acquired with regard to the settlement, they became very closer and details were discussed accordingly and a day had to be fixed for the final settlement.

Like initiation, in negotiation also participated elderly ladies, close friends and near relatives. Apart from them an unique personality know as 'Mushata'[147] was accustomed to play a great role in the marriage discussions and was paid handsome reward for her services. Marriage relatings were thus established mainly in consultation with the kinsmen of both the parties.

While arranging the marriage, in some cases, the guardians of the bride proposed to keep the daughter and the son-in-law in their own house after the marriage. This system is continuing today also and the bridegroom is called a '*Ghar Damad*'. Mirza Shah Husain, in his old age, asked for the hand of Yadgar Nasir Mirza with the same condition, for his daughter.[148] This practice was especially prevailing in wealthy families and in families having the bride to be the only daughter.

During the Mughal age, in certain cases, matrimonial alliances were settled on a mutual basis when a boy of one family married a girl of the other family and the latter's family married a girl from the former. Such marriage was called '*Golat*' or '*Golawat*'. Same happened in imperial household also. Aurangzeb's daughter Zub-datun-Nisa and his son Mohammad Azam were married to Dara Shukoh's son Siphr Shukoh and daughter Jahan Zeb Banu.[149] Sometimes two sisters were also married to two brothers in the same house. Babur's two daughters Gulrang Begum and Gul Chihra Begum were married to two brothers, Isan Timur Sultan and Tukhta-bugha Sultan on following the same tradition.[150] Also Maham Anaga's two sons, Adam Khan and Baqi Mohammad Khan were married to two daughters of Baqi Khan Baqlani.[151] Aurangzeb and Murad Baksh were also married to Shah Nawaz Khan Safvi's two daughters[152].

Before organising the marriage of their children, some pious people observed 'Istikhara'[153] (application for the favour of God), only after which the negotiation was considered complete. In this ceremony generally the father or mother or any other pious man sought the permission of God about the marriage, scheduled to be held, with the help of *'Tasbih'* (Rosary) or the *Quran* or the slips of paper placing them under the *'Ja Namaz'* (prayer carpet) or by reciting two *'Rakat'* prayers before retiring to rest at night.

Sometimes the verses composed by the poet Hafiz was also consulted as 'Fal' or omen,[154] which was treated as a leading book for many purposes. When the *'Istikhara'* was in super affirmative the marriage was finally settled. Immediately after 'Istikhara' the youth's pedigree or Shijrah was sent to the girl's house by the boy's parents.[155] If the poposal was rejected, the horoscope was returned forthwith immediately received back by the sender as a tacit proof of suitor's rejection. No further explanation was ever given. But in regard to the rejection if the proposal was in affirmative the pedigree was retained at the bride's side for good.

In some families when te pedigree was found to correspond and the parties agreed to the union, astrologers were consulted to predict, destiny of the boy as well as the girl. So horoscopes of the paircast were examined.[156] Finding destiny favourable, an auspicious day was fixed for the betrothal ceremony.

On getting approval from both sides, the ceremony of betrothal was performed accordingly.

Mangni **or Betrothal Ceremony**

'Mangni' was the first contract binding on the bride and bridegroom's parties to accomplish their engagement at an appointed time and period. This ceremony, being an expensive affair, bore different names such as 'Imam Zamim', 'Nisbat', 'Sherbat *Khori* and '*Lahri Bel*' (green creeper). In the ceremony of the mother of the youth, accompanied by his relatives and friends paid a visit to the house of the girl on the appointed date.[157] They carried several *khwans* (trays) full of gifts for the bride and her parents. These gifts contained costly dresses, jewellary, cosmetics, perfumes, betal leaves, fruits and sweets, according to the status of the youth. In royal families, articles worth thousands and lakhs were presented to the girl.

When Sultan Murad's daughter was engaged to prince Parwez,

one lakh thirty thousand rupees with varieties of articles were sent to her.[158] Also for the *mangni* of Shahriyar, with Nur Jahan's daughter Ladly begum, Jahangir sent presents worth rupees one lakh.[159]

When lady guests would reach the bride's house they first entertained them with *Sherbat* followed by refreshment, in accordance with the custom. At the close of the refreshment, lady guests were expected to offer some money as tip, called *'Thal'*[160] or tray.

Now the girl was called to the assembly of lady guests wearing clothes brought from the bridegroom's side. Then they would anoint her hair with perfumed oils and adorned with jewels and jewellery brought from the bridegroom's house. After this, the bride's face was shown to all lady guests who having seen her offered money according to custom on the occasion at first look. Then they would take her *'Balayen'* (evils) on their own temples so as to take away any ill luck of the girl, on their own heads.[161] It was also traditional to place a ring[162] on the forefinger of the girl's right hand which she was expected to wear from that moment onward till her death, being the first present from her husband's house. Following this custom, Jahangir on the *Mangni* ceremony of his son Khurram with Arjumand Banu Begum, placed a ring on the finger of his prospective daughter-in-law.[163]

It was also traditional to feed seven places of sugar candy or sweets to the girl through the hand of the chief lady guests.[164] After the guests had left, the mother of the bride distributed sweets of her son-in-law's house to all the relatives, friends and neighbours.

On expiry of a few days, in return, the parents of the bride used to send clothes, sweets, fruits, ring and other gifts to the bridegroom's house, with the same care and rejoicings[165] on the eve of the betrothal.

During that period, poor people could not afford this expensive ceremony. They performed another ceremony known as 'Imam Zamim'. This ceremony required only sweets and *'Imam Zamim'* a silver or gold coin wrapped in a silken cloth. The mother of the youth among other ladies visited the girl's house and tied the *'Imam Zamim'* round the upper portion of girl's right arm.[166]

Between the engagement and nuptial ceremony gifts were exchanged on every important occasion, by both the bride and bridegroom's houses.[167] In Idul-Fitr, *'Sewai'* with sweets, fruits, clothes and money was exchanged. Similarly in Id-ul-Zuha sheep were offered alongwith other goods. In Muharram, *'badhi'* (necklace of coloured thread) and embroidered *'batwa'* (purse) at *'Akhri-Chahar Shamba'*, sweets and at Shab-e-Barat, bread and 'Halwa' with fire works were exchanged. In order to keep the custom in full force the trays were never returned even without some trifle things.

Even after the fixation of marriage it was not necessary in every case that the marriage could be certainly materialised as agreed upon between the parties. The betrothal ceremony could be broken in case of some dislike expressed even after negotiation by either party for causes not suiting the interests of the bride and the bridegrooms.[168]

Fixation of Marriage Date

Like today, during the Mughal age, generally at the time of engagement, the month and years for the marriage was settled. The Muslims preferred to marry their children in the month of *'Rajab Shaaban'* and after the tenth of 'Idul-Zuha' and in the second half of *'Rabi I'*. Marriages in the month of 'Muharram', 'Safar' and the first eight days of *'Rabi I'* were deemed to be unauspicious.[169] The marriage of Shah Jahan was postponed for two months[170] due to this reason.

Islam imposes no restriction on any one binding him to marry within any particular month of the year. Hence, few marriages were celebrated by the Mughals in the month of 'Muharram' also.[171]

The day of a Muslims marriage was always declared with the first visibility of the moon and generally first and last weeks of a moon were preferred. It was a common practice during those days to consult astrologers.[172] Humayun in his marriage with Hamidah Banu Begum himself took the astrolobe and calculated the auspicious hour for the marriage.[173] Thus the date was being fixed orally or in writing for the marriage celebration.

Announcement of the date of marriage produced delightful atmosphere in both the houses. Women relatives and neighbours assembled in order to sing famous wedding songs to the accompaniment of drum.[174] Thus till the marriage day their afternoon and evening became more entertaining by their jokes, songs and dances.

Like today, during the Mughal age, no invitation cards were used but the invitation of marriage duly written in Persian on red paper was sent to relatives and friends usually through barbers.

Ceremonies Preceding Marriage

Several ceremonies like *'Maniha,'* 'Henabandi,' 'Sachaq' and Baral preceded the actual marriage.

Manjha. Manjha was purely a Hindu ceremony in which *'Butna' (Ubtan)* was rubbed on both bride and bridegroom's bodies in their own houses. This ceremony was celebrated generally eleven, nine, seven, five or at least three days befoe *'Nikah'.* For *'Manjha'* yellow dresses, utensils, oil, sweets and *pindis*[175] were exchanged between the parties.[176] At a fixed date and hour women of the neighbourhood and other female friends and relatives gathered in the houses of both the bride and the bridegroom.

In the bride's house, she was made to sit on a wooden portable platform covered with a red carpet. Ladies assembled and rubbed her body with *'ubtan'*. Her hair was anointed with oil and colliriurn *(Kajal)* was applied to her eyes. Singing continued all the time during the course by the participant ladies. The Muslim ladies took interest in playing with *ubtan* and coloured water.[177] This could be included by the Muslims only due to their long standing harmonial relations between the Hindus and Muslims.

From the *Manjha* till the marriage, the barber's wife in case of the bride, and barber in case of bridegroom, rubbed *'ubtan'* on their bodies twice or thrice a day. When this was over the bride remained confined in a separate room where the entry of male members including father and brothers was strictly forbidden. Similarly, the bridegroom was forbidden to move outside his house. During this period the bride had to eat rice, sweets, milk, fruits, pulse and bread only, to enhance her beauty and restore good health.

Sachaq. Marriage itself embraced several minor observances. *Sachaq* being the first,[178] one. It was a Turkish custom in which wedding presents were sent from bridegroom's party to the bride and her family. Gifts as received were used in course of the *'Nikah'* and *'Chawthi'* periods. Its preparations generally begun just after the fixation of marriage date. To make it incomparable in the bride's house the chief lady friends and relatives prepared and adorned the *sachaq* carefully and skillfully. Other ladies, too, enjoyed themselves with native songs. After completing the preparations, an exhibition[179] of these wedding presents was arranged to show the male and female guests.

According to the custom, two days[180] before *'Nikah' Sachaq* procession started from the bridegroom's house. But in some cases the marriage was celebrated few months after *sachaq* procession.[181] This procession generally started in the evening, accompanied with music and drumming.[182] Torch bearers also joined the great procession to light to roads. In this procession, the male relatives, friends and the father of the bridegroom undertook the journey on horseback, elephants and in palanquins. Ladies also attend the parade in covered and decorated conveyances. On the marriage of Dara Shukoh ladies of the royal household—the mother, sisters and paternal aunts of Mumtaz Mahal went to bride's house with *Sachaq.*[183]

Sachaq was sent in golden, silver or ornamented wooden *khwans* (large trays) covered with gorgeous wrappings through richly dressed servants and slaves alongwith the procession.[184]

Sachaq included[185] articles like gold, embroidered dresses, jewelleries, *suhag chura* (make up goods), perfumes, betel leaves in gold and silver foil, garlands, dried fruits, sweetmeats, 'Nuqals' (a variety of sweet meat) etc. compulsarily. Besides these, money was also sent to the bride according to the status of the bridegroom's family. Khafi Khan writes that Shah Jahan sent one lakh and sixty thousand rupees including other gifts as *sachaq* to the daugther of Shah Nawaz Khan who was betrothed with Aurangzeb.[186] Jhan Zeb Bahu Begum, daughter of Dara also got the same amount in sachaq from Aurangzeb as she was betrothed with his son Mohammad Azam.[187] Thus, in royal families the cost of *sachaq*[188] generally reached thousands and lakhs which was impossible for the then other classes of Muslim society. But yet the parents or guardians of the bridegroom always cared to send expensive *sachaq* as far as possible suiting their financial position.

As soon as the *sachaq* procession arrived within hail of the bride's village or *Mohallah*, the people awaiting them, welcomed and conducted them to the bride's house. The *sachaq* was then received and welcomed by the bride's party and taken into the female apartment where ladies watched them with critical eyes keenly and with great interest.

In the bride's house, as a custom, *'sherbat'* was served first to all the guests from the bridegroom's side.[189] There the guests enjoyed music and dancing parties, especially arranged for this occasion. After a few hours of merry rich dishes were served then in male as well as female apartments. At last, after taking dinner, the procession returned at night.[190]

In poor families guests were generally served with *'Sherbat'*, *'pan'* (betel) and sweets on the occasion. From the day of *sachaq* the bride and the bridegroom were designated with various names such as *'Dulhan'* and *'Dulha'*, *Nawshih* (New Empress) and *'Nawshah'* (New Emperor), *'Bani'* (Bride) and *'Bana'* (Bridegroom).

Hena Bandi. *'Hena Bandi'*, an Arabic custom, was the next stage of a Muslim marriage. In this ceremony the hands and feet of the bride and bridegroom were dyed in their own houses, with *'hena'* (Mehandi). As it was performed in the night it was also called Night of *Mehandi*.[191] For the bride *Mehandi* was sent from the bridegroom's family on the day of *Sachaq,* while for the bridegroom from the opposite concerned party on the eve of *'Hena Bandi'*.[192] Hena with other goods was sent to the bridegroom in a stately procession,[193] one day before the marriage.[194]

The procession started in the evening with several guests. Male guests seated on horse back, elephants or in open carriages, and the ladies in covered litters.[195]

Like a *Barat* party mace bearers and retainers walked on either side of the procession. Torch lights and a band of music also accompanied them to light the dark streets making the environment happy. With the procession there was also a representation made of cotton, satin and paper in the form of ships or boats ornamented with tinsel of different shades of flowers.[196]

Also, to promote pump and grandeur of the procession there was an enchanting display of fireworks.[197]

This procession contained several gold or silver *'Khwans'* with *'hena',* a magnificent suit for the bridegroom, goods of toilet, sweets, dried fruits, betel leaves in gold or silver foil, sugar candy, strings of flowers, scents and fire-works hidden in flowers formed in the transparent ubreck[198] (mica).

In Imperial families, besides these trays, several trays of costly dresses and jewels covered with beautiful costly *khwanposh* (wrappings) for all members of the family were sent.[199]

When the *mehandi* procession reached the bridegroom's

house, the ships and boats they had brought with them were put on the roof. New mirth prevailed in young ones of both parties who wanted to snatch these ships and boats for the sake of fun. In the efforts, as a result usually it soon fell to pieces, which amused all.[200] After that the guests took their seats in their respective assemblies and were served *sherbat,* betel, cardamoms and dried fruits etc.

After refreshment the ladies from the bride's side requested to bring the bridegroom to their assembly duly dressed in expensive clothes (brought from the bride's house). Then he was brought to female apartment and assigned a proper seat.[201] Due to *Pardah* system all the lady guests of the bride's party remained behind the curtain, very near to the seat of the bridegroom,. Really it was a crucial time for the bridegroom who was expected to obey various commands, received showers like from the women behind very near to the seat of the bridegroom. Really it was a crucial time for the bridegroom who was expected to obey commands, received shower like from the women behind the curtain with child-like docility. Grinded Mehandi was applied to the hands and feet of the bridegroom,[202] and tied with red bandages of gold embroidered cloth. They also sprinkled, scents over the bridegroom. But all was done behind *purdah.*

Then the sister of the bridegroom arriving there would put a piece of sweet in his mouth, wishing him happy married life. Soon other ladies of near relation followed this custom.[203]

To entertain the bridegroom and themselves, the ladies observed another interesting custom. In this custom, small pieces of sugarcandy were presented before the bridegroom. Thinking it a sign of good luck (as it was from his bride's house) he made great efforts to eat it up. But due to *hena* he could not use his hands. So the ladies tantalised him by bringing a lump of sugar candy near his mouth and suddenly withdrew it just when he opened his mouth or tried to snap at it. Thus the futile efforts amused all the ladies.[204]

To fix the dye bright and permanent on the hands and feet of the bridegroom at least one hour was required. Therefore, during this period the lady singers of both sides[205] started to sing appreciating their bride and the bridegroom. Such competition of songs and their dances greatly entertained the guests.[206] Fingers of the lady guests were also dyed with hena.[207]

After an hour the bridegroom's hands and feet were washed off with rose water.[208] Moreover, as a sign of confirmation, the bridegroom had to drink a glass of water according to the custom. If he refused, the ladies made strong arguments, besides oaths, and pressed him to drink the desired glass of water so that he would be frantically enamoured of his bride.[209]

On *'hena bandi'* ceremony offerings *(Nuzzas)* were presented to the bridegroom by the guests. At last, wearing the flower garland, he would return to his male apartment, where he was embraced and greeted by his friends. The guets also, after enjoying the banquet, would depart at night,[210] with suitable gifts presented to them.

***Barat* (Marriage Procession).** The most dominant procession connected with marriage was *'barat'* for which invited guests started to assemble in the bridegroom's house a few hours before the fixed time. On that day no one was expected to come empty hand and they carried *'Kishti'*[211] *(Khwans)* full of presents with them there. All guests were welcomed and encouraged to amuse themselves with Pan, *'huqqa', 'sherbat'* and music notes till the appointed hour for setting out of the *barat* procession.

The bridegroom after taking his bath dressed himself in wedding suit either of red[212] of saffron colour.[213] To enhance his beauty *'afshan'* (tinsel) was applied on his cheeks, *'missi'* (dentrifice) on his teeth and *'surma'* (antimony) on his eyes. Costly perfumes were also sprinkled over his garments. A turban was tied on his head in 'Raja Shahi' style, only by an old man of his family having wife alive. The old man first twisted the turban two or three times round his own head (signifying that the bride and the bridegroom might enjoy long and happy married life, like him) and then tied the turban on the bridegroom's head with attractive garland flowers.[214] He had also to wear *'sehra'* (chaplet) on his forehead, covering the eyes like a veil falling down upto his chest or waist.[215] Generally, it was prepared with flowers, but in imperial families it was made of gold, silver, pearls, emeralds, rubies and diamonds.[216] Among commoners the brother-in-law tied *'sehra'* on the bridegroom's forehead and received some cash from the family elders. The amount received thus was also shared by other brothers-in-law. But on the contrary, in royal families, it was a custom and the father of the bridegroom tied *sehra* on his son's forehead. Following this practice Jahangir tied a *'sehra'* on Shah Jahan's forehead and

Shah Jahan tied it to Dara[217] and Aurangzeb,[218] their sons, and Aurangzeb too tied it to prince Mohammad Sultan.[219] *'Sehra'* was quite unknown in Islamic countries and was originated in Indian soil and adopted by the Muslims at a later stage. Over *'sehra'*, a *dupatta* of thin cloth known as *Maqna* was worn over the turban which hung down the waist of the bridegroom, to protect him from the evil eye.[220] After wearing *'sehra'* and *'Maqna'* the bridegroom saluted his parents called *'Taslimat-i-Sehra'* which entitled him to receive gifts from his elders. Aurangzeb's son Mohammad Muazzam, on his marriage with the daughter of Roop Singh, got one lakh rupees with several elephants and horses for solution of *'sehra'* from Aurangzeb.[221] Before departure of *'Barat'* the tutor of the youth, the family barber, sweeper, gardener, washerman, tailor and household servants were rewarded suitably with money and clothes to mark the auspicious occasion. Relatives and friends also got dresses from the bridegroom's parents. The poor and needy persons were also offered gifts. When prince Shuja was married to the daughter of the Rustum Mirza Safvi, relatives, friends and the needy received gifts of several lakhs.[222]

After making 'Nishar' (showering of money) on the bridegroom the 'barat' proceeded to the bride's house. Unless the distance between the two houses was very great, all the men attending, walked on foot except the bridegroom who alone rode on a well decorated[223] horse or elephant's back.[224] Sometimes, an umbrella prepared by flowers or papers ornamented with mica, was twirled round his head. The ladies followed either in close carriages or palanquins richly decorated and closely curtained.[225] Similarly, the ladies of Akbar's *harem*, in Jahangir's *barat'*, visited the house of *Raja* Uday singh as his daughter was going to be married to Jahangir.[226] In the *barat* elephants, camels, floral troples, umbrellas and banners of painted papers[227] were requisitioned from wherever possible to add to its pomp and grandeur. A blaze of torch lights brightened the streets and a group of musicians led the procession.[228] Thus women, singing and dancing and men playing upon elephants and camels, making a great noise, followed the *barat.*[229] Various kinds of bombs and fireworks were also let off to enhance its pomp.[230] If the procession had to pass through a town, it perambulated gradually[231] through all its streets, rather than taking a direct course.

On the way to his destination, in some families, the bridegroom had to visit the shrine of a well-known saint.[232] Like today, before reaching the bride's house the bridegroom offered two *'Rakats'* prayer in a mosque[233] falling on the way. As the *'barat'* reached the bride side offered a ceremonial welcome to the *'baraties'*.

The entry of the bridegroom at the bride's door was greeted by a fun of resistance, made by the bride's party. They stopped him and his men with bamboo, oranges, lemons, eggs, plants, turnips, radishes and many other things, till the bridegroom paid some money as an entrance fee.[234] In the house, ladies again presented him with garlanded rods.[235] When the fun was over, hearty welcome was paid to all. As a mark of respect, the bridegroom was helped to dismount and was carried in on some one's back and was offered, like today, a glass of milk or *'sherbat'* as a sign of making his married life sweet.

The guests were ushered inside and were served *'sherbat'*[236] and 'pan'. With the Hindu influence, on this occasion, the dominies (household dancing girls) recited satirical and facetious songs relating to the guests and relatives of the bridegroom,[237] thus to entertain the listeners. They also cracked jokes at the cost of *'samdhans'* (close female motherly relatives of the bridegroom). In the femle apartment, a recreation of music and dance of dominies was organised.[238] Thus, till the *'Nikah'* ceremony, both men and ladies in their own apartments enjoyed singing, dancing and other pastimes, but the bridegroom had to sit silent[239] covering his mouth with the help of a handkerchief,[240] as today.

Ceremonies During the Performance of Marriage

Several ceremonies were observed during the marriage including the *'Nikah'*, *'Arsi Mushaf'*, 'Robbery of bridegroom's shoes', *'Salami'*, *'Jalwa'*, *'Nabat chunna'*, *'Rukhsati'*, *'Kheer Chatai'* and *'Ru-numai'*.

Nikah Ceremony. The most important ceremony concerning marriage was *'Nikah'*, the celebration of the marriage contract. By this *Nikah* ceremony Islam seeks the permission of both the bride and the bridegroom without which the marriage is null and void in accordance with the principles prescribed by the religion.

During this period, *Nikah* ceremony was performed mostly by one *Qazi*,[241] in presence of at least two witnesses as per the instructions of Islam, to prove that a man and a woman had entered into marriage contract. In the marriage of Jahan Zeb Banu Begum with prince Mohammed Azam, *Qazi* Abdul Wahab tied the knot in the presence of two witnesses—Mulla Auz Akhsikhti and Shaikh Saifullah Sirhindi.[242]

In upper India the father of the bride was not expected to be present at the time of *Nikah.*[243]

Dower or Mehar

Without dower or Mehar, which was considered an essential ingredient Muslim marriage, marriage is not legalised in Islam. Dower means a certain sum of money paid by the bridegroom to the bride immediately after *'Nikah'*. This system is an ancient custom traced back to the pre-Islamic days in Arab, where a cost for a bride was paid at the time of marriage. When the seed of Islam germinated and developed fully. In Arabia, this custom, continued altogether and a legal right over this was permitted, and it was made mandatory for legalising marriages. During the Mughal age, like today, the amount of *mahr* was fixed by mutual agreement of the couple concerned, but practically the guardians considered it their duty to settle the sum and the couple were informed of it for getting their final permission, and it was communicated to the religioius heads (Qazi) prior to reciting Nikah.

Islam has not fixed any amount of dower as the only object is to make the wife economically and financially sound so that she may not find herself helpless as against her husband, and feel confident enough to defend her rights. However, according to Islam the amount of dower should conform to the financial position of the bridegroom, but practically, during the Mughal age, it never generally matched the means of the bridegroom, chiefly due to the family status, customs and as a safeguard against divorce. It was, therefore, also interpreted as a mark of respect given to the bride.

Among royalty and nobility, the fixation of very high dower was customary which, usually, was according to the status of the bride's families. Jahangir while marrying Mehrun Nisa, assigned eighty lakhs of *asharfis* of five misqals, having the value of 7 crores and 20 lakhs of rupees. In Shahjahan's marriage with Arjumand Bano Begum, the dower was fixed at Rs. 5 lakhs. Similarly, in Dara's marriage with Sultan Parwez's daughter, Nadira Bano Begum, *Mehar* was 5 lakhs of rupees.

In Aurangzeb's marriage with Dil-ras-Bano Begum, daughter of Shah Nawaz Khan Safvi, the *Mehar* was 4 lakhs of rupees.

Even among commoners also it was the custom to fix a handsome amount as dower as to check the possibilities of divorces in society by high dowers. Emperor Akbar also supported the same idea. High dowers were also preferred by the Muslims because in case of unwarranted divorce, the wife could pass her life comfortably. With the amount she got in lieu of her *Mehar*. Islamic rules entitle a divorced wife to get the entire amount of dower fixed at the time of *Nikah.* Following this Islamic injunction, Ali Khan, the ruler of Kashmir, following his daughter's divorce, demanded her dower. The custom of fixing heavy *mehar,* generally, beyond the husband's means, seems to be based upon the intention of refraining the husband from ill treating his wife, and, above all, from his marrying another woman.

Though high dowers were preferred, people generally, were incapable of paying the large amount fixed, either at the time of *Nikah* or afterwards. In India, the dower remains unpaid, and so like an on-demand obligation remained due at all times and the wife's right to the same not being fulfilled by lapse time. Therefore, a wise emperor Akbar disapproved of high dowers. Among poor Muslims, high dowers could not be fixed and so they generally settled dowers as per the resources of the bridegroom. Islam does provide no measures against low dower, and hence there is permission to accept even low dower, but its minimum is never less than ten dirhams. Keeping in view the needs of the poor, Prophet Mohammad set an example himself by demanding a small amount from his son-in-law, Hazrat Ali, for his daughter Bibi Fatima Zohra, which is now equal to Rs. 1,100 only. The smallest dower amount, as accepted by the Prophet Mohammad, termed as *Sharayee Mehar* or *Mehar Fatimi,* is considered to be very auspicious by all the Muslims. In the early period of Islam, it was commonly followed. With increase in wealth and standard of living it began to rise, and so the customary dower prevailed over Sharayee dower. Therefore, during this period, dower used mostly to be in crores, lakhs and thousands of rupees, and till it is in lakhs and generally in thousands, with the exception, however of very poor people.

The amount of dower could be paid immediately after *Nikah* or at any time thereafter. In fact, dower was the first claim of a wife over the husband's property and a debt a husband owing to his wife. The wife also could claim it at any time in her life time. Among royalty and nobility generally the amount was paid at the time of the contract was entered into and was known as *Mehar Muajjal* or prompt dower. But the dower remained unpaid at the time of *Nikah,* was called *Mehar Muwajjal* or deferred dower, and could be demanded at anytime by the wife. The husband could also pay it whenever he liked. Thus, the payment of dower was binding even after divorce or on the death of either party.

In case of deferred dower, the wife generally was free to forego the amount, either at the time of her death or at the husband's or during his life time but it was, very rare. In the event of the death of the husband, the payment of the *mehar* has the first claim on the estate after funeral expenses, the law regarded it as a just debt. Therefore, during the Mughal period, a lady after her husband's death also could claim her dower, if she so desired. In case the wife died, her successors might claim the dower from the husband.

Thus, *Mehar* was of prime importance in a Muslim marriage and not a price for the bride but a mark of respect for her. It was also a preliminary provision and a primary condition, safeguarding her future up-keep in life.

After getting the bride's approval, the *Qazi* returned to male apartment and asked three times, one by one, from the bridegroom in the earlier manner whether he accepted the lady concerned as his wife with such and such amount of *Mehr* as settled and he also replied in the affirmative. On having been satisfied that both the bride and the bridegroom had agreed upon, the *Qazi* recited the religious discourse as per religious rule known as *'Khutbai-Nakah.'*[244] Afterwards, the witnesses signed on the *'Nikah Namah'*[245] (marriage deeds). The *Qazi* and all the guests prayed for the happy and prosperous married life of the newly wedded couple.[246] After the prayer was over, the relatives and friends congratulated[247] the couple and their guardians or parents. On completion of *Nikah,* the people made a display of fire works token of happness.[248]

After 'Nikah' the bride wept or was supposed to weep, thinking that she had now formally and legally passed into another family being no more a part of her parental home or even master of herself.

Consequently, therefore, the mother and sister of the bride and other near relatives wept with the bride. During the Mughal age, after the *'Nikah'*, money was showered as *Nisar* over the married pair. In imperial families, gold and silver coins and diamonds were showered. When Arjumand Banu Begum was married to Shah Jahan, diamond was showered on Nisar.[249] Similarly, in Dara's marriage with Nadira Begum, gold and silver coins were showered.[250]

Like today, on this rapturous occasion, poets would recite 'Sehra' (a sort of poetry) in praise of the married couple and their families.[251] Thereafter, dried dates, sugar candy and *'Nuqals'* were showered which ensured a tussle between the younger generation of both the parties because every one tried to get as much of it as possible amusing the guests thereby.

At the close of this tussle, the *'baraties'* were first entertained at dinner[252] and then relatives, friends and the neighbours of the bride's family were fed. The poor and needy were also not neglected altogether.

To mark this auspicious hour, in royal families *'Khilats'* with other gifts were distributed amongst the relatives, friends, Amirs and Nobles. *'Zarbaft'* and *'Deeba'* were distributed to all and sundry in Khuram's marriage with Arjumand Banu Begum.[253] Sometimes people preferred to tie the marriage knot *(Nikah)* in a mosque.[254] *Nikah* of prince Mohammad Azam, Mohammad Akbar, Mohammad Sultan, Siphr Shukoh and Mura Bakhsh's daughter were performed in mosques.[255]

After Nikah other important ceremonies were observed during the period under review which are given below separately.

Salami and Stealing of Bridegroom's Shoes. The bridegroom was called in the female apartment after *Nikah* for the *taslim* or salutation.[256] After the *taslim/*salutation to the ladies, he was seated there in the room, and for the first time, all ladies assembled before him unveiled with the conception that *purdah* before a king (Shah) and a bridegroom (Newshah) was not needed. On having a look to the bridegroom all offered him either money or gifts or both known as *'salami'*.[257] Provision was also made for music and native songs.[258] In the meantime, the sisters of the bride concealed bridegrooms shoes secretry.[259] It was a custom, just for the sake of fun, and the shoes were restored only when he paid some cash or present to the holder(s).

Salami was followed by another ceremony known as 'Arsi Mushaf'

Ceremonies After Marriage

Arsi Mushat.[260] In this ceremony the birdegroom, for the first time, saw his bride's face with the help of a mirror. For divine blessings for the couple, of course, the *Quran* was also placed there alongwith the mirror. Now, a candle was held under the shawl spread over the heads of the pair as a shield. The bridegroom was permitted to see the face of his bride thereafter through the mirror in privacy, though the ceremony took place publicly. Now, the veil of the bride was removed from her face. It was very critical time for the bride, who kept her eyes constantly closed. The bridegroom was asked to say, "O my dear wife, open your eyes", and on insistence of others, she had just a look at the face of her bridegroom through the mirror, as the shawl was not removed as long as this custom was observed altogether. When it was over, the bridegroom was asked to write 'Sura-I-Ikhlas (a Holi verse of the *quran*) on the forehead of his bride with his right and pointer finger *(Kalme-ki-ungli)*. With this, the ceremony concluded and *'Jalwa'* started.

Jalwa.[261] *Jalwa* ceremony (face displaying ceremony of the bride) commonly held in her own house, was adopted from the Hindus.[262] In this ceremony, the couple were allowed to take their seats opposite each other, and a red screen hung between them. Now the *Mushata* (tire-woman) holding the bride's *'sehra'* (flowery veil) would start singing a special song for such occasion. At the close of the song, she tied the *sehra* on the bride's forehead. The Mushata after his, holding a piece of string, put it with some raw rice in the bride's hand, helped her in throwing it over the curtain leading to her husband's head. On the opposite side, the bridegroom's sister tied a ring to the end of the special thread and put the same with some raw rice in her brother's hand, made him throw these over the curtain where the bride was seated. The ring was thrown backwards and forwards thrice amusing the ladies and the children greatly. Songs continued all along in the midst. Before *Rukhsati* (departure), another cermony known as *'nabat chunna'* was performed.

Nabat Chunna.[263] In this ceremony, in the presence of the bride and the bridegroom, the *'mushata'* put a piece of sugar candy *(nabat)* on the bride's head and ordered the bridegroom to pick it up with the help of his lips. This was repeated twice, by keeping *'nabat'* on the bride's shoulder, knees and feet. Eventually, instead of taking the sugar candy in his mouth, he tried to do with his left hand and then, finally, he had to take it up with his right hand. Now the *'mushata'* taking hold of the couple's heads, moved backwards and forwards twice or thrice. Thus, the ceremony added extra mirth and joy among the ladies.

Rukhsati. Like today the bride's departure from her parental home generally took place on the next morning[264] called *'rukhsati'*. The parents or guardians of the bride despatched a number of articles for the use of their daughter and son-in-law in the form of dowry *(Jahez)* at the time of *'rukhsati'.* These articles generally consisted of dresses, ornaments, furniture, utensils etc. In imperial families, vessels of gold and silver cards of horses, elephants and even girl friends of the princesses were sent as dowry.[265] The bride of the royal household brought heavy dowries worth rupees several lakhs.[266] People, in general, provided heavy dowries, which were beyond their means, these things were exhibited to all the guests first and packed up finally.

Now the bride and the bridegroom, with *'barat'* party were made ready to depart. Finally, after some picturesque ceremonies and humorous and lively songs, the bridegroom took his bride in his arms[267] and brought her in the palanquin. The bride at the time of her departure, was instructed by her parents regarding her duties and responsibilities of a married life so as to follow them for cordial relationship with all concerned at her husband's house.[268] They also instructed and advised the bridegroom, and pleaded him to keep their daughter happy. Every one wept, and thus, the bride took leave from her parental roof, with a heavy heart and tearful eyes. In royal families, gold was showered on the bride's palanquin as soon as it started its journey.

When the houses of the bride and the bridegroom happened to be near, the dowry was sent usually before the bride's departure[269] and arranged in the bridegroom's house prior to their reaching. As soon as the *barat* party reached near the residence of the bridegroom, the neighbours threw rose water and other sweet perfumed water upon the bride and the bridegroom.[270] The sisters of the bridegroom, accompanied by other ladies, temporarily resisted the entry of bride and the bridegroom. They demanded their fee and let them enter the house only after getting the desired money.

Khurram on this marriage with Arjumand Banu Begum gave jewellery to the Begums and other ladies of his house too.[271]

As soon as the bride entered her husband's house, her feet were washed in a basin and the water was sprinkled in all corners of the house for retaining prosperity.[272] As the bride remained still under veil, another Turkish ceremony was observed for unveiling the bride. According to this, a child was told to pluck off the bride's *purdah* and run away. Babar says that when he was five years old, he was told to uncover the veil of Khanzada Begum who was then married to Sultan Ahmad. There was a firm belief that this led to the child's own successful marriage.[273] It was known as *'burka koshan'*.[274]

For the first time in her husband's house, the bride was served a sweet dish requesting to eat it up. She also received presents from her mother-in-law in course of it. The bridegroom generally offered two *rekat* prayer as *shukrana* (thanks) to God, on achievement of something. On the *dupatta* of his bride itself as per custom[275] runumai (face showing ceremony) would begin only after the *rukhsati* was over.

Ru-Numai[276] **(Face-showing Ceremony).** In this ceremony the male members of the family, close relatives and the male friends of the bridegroom were entitled to see the bride's face for the first time. On having seen her face, they would present her jewellary, money and other gifts, regarded as the personal property of the bride. Following this Islamic custom,[277] Jahangir gifted the bride of his son, Sultan Parwez, one lakh fifty thousand rupees.[278] Aurangzeb also presented jewels worth rupees one lakh to his son Mohammad Muzzam's bride (daughter of Roop Singh) on her *runumai*[279].

***Walimah* (Marriage Feast).** *Walimah* was the nuptial feast involving religious significance. In all Islamic countries the Muslims consider the feast as *'sunnah'* attached with Mohammad himself, who performed it once the marriage with Sufiyah-un-Salma and Zainab.[280] Regarding this reception as a divine authority he commanded, one must accept the invitation when invited on such an occasion". Therefore, during the Mughal period this reception was arranged on wide scale by the parents or guardians of the bridegroom at their place,[281] generally on the next day of 'rukhsati.[282] But in some exceptional cases it was observed after a few days of the marriage. When Hindal was married to Sultanam Begum, his marriage feast was postponed due to the death of Maham Begum (Babar's wife) who had adopted him. But later on it was performed by the order of Humayun.[283]

In royal families, 'tu-i-shadi' (marriage feast) was celebrated with great pomp and show.[284] The whole city was decorated and illuminated on this occasion. Music and dancing parties were also arranged with great enthusiasm. Different kinds of fireworkers were also displayed. Relatives and courtiers attending the feast were honoured with gifts. At the marriage feast of *Khurram,* Jahangir presented *'Khilats'* (robes) to his Nobles.[285] Rich dishes were prepared and served to all the guests in their honour. Jahangir, in his memoires, writes about the marriage reception of prince Parwez, "All who were present were exalted with all kinds of honour and civilities.[286] During the Mughal age, for the welfare of the newly married couple alms were distributed. In prince Parwez's 'Walima' nine thousand rupees were given to Sharif Amuli to distribute amongst the poor people.[287] In view of the Prophet Mohammad's advice, "The worst of feasts are marriage feasts to which the rich are invited and poor left out".

On the day of 'walima', the bride's parents, guardians and relatives were particularly invited, who always visited their duaghter's conjugal home with various presents, both for the daughter and son-in-law.[288]

Chowthi.[289] *Chowthi* was the last of the ceremonies of a Muslim marriage. It celebrated on the fourth day after the marriage, counted the day of the arrival of the bride and the bridegroom, at the latter's house. Both, after taking their bath, put on their dresses, especially made for that occasion. On the eve of *chowthi* people from the bride's house visited the bridegroom's house to take back their daughter with them. Then, there, the *chowthi* was played. At this ceremony, the couple was seated opposite to each other, and a friend of the bride put some vegetables and fruits in the hands of the bride, and then, holding her wrists, threw them in the lap of the bridegroom. The bridegroom, too, repeated the same in the similar manner. Then the young ones from both sides divided themselves into two opposite groups and made competitions with fruits and vegetables, which ended only by the interference of the elderly ladies. Also, on this occasion, ladies of both the parties played with coloured water sprinkling on one another. After feasting, the bride returned to her father's house alongwith her husband.

The bridegroom, generally, stayed in his father-in-law's house for about nine or ten days according to the tradition and this period was called *'ayyam urusi'*[290] (days after marriage).

Chalas.[291] Feast arrnaged by the close relatives, especially from the bride's side to the newly married couple, was called 'chalas'. The brothers, married sisters, uncles and aunts invited separately the pair to their houses, recreated them with banquets, and presented gifts to ensure close intimacy with one and all.

References

1. Refer to Humayun Namah for Maham Begum's great longing and desires to see a son of Humayun. Gulbadan Begum, *Humayun Namah,* Parsian, edited by Mrs. A.S. Beveridge (India, 1972), p. 27.
2. Niccolo Manucci, *Storia Do Mogor,* Vol. II Tr. by W. Irvine, Indian Test Series, (London, 1907), p. 11.
3. *Diwan-I-Talib Amuli,* Persian, MS. Buhar collection, National Library, Calcutta, p. 53: Also Abul Fazl, *Akbar Namah,* pers Text. Bibliotheca indica, Vol. II, pp. 350-351; Also Nizamuddin Ahmad, *Tabqat-i-Akbari,* Eng. Tr. by B.De. Pub. by A.S.B. (Calcutta, 1936) pp. 358, 361; Also Khafi Khan, *Muntakhab-ul-Lubab,* Vol. I. Urdu translation by Mahmud Ahmad Farqui, First edition (Karachi, 1963), p. 257.
4. Bikram Jit Hasrat, *Dara Shukoh, Life and Works,* First Published (Allahabad, 1953), pp. 1-2.
5. Manucci, *Storia Do Mogor,* Vol. II, p. 343.
6. *Akhbarat* (Aurangzeb's reign) 28, Rabi 11 and 1st Jamda 11, 8th R.Y. 25, Rabi 1, 38, R.Y.
7. On the birth of one of her sons, Mumtaz Mahal was presented Seem-o-Zar (gold and silver), Qazwini, *Padshah Namah,* Pers MS No. 69.
   Buhar Collection, N.L. Calcutta, p. 126; Jahangir says that he presented Mumtaz Mahal 40 thousand rupees *Tuzuk-i-Jahangiri,* Pers. Text, Nawal Kishore Press, Lucknow, p. 287.
8. Shah Nawaz Khan, *Massir-ul-Umarah,* Eng Tr. by H. Beveridge, First reprint (Patna, 1979) Vol. II, part II, p. 687.
9. *Babar Namah,* Eng. Tr. by Mrs. Beveridge (London, 1921). Vol. I, p. 374.
10. Abul Fazl, *Akbar Namah,* Persian Text. Vol. I, p. 43; Also Eng. Tr. by H. Bev. First Indian reprint 1972 Vol. I, p. 129.

11. On her birth Jahan Ara was brought to Jahangir in the male apartment. Qazwini, *Padshah Namah,* MS, p. 15.
12. Thomas Patric Hughes, *A Dictionary of Islam* (1973), p. 50.
13. *Mishkat,* Book XVIII, Chapt. IV, p. 2.
14. Mohammad Umar, *Hindustani Tahzeeb K Mussalmano Par Asar* (Urdu) (Delhi, 1975), p. 126.
15. Jafar Sherif, *Qanun-i-Islam,* Tr. by Herklots, revised and rearranged by W. Crooke (1972) p. 25; also Hughes' *A Dictionary of Islam,* p. 50.
16. *Mishkat,* Book XVIII, Chapt. IV, p. 1; also *Muslim, Bokhari,* Tr. by Mirza Heyat, in Urdu, pp. 127-128.
17. Abul Fazl, *Ain-I-Akbari,* Vol. III, Tr. by H.S. Jarett, Pub. by A.S.B., 1894, p. 136.
18. Abul Fazl, *Akbar Namah,* Pers. Vol. I, p. 43; also Tr. by H. Bev. (1972), p. 129; see also F.n. 8 pp. 129-130.
19. Jafar Sharif, *Qanun-i-Islam,* Tr. by Herklots, revised and rearrangement by W. Crooke, p. 36.
20. Frederick Augustus, *The Emperor Akbar,* Vol. I, Tr. and edited by A.S. Beveridge (1973), p. 54.
21. *Tuzk-i-Jahangiri,* Tr. by A Rogers, edited by H. Beveridge (Second edition, Delhi, 1968), p. 36.
22. Qazwini, *Padshan Namah* Pers., M.S. p. 46; also Lahori, *Badshah Namah,* Persian Text, edited by Kabir, Bibiotheca Indica (Calcutta, 1867) Vol. II, 254.
23. When Aurangzeb was born, Jahangir distributed one thousand Ashrafi as Nazr Qazwini, *Padshah Namah,* M.S. p. 59; On the birth of Mohammad Sultan, Shahjahan offered in *Nazrana* thirty thousand Ashrafi, diamonds of worth rupees 6 lakhs and fifty elephants. Khafi Khan, *Muntakhab-ul-Lubab,* Tr. (Urdu), Vol. II., p. 157; In the birth of Sapahar Shikoh one thousand Mehr was distributed as alms (Nazr), Abdul Hamid Lahori, *Badshah Namah.* Persian Text, Vol. II, p. 388; also Abul Fazl, *Akbar Namah,* Vol. I, Tr. Bev. pp. 609-635.
24. Qazwini, *Padshah Namah,* M.S. p. 59; Manucci, Storia Do Mogor, Vol. II, Tr. p. 343, also F. Augustus *The Emperor Akbar,* Vol. I, p. 53.
25. Gulbadan Begum, *Humayun Namah,* Tr. by A.S. Bev. Introduction p. 143. it says that hearing the news of the birth Kamran's son Al-Aman, Babar sent congratulatory gifts; also *Manuccl Storia,* Vol. II, Tr. p. 343; and Vol. III, *Ibid,* p. 105.
26. Gulbadan Begum says that on the birth of Akbar, when Tardi Mohammad Khan informed Humayun, he became so happy that by way of reward and *Nisar,* for the tidings, that he forgave all so ever of Tardi's past offences. *Humayun Namah,* Pers. p. 59; also

Tr. Bev. p. 158; Abul Fazl gives Mehtar Sumbul's name in place of Tardi Mohammad Khan. Akbar Namah, Vol. II, Pers. p. 20; when Mah Jujak gave birth to a son Md. Hakim, Shah Wali brought this news to Humayun. Hearing the news of the birth of a son, Humayun rewarded Shah Wali for this news, with the title of Sultan. *Akbar Namah,* Vol. I, Tr. p. 609.

27. Gulbadan Begum, *Humayun Namah,* painting to face pages 160 and 162.
28. Abul Fazl, *Akbar Namah,* persian Text Vol. I, p. 47.; also Vol. II Tr. by (Bev) pp. 357, 515; Qazwini, *Padshah Namah,* MS p. 49.
29. Gulbadan Begum, Humayun Namah, Persian, p. 27. It says that when Humayun's two wives Bega Begum and Mawa Jan were expectant, Maham Begum, Humayun's mother prepared fruits of gold and silver.
30. Abul Fazl, *Ain-i-Akbari* Tr. (Blochmann) 1965, second edition, p. 338; see also *Akbar Nama,* Tr. (Bev.) Vol. I, p. 134; also V.A. Smith, *Akbar the Great,* p. 20; also Elliot and Dowson, Vol. V. p. 231.
31. *Quran:* Book II, Surah Baqr.
32. Mutamid Khan, *Iqbal Nama-i-Jahangiri,* Urdu Translation by Md. Zakariya Mail (Karachi, 1963). Second edition. p. 63.
33. *Quran:* Book II, Surah Baqr, I.
34. Mir Hassan, *Masnavi Mir Hasan* (Urdu), Pub. by Pustak Bhandar, Patna, p. 30.
35. Qazwini refers to Jahanara's naming on the day of her birth, *Badshah Namah,* Persian M.S. p. 40; For naming on the day of birth see also Manucci, Storia, Vol. II, Tr. (Irvine) p. 343.
36. Muslim, Bokhari, Urdu translation, pp. 127-128.
37. Mumtaz Mahal's first daughter was named by Jahangir Ra-Hurun-Nisa Begum. Jahan Ara received her name by her grandfather Jahangir. *Qazwini, Badshah Namah,* M.S. pp. 31-40; see also Mutamid Khan, *Shahjahan Namah* Pers. MS No. 74 Buhar collection N.L. Cal., p. 15; also G. Yazdani, "Jahan Ara" *Journal of Punjab Historical Society,* Vol. X, p. 1; also Iqbal *Nama-i-Jahangiri* (Urdu) p. 78; also for naming Parhez Bano Begum by Jahangir refer to Iqbal, *Nama-i-Jahangiri* (Urdu) p. 58; also Khafi Khan, *Muntakhab-ul-ubab* Tr. (Urdu), Vol. II, p. 93; It says that when a daughter was born to Shuja, Shah Jahan gave her the name Dil Pazeer Bano Begum; also Lahori, *Badshah Nama,* Persian Text, Vol. II, p. 2, refers to the naming of Zinat-un-Nisa (Aurangzeb's daughter) by Shahjahan.
38. Gulbadan Begum, *Humayun Namah,* Tr. (Bev.) p. 92.
39. Abul Hamid Lahori *Badshah Namah,* Vol. II, Pers. Text, p. 245; refers to the naming of Dara's daughter, Pak Nahad Banu Begum;

also Gulbadan, *Humayun Namah* Pers. edited by (Bev.) p. 27 for naming of Bega Begum's daughter Aqiqa Begum.

40. K.M. Ashraf, "Life and conditions of the people of Hindustan" Journal Asiatic Society of Bengal, Art. No. 4, 1935, p. 249.
41. Jafar Sharif, Qanun-i-islam, Tr. (Herklots) p. 28.
42. Among Babur's relations, Abu Said Mirza's daughter and Grand daughter had the same name, Afaq Begum, refer to Gulbadan Begum, *Humayun Namah* Tr. (Bev.) pp. 118 and 120; also Appendix A, pp. 203-204; Likewise Babur's first cousin and Kamran's daughter had the name Ayisha Sultan Begum, *Ibid,* p. 119; also Appendix A, pp. 215-16-17-18 for the name Bega Begum. One was Babur's cousin and the other was Humayun's cousin who later on became his wife. One of Babur's wives was also named Bega Begum.
43. Names related to flowers were mostly liked, as Gulbadan, Gulchihra, Gul Rang, Gul Barg, Gul Anar, Naz Gul, Gul Begum etc. Gulbadan Begum, *Humayun Namah* Tr. (Bev.) pp. 121-123.
44. Names, such as Dukhi, Kaki, Bhikhi etc. *Qanun-i-Islam* Tr. (Herkiots) p. 34.
45. When Jahan Ara was given her name, all people took part in rejoicings, refer to Qazwini, Padshah Namah, Pers. M.S. p. 40.
46. Abul Fazl, *Akbar Namah,* Vol. II Tr. pp. 514, 542.
47. Abul Fazl, *Ain-i-Akbari,* Tr. by Jarret, Vol. III, p. 317.
48. Manucci, *Storia,* Vol. III, p. 150; Abdul Halim Sharar, *Guzashta Lucknow* (Lucknow, 1965), p. 332; also see E. Dension *Ross Feasts and holidays of Hindu and Muhammadans* Imperial Record Department, Calcutta, 1914, p. 100.
49. E.D. Ross, *Feasts and Holidays,* p. 100; also Women in Indian Folklore edited with an introduction by Sri Sankar Sen Gupta, First Published August 15, 1969, Indian Publication, Calcutta-1, p. 270; also *Qanun-i-Islam* (Herklots) p. 35.
50. *Qanun-i-Islam* (Herklots) p. 35.
51. K.R. Qanungo, *Dara Shukoh* (Calcutta), Vol. I, p. 18; in Sapahr Shukoh's birth Shah Jahan gave two lakh rupees for birth celebration, Lahori, *Badshah Namah,* Vol. II, Persian Text, p. 339.
52. Sharar, *Guzashta Lucknow,* p. 332; also E.D. Ross, *Feasts and Holidays,* p. 100; also Ashraf Ali, *Behishti Zewar* (Delhi), Vol. VI (Urdu), p. 13.
53. When a son was born to Shah Jahan, he offered forty thousand rupees to his mothers and presented gifts to Jahangir worth Rs. 1 lakh and 30 thousand. *Iqbal Nama-i-Jahangiri* (Urdu), p. 123; on another such occasion Jahangir was presented fifty elephants and gifts worth Rs. 2 lakhs, by Shah Jahan, *Iqbal Nama-i-Jahangiri* (Urdu), p. 113; when Mohammad Sultan was born,

Shahjahan presented gifts worth Rs. 2 lakhs to Ali Marden and other courtiers. Khafi Khan, *Muntakhab-ul-Lubab,* Tr. (Urdu) Vol. II, p. 157.

54. Khafi Khan, *Muntakhab-ul-Lubab* (Urdu) Vol. II, p. 157.
55. Md. Umar, *Hindustani Tahzeeb Ka Mussalmano Par Asar,* p. 129.
56. *Qanun-i-islam* (Herklots) p. 36; also see Sankar Sen Gupta, *Women in Indian Folklore,* p. 270.
57. Md. Umar, *Hindustani Tahzeeb ka Mussalmano Par Asar* (Urdu), p. 129.
58. *Qanun-i-Islam* (Herklots), p. 36.
59. Munucci, *Storia,* Vol. III Tr. (Irvine) p. 150.
60. Md. Umar, *Hindustani Tahzeeb Ka Mussalmano Par Asar* (Urdu) p. 130.
61. John Fryer, *A New Account of East India and Persia,* (London 1909) *MDCXC VIII,* p. 94; see also Ovington, *A Voyage to Surat in the Year* 1689, edited by H.G. Rawlison (Oxford University Press, London, 1929) p. 197.
62. Ovington, *A Voyage to Surat* in the year 1689, p. 197.
63. Mrs. Meer Hassan Ali, *Observations on Mussalmans of India,* Indian reprint 1973, p. 9; see also Herklot's *Qanun-i-Islam* p. 37.
64. Amir Khusro, Kulliat-i Khusravi, (Aligarh, 1918), p. 756; Khamsah-i-Sarfi, Pers. M.S. Buhar collection, N.L. Cal. p. 8.
65. *Mishkat,* II, p. 515.
66. *Zarur-ul-Muslemin* (Urdu), edited by Md. Tahir Ali, (Bombay) p. 19; see also *Behishti Zewar,* Tr. (English) by Md. Masroor Khan (Delhi 1979, second edition) Part VII, p. 130; also Maulana Sayyad Abul Hasan Ali, *Hindustani Musalman Ek Nazr Men* (Urdu) (Lucknow, 1974 second edition), p. 22.
67. K.M. Ashraf, Journal A.S.B. 1935, Art No. 4, pp. 248 249; also E.D.Ross, *Feasts and Holidays,* p. 97; also Herklot's *Qanun-i-Islam,* p. 38.
68. When Babur was born, his mother's father, Younus Khan was invited to Fargana and he joined heartily in the rejoicings of feasts with which the ceremony of shaving the child's head was celebrated. S.Lanepoole, *Babar,* pp. 21-22.
69. Mishkat, Book XVIII, Chapt. IV Part 2.
70. *Bahisti Zewar* (Urdu) Vol. VI, p. 14; *Qanun-i-Islam* (Herklots') p. 39; also E.D. Ross, *Feasts and Holidays,* p. 109.
71. *Muslim, Bokhari,* Urdu translation, Vol. III, p. 128.
72. *Ibid.,* also *Mishkat,* Book XVIII, Chapt. 3.
73. *Bahisti Zewar* (Urdu) Vol. VI, p. 14; also Mohammad Tahir Ali edition, *Zarur-ul-Muslemon (Urdu)* Pub. in Ali Bhai Sharf Ali and Company Pvt. Ltd. Bombay, p. 19; also *Qanun-i-Islam* (Herklots) p. 39.

74. *Behishti Zewar* (Urdu) Vol. VI, p. 14.
75. Maulvi Mohammad Hussain Azad, *Darbar-i-Akbari* (Lahore, 1921) p. 18.
76. *Qanun-i-Islam* (Herklots) p. 135, see also E.D. Ross *Feasts and Holidays,* p. 109.
77. Abul Fazl, *Akbar Namah,* Tr. (Bev.) Vol. I, p. 397.
78. *Ibid.,* p. 396.
79. *Ibid.,* p. 397.
80. Abul Fazl, Ain-i-Akbari, Tr. Jarret, Vol. III, p. 317.
81. Abul Fazl, *Ain-i-Akbari,* Tr. Jarret. Vol. II, p. 317; see also Manucci, Storia, Vol. II, Tr. Irvine, p. 346.
82. Manucci, Storia, Vol. II, p. 346.
83. *Behishti Zewar* (Urdu) Vol. II, p. 14; also E.D. Ross Feasts and Holidays, p. 111; also *Qanun-i-Islam* (Herklots) p. 47; see also Mrs. Meer Hassan Ali, Observations, pp. 10-11.
84. Manucci, Storia, Vol. II, pp. 345-346.
85. For Jahan Ara's birthday celebration see Muntakhab-ul-Lubab (Urdu) Vol. II, p. 176.
86. Lahori, *Badshah Namah,* Vol. II, Persian Text, p. 363; also Chandra Bhan Brahman, *Chahar Chaman,* Persian, MS. No. 67 Buhar collection, N.L. Cal.p. 2.
87. Manucci, Storia, Vol. II, pp. 345-346.
88. John Albert De Mandelslo, *The Travels of East Indies,* (London, 1669 second edition), Vol. I, p. 42.
89. Manucci, Storia, Vol. II, p. 346.
90. *Ibid.*
91. Mandelslio, Travels, Vol. I, p. 42; also Abul Fazl, Ain-i-Akbari, Vol. I, Tr. Biochmann, p. 256 etc.
92. W.Hawkins, *Voyages during the Reign of Henry VII, Queen Elizabeth and James I,* edited by C.R. Morkham, London, printed for Hakluyt Society, MDCCC LXXXIII, p. 440.
93. E.D. Ross, *Feasts and Holidays,* p. 103; see also *Qanun-i-Islam* (Herklots) pp. 41-42.
94. *Qanun-i-Islam* (Herklots) p. 43, also E.D. Ross Feasts and Holidays, p. 99.
95. *Ibid.*
96. Ain-ul-lim Manbasat Ibn Hajar, *Al-Nikah* (Risala) Arabic MS. No. 3229 Khuda Buksh Oriental Public Library, Patna, p. 214.
97. Humayun paid 2 lakh rupees at the time of his Nikah with Hamida Bano Begum, Gulbadan Begum, *Humayun Namah,* Pers. (Bev.). p. 53.
98. Humayun's marriage with Hamidah Bano Begum was a Sharayee marriage.
99. Qanungo, Dara Shukoh, Vol. I, pp. 165-166.

100. Abul Fazl, *Ain-i-Akbari,* Vol. I, Tr. (Bloch) p. 288.
101. Maham Begum, Humayun's mother selected, Maywa Jan for her son, Gulbadan Begum, *Humayun Namah,* Pers. (Bev.). p. 27; also Mah Chuchak (one of the wives of Humayun) selected Abul Maali, for her daughter Fakhrun-Nisa, Abul Fazl, Akbar Namah, Vol. II, Tr. (H. Bev.), p. 318, Maham Anaga also selected daughter of Baqi Khan Baqlani for her son Baqi Mohammad Khan. Abul Fazl, *Akbar Namah,* Vol. II, Tr. pp. 204-205.
102. Masuma Sultan's marriage with Babar was a love match on both sides. Gulbadan Begum, Humayun Namah, Translation (Bev.) p. 262; Manucci refers that the daughter of Qazi Abdul Wahab married with her own choice Storia, Vol. II, Tr. pp. 188-189.
103. Manucci, Storia Do Moger, Vol. III, Tr. p. 152.
104. *Quran,* Chapter IV and V.
105. Gulbadan Begum, *Humayun Namah,* Pers. (Bav.), p. 27.
106. Ganun-i-islam (Herklots) p. 58.
107. Bernier, Travels in the Mughal Empire, translated by A Constable, 1963, second Edition, p. 259; also Pelsaert's *Jahangir's India,* Tr. by Moreland and P. Geyl (c) 1972; p. 60; also, Ovington, p. 165; also purchas' Pilgrimage, (Calcutta, 1864) p. 90; J.N. Sarkar, *Anecdotes of Aurangzeb* 3rd edition, 1949, p. 122; It refers 'In order to please Aurangzeb Ruhullah Khan, a Shia had adopted Sunnism and wrote in his will that his two daughters be wedded to Sunnis. Aurangzeb made order to give first to his son Mohammad Azam and the younger to Siadat Khan. But Siadat Khan objected the girl's religious thought and submitted "How do we know that she too holds "the cried of Sunnism"?
108. Amir Khusrau's father was a Turk while his mother was Indian, Prof. Khalique Ahmad Nizami, *Tarikhi Maqalat* (Urdu) Delhi, 1966, first edition. p. 48.
109. *Babur Namah,* Tr. (Bev.) p. 245.
110. Gulbadan Begum, Humayun Namah, Tr. (Bev.). p. 85, also S. Lanepoole Babar, pp. 59-60.
111. It includes mother, grandmother, sister, niece, aunt etc. *Quran,* Chapt. V, Surah Nisa.
112. It includes mother-in-law, step-grand-mother, daughter-in-law, step-grand-daughter. *Ibid.*
113. A man cannot marry his foster mother nor foster sister unless the foster brother and sister were nursed by the same mother at intervals widely separated. But a man may marry the mother of his foster sister or the foster mother of his sister. *Ibid.*
114. *Quran* strictly orders that under no circumstances a Muslim woman can marry any, but a Muslim, otherwise the marriage wll be invalid.

Quran, Chapt. V, Surah 6; also *Muslim Bokhari* Tr. (Urdu) Vol. III, Kitab-un-Nikah, p. 58.

115. Jahangir refers, "They ally themselves with Hindus and both give and take girls. Taking them is good but giving them, God forbid". Tuzk-i-Jahan in, Tr (RQB) Vol. II, p. 181.
116. Abul Fazl, *Akbar Namah,* Vol. I, Tr. (Bev.) p. 113.
117. *Tuzk-i-Jahangiri,* Vol. I, Tr. (R & B), p. 113.
118. Badaoni, *Muntakhab-ul-Twarlkh,* Vol. II, Tr. (Loew) p. 352; also Khafi Khan, *Muntakhab-ul-Lubab* Tr. (Urdu) Vol. I, pp. 213; 257.
119. Mutamid Khan; *Badshah Namah,* Pers. MS. p. 1; also Khafi Khan *Muntkhab-ul-Lubab* (Urdu) Vol. I, pp. 257-258; Manrique refers her name Balmati Begum, *Travels of Fray Sebastlen Manrique,* Oxford, MCM XXVII, p. 201; also F.n. 3; also A.I. Shrivastava, *Akbar the Great,* Vol. III (1973 1st edition) p. 203; also *Bazm Taimurla,* edited by Sayyed Shahbuddin Abdur Rahman (Urdu) First edn. 1973, p. 72.
120. Qanungo, *Dara Shukoh,* pp. 163-165.
121. In 1672 Murad's daughter Aisha Banu was married to Mohammad Salih. a noble belonging to a Persian family, *Massir-i-Alamgiri,* Tr. (J.N. Sarkar) (Cal., 1947), p. 120; also M. Athar Ali, *The Mughal Nobility under Aurangzeb,* 1966, p. 143.
122. Mutamid Khan, *Iqbal Nama-i-Jahangiri* (Urdu), p. 64, also Khafi Khan, *Muntakhab-ul-Lubab,* Vol. I, Tr. (Urdu), p. 276.
123. *Bazm Taimuria,* pp. 4-5.
124. Gulbadan Begum, *Humayun Namah,* Tr. (Bev.) Appendix A, pp. 209, 215, 295.
125. *Ibid.* p. 218.
126. Shah Nawaz Khan, *Maasir-ul-Umara,* Tr. Vol. II, Part I, p. 383.
127. *Ibid.,* p. 562.
128. Manucci, Storia, Vol. II, Tr. pp. 393-394; also Qanungo, Dara Shukoh, pp. 18-19 and 331.
129. J.N. Sarkar, Tr. *Massir-i-Alamgiri,* p. 77; also Qanungo, *Dara Shukoh,* p. 330; Manucci, *Storia,* Vol. II, Tr. p. 58.
130. Khafi Khan, *Muntakhab-ul-Lubab,* Vol. III (Urdu), p. 99; also Qanungo, *Dara Shukoh,* p. 165.
131. Badaoni, *Muntakhab-ul-Twarikh,* Vol. II Tr. (Lowe) (India, 1973), p. 315; also Abul Fazl, Ain-i-Akbari, Vol. I Tr. (Bloch) p. 288, also *Bazm Talmuria,* Vol. I, p. 72; also Frederick Augustus, The emperor Akbar, Tr. and edited by A.S. Bev. (Patna, 1973), Vol. I, p. 338.
132. Mandelslo. *The Voyages and Travels* (second edition, Oxford, 1669) Vol. I pp. 51 and 115, also Linschoten, *Early travels of India* Cal. (1864) p. 197; Purchas, p. 106; also Thevenot, *Indian Travels,* ed. by S.N. Sen (1949) pp. 72; 248; also Fitch, *Early*

Travels in India, ed. by Foster (Oxford 1921) pp. 16-19 Withington, *Early travels,* p. 221.

133. Babur on his death bed commanded to arrange for his daughters' Gulrang Begum and Gul Chihra Begum, Gulbadan Begum, *Humayun Namah,* Pers. ed. by Mrs. Bev. p. 23; also Tr., pp. 106-107.
134. Pelsaert, refers a youth of 15 to 18 years was regarded marriageable. *Jahangir's India,* p. 81.
135. Pelsaert, refers a youth of 15 to 18 years was regarded marriageable, also Terry, Early Travels, ed. by Foster, (Oxford 1921), it refers that they generally married their children at the age of twelve or thirteen, pp. 320-321.
136. Jahangir was married in his fifteen years with Man Bai. Khafi Khan, *Muntakhab-ul-Lubab* (Urdu) Vol. II, p. 257; Badaoni refers Jahangir's age 16 years. *Muntakhab-ul-Twarikh,* Vol. II Tr. (Lowe) p. 352; also Shah Jahan's first marriage was conducted in his 15 years. Tuzk-I-Jahangirl, Vol. I, Tr. (R and B) p. 224; F.n. 2; Aurangzeb was married in his eighteen years and seven months age. Sarkar, Studies in Aurangzeb's reign (second edition, Cal. 1933), pp. 1-2.
137. Qazwini, *Padshah Namah,* Pers. MS. p. 30; Shah Nawaz Khan, *Maasir-ul-Umara,* Tr. Vol. I, 294; also *Tuzk-i-Jahangiri,* Tr. (R&B) Vol. I, p. 224; F.N. 2. It has mentioned 19 years 1 month instead of 19 years 7 months and 25 days.
138. Humayun was nineteen years older than Hamidah Banu Begum, S.K. Banerjee, *Humayun Badshah,* (Oxford 1938), p. 37.
139. Badaoni, *Muntakhab-ut-Twarikh,* Vol. II Tr. (Lowe) p. 405; also Abul Fazl, *Ain-i-Akbari,* Vol. I, Tr. (Bloch), p. 288.
140. Abul Fazl, *Ain-i-Akbari,* Vol. III, Tr. (Jarret) p. 311; It refers "until the elder brother is married the younger may not lawfully be so".
141. Humayun sent Khawaja Jalal-uddin Mahmud and Bibi Fatima (Urdu Begi) to ask for Shahzada Khanam's hand from her mother Haram. Gulbadan Begum. *Humayun Namah*, Tr. (Bev.) p. 50; also Abul Fazl, *Akbar Namah,* Vol. I, Tr., p. 575.
146. Mirza Shah Husain sent his seal bearer, Babur Quli to Yadgar Nasir Mirza, for the marriage of his daughter, Abul Fazl, *Akbr Namah,* Vol. I, Tr., p. 363.
147. A *Mushatta* was working woman—visiting well-to-do families to help young girls to complete their toilet etc. Due to their close and deep knowledge of the status of the different families, the character of the individual and their behaviour it was customary to send letters from both parties by these Mushatta. Abdul Halim Shrar, *Guzashta Lucknow* (Urdu) pp. 338-339; also Nazir Ahmad, *Maratul Urus* Urdu (Delhi, 1951), p. 227; also G.A. Gnerson,

Bihar Peasant Life (Delhi, 1975), p. 375.
148. Abul Fazl, *Akbar Namah,* Vol. I, Tr. p. 368.
149. Mutamid Khan, *Massir-i-Alamgiri,* Tr.p. 77; also Qanungo, Dara Shukoh, Vol. I, pp. 18-19 and 330-331.
150. Gulbadan Begum, *Humayun Namah,* Pers. ed. by Mrs. Bev., p. 23.
151. Abul Fazl, Humayun Namah, Vol. II, Tr. pp. 204-205.
152. Shah Nawaz Khan, Mansi-ul-Umara, Tr. Vol. II, Part II, p. 768, also Khafi-Khan, *Muntakhab-ul-Lubab* Vol. II. Tr. (Urdu) pp. 131 and 172.
153. *Mishkat* Book IV. Chapt. XI also Ajoul ilm Mansabat ibn Hajar. Al-Nikah (Risala) Arabic MS No. 3229 Khuda Buksh O.P.L. Patna, p. 23; also *Qanun-i-islam* (Herklots), p. 61; Mrs. Meer Hasan Ali, *Observations,* pp. 61-62.
154. Aurangzeb took omens from the writings of Hafiz, *Storia,* Vol. II. Tr. p. 148.
155. Harklot's, *Qanun-i-Islam,* p. 58; Mrs. M. Ali, *Observations,* Vol. I, pp. 355-356.
156. *Ibid.*
157. Palsaert, Jahangir's India, p. 81; also Abdul Halim Sharar, *Guzashta Lucknow* (Urdu), p. 338.
158. Mutamid Khan, *Iqbal Nama-i-Jahangiri,* Tr. (Urdu) p. 32.
159. *Ibid.,* p. 162.
160. Mrs. Meer Hassan Ali, *Observations,* p. 363; also Grierson, *Bihar Peasant's life,* Reprinted in India, 1975, p. 375.
161. *Qanun-i-Islam* (Herklots) p. 63; This custom is also prevalent today.
162. Palsaert, *Jahangir's India,* p. 81; also Abdul Halim Sharar, *Guzashta Lucknow,* p. 338; also *Qanun-i-Islam* (Herklots) p. 63; also Mrs. Meer Hassan Ali, Observations, p. 358.
163. Saksena, History of Shah Jahan of Delhi, (Allahabad 1938) pp. 8-9.
164. Md. Umar, Hindustani Tahzeeb Ka Mussalmano Par Asar (Urdu) p. 141; also Mrs. Meer Hassan Ali, Observations, p. 359.
165. Md. Umar, *Ibid.*
166. Md. Umar, Hindustani Tahzeeb Ka Mussalmano Par Asar (Urdu), p. 141; also Mrs. Meer Hassan Ali, Observations, p. 359.
167. Abdul Halim Sharar, Guzeshta Lucknow (Urdu) p. 338; also Md. Umar, *Ibid.* also Dr Nazz Akbarabadi, *Maaratul-Urus* (Urdu), p. 79; also *Qanun-i-Islam* (Herklots) p. 65; also Mrs. Meer Hassan Ali, Observations. pp. 364, 366.
168. Prince Akbar's marriage could not be carried out even after betrothal, because the girl was made captive by the Pathans which was an indignity for a prince of royal blood to marry one who had been taken and put to ransom. *Storia,* Vol. II, Tr., p. 201.

169. Pelsaert refers that during the two ids 'few or no marriages are allowed to take place", Jahangir's India, p. 73.
170. Qazwini, *Padshah Namah,* pers. Ms. No. 622, Daftar-i-Diwani Wa Mulki, Library, Hydrabad, 219 b. 220a.
171. The marriage of prince Bidar Bakht was celebrated on 15th Muharram 1098 A.H. with the daughter of Qamar-uddin, Shah Nawaz Khan, *Mansir-ul-Umara,* Tr. Vol. II, Part I, p. 255.
172. Manucci, *Storia,* Vol. III Tr. (Irvine) p. 59; also Bernier, *Travels in the Mughal Empire,* pp. 151-162; also *A Dutch Chronicle of Moghul India* translated and edited by Brij Narain and Sri Ram Sharma, 1957, p. 42; also Bazm-i-Taimuria, p. 52; also *Diwan-i-Nazir Akbarabadi* (Delhi, 1942), p. 153; also Meer Hassan, *Masnavi Sihrul Bayan,* p. 142.
173. Gulbadan Begum, Humayun Namah, Tr. (Bev.) p. 151; also Abul Fazl, *Akbar Namah,* Vol. I, Pers. Text, p. 174.
174. *Pelsaert, Jahangir's India,* pp. 81-82.
175. It was a kind of sweet meat made of fruits 'kernels and gum.
176. Sharar, Guzashta Lucknow, p. 338.
177. Md. Umr, *Hindustani Tahzeeb Ka Mussalmano Par Asar* (Urdu) p. 143; also Khwatoon (Urdu) edited by Md. Aslam (second edition, Delhi, Nov. 1951), p. 219.
178. Paisaert, Jahangir's India, p. 82; Khafi khan, Muntakhab-ul-Lubab, Vol. II, Tr. (Urdu), pp. 131-172.
179. Saksena, *History of Shah Jahan of Delhi,* p. 311, also Ashraf Ali Behishti Zewar (Urdu) Vol. VI, p. 29.
180. Pelsaert, p. 82; alsc Saksena *Ibid.*
181. Marriage festivities of Dara were performed three months after Sachaq. Lahori, *Badshah Namah,* Pers. Text. Vol. I, p. 453.
182. Pelsaert, p. 82; also Sharar, *Guzashta Lucknow* (Urdu), pp. 338-339.
183. Lahori, *Badshah Namah,* Pers. text. Vol. I, p. 453. also Eanungo Dara-*Shukah,* p. 12.
184. Pelsaert, p. 82.
185. Tuzk Jahangiri, Vol. I. Tr. (R and B), p. 157. also Saksena History of Shah Jahan of Delhi, p. 311, and Pelsaert, p. 82. also Ashraf Ali, Bahishti Zewar (Urdu) Vol. VI, p. 29.
186. Muntakhab-ul-Lubab (Urdu) Vol. II, p. 131.
187. *Maasir-i-Alamgiri,* Tr. J.N. Sarkar, p. 47.
188. Lahori, *Badshah Namah,* Vol. II, Pers. Text. p. 305; also Tuzk-i-Jahangiri (Urdu), p. 49.
189. Mirza Mohammad Hassan Qateel, *Haft Tamashah,* Pers. Text Nawal Kishore, 1875, p. 139.
190. Pelsaert, *Jahangir's India,* p. 82.
191. Pelsaert, *Jahangir's India,* p. 82., also Sharar, Guzashta Lucknow

(Urdu) p. 340.
192. Khafi Khan, *Muntakhab-ul-Lubab,* Tr. (Urdu) Vol. II, p. 133.
193. *Ibid.* Pelsaert, p. 82.
194. Lahori, *Badshah Namah,* Pers. Text, Vol. II, p. 305; Pelsaert, p. 82; Khafi Khan, *Muntakhab-ul-Lubab,* Tr. (Urdu) Vol. II, p. 133.
195. Pelsaert, p. 82; Sunity Devi, *The Beautiful Mughal Princesses* Pub. in 1918, pp. 52-53.
196. Pelsaert, p. 82.
197. Khafi Khan, *Muntakhab-ul-Lubab,* Tr. Urdu Vol. II, p. 133.
198. Sunity Devi, *The Beautiful Mughal Princesses,* p. 53; also Abdul Halim Sharar, *Guzashta Lucknow* (Urdu), p. 340; also E.D. Ross, *Feasts and Festivals,* p. 105; also Mrs. Meer Hassan Ali, *Observations,* p. 378.
199. Sunity Devi, *The Beautiful Mughal Princesses,* p. 53.
200. Pelsaert, *Jahangir's India,* p. 82.
201. Lahori refers that Murad was brought in the Mahfil-i-Hena bandi, *Badshah Namah,* Vol. II, Pers. Text, p. 305.
202. Manucci, *Storia,* Vol. III, Tr. (irvine) pp. 151-152; also Pelsaert, p. 82; also Qanungo, *Dara Shukoh,* p. 13.
203. Sunity Devi, *The Beautiful Mughal Princesses,* p. 54.
204. Mrs. Meer Hassan Ali, *Observations,* pp. 380-381; also E.D. Ross, *Feasts and Holidays,* p. 106.
205. Manucci, *Storia,* Vol. III (Irvine), p. 151.
206. Khafi Khan, *Muntakhab-ul-Lubab,* (Urdu), Vol. II, p. 133.
207. "Qanungo, Dara Shukoh, p. 13.
208. Manucci, *Storia do Mogor,* Vol. III (Irvine), pp. 151-152.
209. *Ibid.,* p. 152.
210. Peisaert, Jahangir's India, p. 82.
211. Manucci, Storia, vol. III (Irvine), p. 150.
212. Pelsaert, *Jahangir's India,* p. 82.
213. Johan Fryer, *A New Account of Esst India and Persia in Eight Letters* (London), p. 94.
214. Manucci, *Storia do mogor,* Vol. III, Tr., p. 150.
215. *Ibid.* also Mandelslo, Vol. I, p. 62.
216. Lahori, *Badshah Namah,* Vol. I, p. 388; Shah Nawaz Khan, *Maasir-ul-Umara,* Vol. I, Tr. pp. 512, 799; also Manucci Storia, Vol. III, Tr. p. 150; also Thevenot, *Travels,* p. 32.
217. Lahori, *Badshah Namah,* Pers. Text, Vol. I, p. 388.
218. Khafi Khan, *Muntakhab-ul-Lubab* (Urdu) Vol. II, p. 134.
219. *Maasir-i-Alamgiri,* Tr. by J.N. Sarkar, p. 77.
220. *Qanun-i-Islam* Herklots), p. 73.
221. Khafi Khan, *Muntakhab-ul-Lubab* (Urdu) Vol. III, p. 128.
222. *Ibid.* p. 76.
223. Shah Abdur Razzaque Banswi, *Malfuzat-i-Razaqi* (Pers). ed. by

Nawab Mohammad Khan Shah Jahan Puri, (Lucknow 1313 A.H.) p. 26 also Purchas, p. 90.

224. Lahori, *Badshah Namah,* Pers. Text. Vol. I, p. 388; also Manucci, *Storia,* Vol. III (Irvine) p. 150; Pelsaert, p. 82; also Terry, *A Voyage to East India,* 1655, p. 285; also Harihar Das, *Norris Embassy to Aurangzeb,* condensed and rearranged by S.C. Sarkar (First edition, Calcutta, 1959), p. 161; also Thevenot, *Travels,* p. 32; Terry, *Early Travels,* p. 320; also Mandelslo, Vol. I, p. 62; also *Maasir-I-Alamgiri,* Tr. p. 73.
225. Pelsaert, *Jahangir's India,* p. 82; also Terry, *Early Travels,* p. 320.
226. Mandelslo Vol. I, p. 62; also Sharar, *Guzashta Lucknow* (Urdu), p. 341.
227. Pelsaert, p. 82; Storia, Vol. III (Irvine) p. 150; *Travels of Thevenot* pp. 31-32; *Norris Embassy to Aurangzeb,* pp. 161-162 Terry, Early Travels, p. 320; Terry, *A voyage to east India,* p. 285; Mandelslo Vol. I, p. 62; Fryer, p. 94; also Khafi Khan, *Muntakhab-ul-Lubab,* Tr. (Urdu), Vol. II, p. 165.
228. *Storia,* Vol. III (Irvine) p. 150.
229. Mandelslo, Vol. I, p. 62; also *see Storia* Vol. III (Irvine), p. 150; Pelsaert, p. 82; Thevenot, p. 32; *Norris Embassy to Aurangzeb,* p. 161; also Khafi Khan, *op. cit.*
230. *Storia,* Vol. III (Irvine), p. 150; also Khafi Khan, *Ibid.* p. 134.
231. *Behishti Zewar,* Vol. VI, p. 31.
232. Linschoten, *Travels of Van Linschoten,* Calcutta, 1864, p. 175, also see *Qanun-i-Islam,* p. 73; also Purchas's *Pilgrimage,* p. 90.
233. Khafi Khan, *Muntakhab-ul-Lubab,* Tr. (Urdu), Vol. I, p. 258.
234. Manucci, *Storia,* Vol. III (Irvine), p. 150.
235. *Storia,* Vol. III (Irvine) p. 150; also *Masnavl Mir Hassan,* p. 147.
236. Mandelslo, Vol. I, p. 62; also *Masnavl Mir Hasan,* p. 148; *Diwan Nazir Akbarabadi,* pp. 140-153.
237. R.R. Diwakar, *Bihar through the Ages,* 1st Pub. in Jan. 1959, p. 535 also Md. Aslam, Khwateen, p. 29; also *Masnavl Mir Hasan,* p. 147.
238. Pelsaert, p. 82; Manucci, *Storia,* Vol. III (Irvine) p. 51.
239. Pelsaert, p. 83.
240. Abdul Halim Sharar, *Guzashta Lucknow* (Urdu), pp. 342-343.
241. Lahori, *Badshah Namah,* Vol. II, Pers. Text. p. 305.
242. Mutamid Khan. *Massir-i-Alamgiri,* Tr. p. 49.
243. Lahori, *Badshah Namah,* Vol. I, Pt. II, p. 270; also Shah Nawaz Khan, *Massir-ul-Umarah,* Tr. Vol. II, Part II, p. 768.
244. Lahori, *Badshah Namah,* Vol. II Persian Text, p. 305; also Muslim Bokari, Urdu translation, p. 66.

245. Pelsaert, p. 83;
246. Mandelslo, Vol. I, p. 62; also Sharar, *Guzashta Lucknow* (Urdu), p. 343.
247. *Khamsa-i-sarfi,* Pers. Ms. p. 19; also Brij Narayan Translation on *A Duch Chronicle of Moghul India,* p. 42; also Jauhar, *Tazkiratul-Waqlat* translated by Charles Stewart (Calcutta 1904) p. 31, also Wahab Asharafi, *Kutub Mushtari are uska Tanqidi Jayeza,* 1977, p. 248; also Saksena, *History of Shahjahan,* p. 312;
248. Lahori, *op. cit.*
249. Qazwini, *Padshah Namah,* Pers. MS. p. 30, B.C.N.L. Cal.
250. Lahori, *Badshah Namah,* Pers. Text Vol. I, p. 453.
251. *Bazm Talmuria,* Vol. I, p. 136; also Saksena, *History of Shah Jahan,* p. 312; also Elliot and Dowson, *History of India* as told by its own Historians Vol. VII, First Indian edition, 1964, p. 119.
252. Pelsaert, *Jahangir's India,* p. 83; also Terry, *Early Travels,* p. 320.
253. Qazwini, *Badshah Namah* MS. p. 30.
254. Linschoten, *Early Travels in India,* pp. 175-176; also Purchas. p. 90.
255. *Maasir-i-Alamgiri,* Tr. Sarkar, pp. 49, 73, 77, 103;
256. Manucci, *Storia,* Vol. III, Tr. p. 151.
257. For *salami* Hindal was presented a number of gifts by his wife's guardians after *Nikah* and at the time of marriage feast. Mahbubullah Mujib, *Moghul Tahzeeb* (Urdu), Allahabad, p. 160.
258. Manucci, *op. cit.*
259. *Bahishti Zewar* (Urdu) Vol. VI, p. 43.
260. *Qanun-i-Islam* (Herklots), pp. 79-80; also Meer Hassan Ali, Observations, p. 388; also E.D. Ross, *Feasts and Holidays* p. 99; also *Masnavi Mir Hassan* (urdu), p. 148.
261. Abdul Halim Sharar, Guzashta Lucknow (Urdu), p. 344; also Wahab Ashrafi, *Qutub Mushtari Aur Uska Tanqidi Jayeza,* p. 248.
262. R.R. Diwakar, *Bihar through the ages,* p. 535.
263. *Qanun-i-Islam* (Herklots) p. 80; also *Masnavi Mir Hassan,* (Urdu) p. 149.
264. Pelsaert, p. 83; also Manucci, *Storia,* Vol. III (irvine). p. 152; also *Maasir-i-Alamgiri,* Tr. p. 49.
265. Khafi Khan, *Muntakhab-ul-Lubab* (Urdu) Vol. II, p. 302, also Vol. II, Tr. 341; also Khwaja Nizamuddin, *Tabqat-i-Akbari,* Vol. II, Tr. p. 599; also Shahnawaz Khan, *Massir-ul Umara,* Vol. I Tr. p. 404; also Pelsaert, p. 83; also *Norris Embassy to Aurangzeb,* p. 253.
266. Khafi Khan refers that Sultan Parwez in his daughter Karima Sultan's marriage gave dowry of seven lakhs, Vol. II, p. 76; also Qutub-u-Mulk gave his daughter the dowry worth rupees 14 lakhs, p. 302.

267. Sharar, Guzashta Lucknow (Urdu) p. 345; also *Masnavl Mir Hasan,* p. 150; also *Qanun-i-Islam* (Herklots) p. 81; also Mrs. Ali, *Observations,* p. 388.
268. Sharar, *Ibid.*
269. Careri, *Indian Travels,* by Surendra Nath Sen, 1949, p. 248.
270. Linschoten, *Early Travels,* p. 176.
271. Iqbal *Nama-i-Jahangiri* Tr. Urdu, p. 72.
272. Sharar, Guzastha Luckow (Urdu), p. 347. also Md. Umar, Hindustani Tahzeeb, p. 154.

276. Khafi Khan, *Muntakhab-ul-Lubab* (Urdu) Vol. III, p. 128; also Nazir Ahmad, *Maratul Urus* (Urdu) p. 80; Bihari Lall refers it 'Munh Dekhai', *Bihari Patrakar*, ed. by Shiwala, Pub, by Mahtab Roy, Nagri Pracharini Sabha Kashi, Banaras, New edition, 1955, Doha, 288, p. 121.
277. *Muslim Bokhari,* Tr. Urdu, Vol. III, Book 21, p. 69.
278. Francis Gladwin, *History of Jahangir,* ed. by K.V.R. Aiyangar (Madras, 1930), p. 36.
279. Khafi Khan, *Muntakhab-ul-Lubab* (Urdu), Vol. III, p. 128.
280. Muslim Bokharil, Tr. (Urdu), Vol. III, Book, 21, Kitab-un-Nikah, p. 71.
281. Khwaja Nizamuddin Ahmad, Tabqat-i-Akbari, Vol. II, Tr. p. 251; also *Iqbal-Nama-i-Jahangiri* (Urdu), p. 55; also Khafi Khan, *Muntakhab-ul-Lubab* (Urdu) Vol. I, p. 275.
282. S.K. Banerjee, *Humayun Badshah,* p. 66.
283. Gulbadan Dogurn, *Hamayun Namah,* Pers. ed. by Mrs. Bev. p. 30.
284. Khafi Khan, *Muntakha-ul-Lubab,* Vol. II (Urdu) pp. 76-165.
285. *Iqbal Name-i-Jahangiri* (Urdu), p. 55.
286. *Tuzkl-i-Jahangiri,* Vol. I, Tr. (R&B), p. 81.
287. *Ibid.*
288. Gulbadan Begum, *Humayun Namah,* Pers. pp. 36-37. It refers that Khanzada Begum and Mehndi Khwaja presented several costly articles to both the bride (Sultanam Begum) and the bridegroom (Mirza Hindal) as they had adopted the bride as their own child.
289. Sharar, *Guzashta Lucknow* (Urdu), pp. 347-348; also Md. Umar *Hindustani Tahzeeb,* p. 155.
290. Khafi Khan, *Muntakhab-ul-Lubab,* Vol. III (Urdu) p. 99.
291. Dr. Nazir Ahmad, *Maratul Urus,* p. 162; also Sharar, *Guzastha Lucknow,* p. 348.

3

Education

Education, a radiant light, illuminates the inner concealed qualities and talents of a human being and conseqently the stream of prudence gushes forth, comes into light and becomes more and more transparent, easy to travel across, offers various opportunities to its seekers and, finally, accomplishes the desired target. It is, therefore a search light, making easy access to the highway. Pushing one ahead, slowly and steadily crossing mile-stones one after another and making him reach at the destination eventually. Contrarily, an illiterate man is like a heap of soil, very dull, totally useless and devoid of beauty and charm.

Based fundamentally, on the aforesaid broad principles Mohammad, the Holy Prophet, vividly said to the Muslims, his followers, the value and aim of education thus:

> 'Education has its great value for all human beings. It is education which enables its possessers to between what is forbidden and what is not. Really it is our friend in the desert, our society in solitude, our companion when bereft of friends. It guides us to happiness, it sustains us in misery.'

He first laid the foundation stone of the learning spirit in the following terms *'Talab-ul-Illmul Farizaton ala Kulle Muslim wa Muslumah'*.[1] Acquisition of knowledge (in the right sense) is incumbent upon all the loyal men (Muslim) as well as women (Muslimah). He further advised,

> 'Seek knowledge right from the cradle upto grave, no matter ye be in China.'

He always used to motivate his pupils every now and then, and proclaimed that the seekers of knowledge shall be welcomed warmly, and greeted by God's angels in Heaven.

In the light of the teachings of Islam, it was obligatory on the parents to impart the best possible education to their children. As Mohammadan himself says:

> "No present or gift of a parent to a child, out of all the gifts and presents, is superior to a good liberal education."

As a result of such impetus provided by thue Prophet, every Muslim considered cbligatory to educate his children. People undoubtedly, believe that the Muslim ladies are forbidden from acquiring education. But as the Prophet Mohammad has set an example in this direction by imparting higher education to his wives as well as his daughter. By his instruction, therefore, unacceptable daughter Fatimah Zohra, and Alyashah, his most favourite wife proved themselves the highly literate ladies of the time. They were so efficiently and effectively equipped with intellectual achievements that even the contemporary leading erudites used to consult them in controversial outstanding topics. There were other unforgetable Muslim ladies too in Arabia, including Zainab, Hafsah, Hamida, Safiya, Maria and Al-kal-leyyeh, being highly educated. It is strange that while prophet Mohammad himself promoted education for his women, the Muslim society does not follow his example.

Marriage being a prominent bond, has been also greatly responsible for the female education. In this regard also, the Prophet Mohammad had emphasised deeply on the education of the fair sex as he stated:

> "Select those girls for marriage who are able, educated and members of a respected family."

Consequently, every Muslim took great care in educating the female, under his own resources, and it became a popular proverb in Muslim society that 'shyness is women's beauty and education is her ornament.'

A great many changes happened in human outlook right from the inception of Islam to the Mughal period, but the central theme of teaching in relation to the Muslim girls remained the same with a few exceptions due to the relationship of Hindu-Muslim culture. Whole educational set-up of the Mughals, basically, had no revolutionary change which could be accepted overnight. The formula of female education was, as such, initiated just to meet the moral requirements of the women folk. Truly the female education, in the modern sense of the term, was almost entirely foreign to the customs and ideas of the age, yet it was neglected altogether. But as far as the question of female learning in the upper classes is concerned, it was not restricted and they could afford it according to their status. Hence, there is resemblance in the education of the Arabs and the Moghals, and the education pattern differed not much. The spirit of female education developed out of religion, and flourished in politics and fashion.

Various Agencies of Education

The agencies of education existing in the Mughal period, differed categorically from the system of eudcation prevalent in modern India. Truly speaking, Muslim education was imparted through the following three told agencies:

(a) Maktab. It was an institution of primary education and resembled very much to the present day elementary/primary school. The floor of a mosque, the rooms or *Varandah* attached to a shrine or mausoleum or the door-way of the teacher's house, served as *'Maktabs'.* They were very common in that period, in cities and towns and even in villages. Such educational institutions were commonly used by the boys as well as girls, and parents put no restriction in sending them to the *maktabs.* In reality, the students receiving their education in *Maktabs,* were of lower ages.

(b) Khanqah[2]. Students of advanced age usually received their secondary education in *'khanqah'*, mostly attached to mosques and run by Muslim missionaries. This was particularly meant for the grown-up boys, because the *'Khanqah'* of the Mughal age was similar to present high schools. Therefore, the grown up girls were never allowed to receive their education in such schools. However, for the grown-up girls separate arrangements were made at their own residences.

(c) Madrasa. This was quite similar to our modern college imparting higher education. 'Madrasas' were mostly attached to mosques, mausoleum of the emperors, nobles and dervishes.

But Muslim girls never received their higher education in *'Khanqah'* and *'Madrasas',* due to the *Purdah* system observed most strictly in those days. Muslim girls were never allowed to mix freely with boys who received their higher education in these institutions, and perhaps no *'Khanqah'* and *'Madrasa'* existed only for girls. But the education of the girls did not end in *'Maktabs'* only, the Mughals were the rulers very inclined to giving polished etquettes and good education to their daughters, and the noblemen were their immediate followers possessing enough wealth to meet their educational requirements at their own discretion and hence, they usually made necessary arrangements for residential education for their girls. Many private houses served as significant agencies of higher education to educate the girls privately.[3]

Medium of Instruction

During the Mughal age Persian was the medium of instruction in India. Persian was first introduced as well as made the language of administration by the rulers of the Turk-Afghan period. Yet people, in general showed no desire to learn Persian. Saints were first attracted towards it and started writing prose and poetry in Persian elegantly.

The year 1526 opens a new chapter in the political and also in the cultural history of India. Now the Persian spirit established itself in the art, literature and culture of the country. It became the recognised language of the court, and of administration. Arrangements were made to teach Persian to children irrespective of caste, creed of sex. Consequently, it became the medium of instruction.

Teaching Method

The method of teaching during the Mughal age was very simple. The children were first taught the Persian alphabets with correct pronunciation, accents and punctuation marks[4] then they were taught the combination of two letters, and then started to study and write short lines of prose or poetry, containing those combinations most frequently. They were also assigned some exercise daily as home task, to progress in the art of reading and writing gradually.

This method continued upto the days of Akbar. He, as a great patron of learning, was anxious to introduce reforms in this field. Consequently, he introduced revolutionary changes in the method of teaching, so that the students could gain proficiency in a much shorter time than was possible prior to his reign. The students were now first taught the Persian alphabets alongwith punctuations and sign of accents. After a few days, they were taught the combination of two letters. Following a week they had to read short lines of prose or verses containing religious or moral sentiment in which those combinations frequently occurred. Care was taken that the students learned to understand everything themselves and the teacher only helped them a little. After a few days, the teacher taught a new hemistich and very soon the students could read with fluency. The teachers assigned them four exercises daily, *viz.* the alphabets, the combinations, a new hemistich or distich and repetition of previous lessons. This method proved very successful as learning took few months [instead of years].

In the primary stage students were also taught numerals and elementary arithmetic[6] and the method was very interesting. To print it in the memory they first recited the chapter in a musical tone and speaking so, they wrote down the same lesson. They learned all chapters one by one similarly.[7]

Writing Method

Besides reading, children were also taught the art of writing. Under the direction of the teacher, the students first practiced the art of writing on the ground covered with sand or dust with their fingers.[8] When the pavement was full of figures, they deleted them with their hand and resumed their practice. Thus they learned writing by easy and cheap method.

When a student qualified himself he was taught to write with red pens or with tubes of some other sort, on plastered wooden board, known as *'takhti'* which could be washed clean with cotton whenever required.[9] Just after acquiring full proficiency in writing a better hand, pupils started the use of pen, lead pencil 'calm I surb'[10] on paper. Bamboo twigs and the quills of bird also served as pens.[11]

Primary Education and its Curriculum

During the Mughal period girls, like boys, received early education in a *'Maktab',*[12] a permanent institution of primary as well as elementary education. As religion was the backbone of education, the *'Maktab'* was generally attached to a mosque. It was maintained through magnificent donations made by the rich people of the vicinity. Few of them received help from the provincial treasury.[13] In these *'Maktabs',* 'Maulvees' were appointed for two purposes—to lead prayers and to teach children. For the female education, separate *'Maktabs'*[14] were arranged. But, usually, upto the primary standard, the system of co-education was prevalent. After this, girls were not permitted to mix freely with the boys and were separated from the boys.

As regards the curriculum, it can be safely said that normally the curriculum of the primary school was very simple. It comprised reading, writing, elementary arithmetic and ethics.

In the primary stage, the Holy *Quran* was chief text book, the entire of which they had to read without knowing its purposes. For this, they were first taught the Arabic alphabets. Certain portions, essential for the daily prayers, were remembered by the students.

Several Muslim girls of different classes generally received their education only upto the primary stage then put under the tuition of some elderly educated ladies. The widows of the middle classes generally imparted religious education to the poor girls in their own houses, and considered it a sacred duty.[19] The masses remained mostly illiterate. Owing to poverty, they had to perform domestic duties, so hardly got time for intellectual pursuits. Those belonging to agricultural and working classes, helped their men in their home industries such as farming, cattle breeding, weaving, dyeing and other professions. Thus the ladies of the poor class had unfortunately, to be occupied too much with domesic and farm work and with children and they hardly found leisure for intellectual pursuits. Among them, if some got time for education, their education was confined only to the reciting of the Holy *Quran,*[20] and that was regarded as their great achievernent in the field of learning.

After completing primary education, they had to face many hurdles. *Purdah* system and child marriage did not let them continue their education. Higher education was considered not only unnecessary, but a crime in the eyes of Puritans. According to them looking after the infants and mastery in home science was sufficient for young girls. This idea proved a great obstacle in the higher education of females.

Higher Education and its Curriculum

During the Mughal age, higher education of Muslim women was mostly confined to the upper classes of society. The kings nobility and higher classes were keenly interested in imparting higher education to their ladies believing that, education brightened the path to the apprehension of truth. They adorned their women with the jewels of *'Ilm'* (Knowledge). These women, unlike their poor sisters, had ample opportunities and leisure for intellectual pursuits. For the education of their girls, well-to-do classes appointed scholarly ladies or meritorious old men[21] in their own houses, while highly paid educated matrons and superintendents[22] were appointed in the royal *harem.* Among the inmates of royal *harems,* those who were very much interested in receiving higher education, had the facility of coaching from various learned scholars.[23]

The curriculum for the secondary and higher education included Ethics, Arithmetic, Accounts, Agriculture, Economics, the art of Administration, Physics, Logic Natural Philosophy, Abstract Mathematics, Divinity, History, Medicine, Morals, Law, Rituals, Rhetorics, Household matters, Poetry, Prose, as the end of novel was not present those days. Astrology, Geography, Scholasticism, Jurisprudence, Tafsir, Fiqhah, Hadith, and traditions Mysticism, Grammar, Syntax, Biography (Lives of Prophets) and Calligraphy.[24]

Books recommended for the aforesaid subjects varied, from time to time, according to the whims of the ruler and the teacher. Whenever any new work was appreciated, it generally got a place in the curriculum. Hence different books were recommended in different periods (reigns) during the Mughal age.

But the aforesaid changes never affected female education, as they were not, after all bound for any higher education, and banned in their homes only where private tutors were appointed on individual capacity. As for their choice of subjects and books, they were very fond of poetry, as per the fashion of the day, the spirit of which came from their Persian lady teachers,[25] who often dictated poems to them. The books of Shaikh Sadi Shirazi's, 'Gulistan' and 'Bostan'[26] written in the form of poetry got much popularity among the students of that time. The ladies of the *harem* enjoyed in reading these outstanding books when free. Persian works, not mere books of poetry, were also treated as a treasured sea, full of knowledge and lessons.[27] Besides the Holy *Quran* and the study of *'Hadis' (Ahadith)* the ladies were taught Persian and Arabic literature, Elementary Arithmetic, Theology, History, Astronomy and Mathemaics.[28] Some of them also gained proficiency in the art of calligraphy.[29] Law was also an interesting subject for them.[30] Many Muslim ladies acquired deep knowledge of medicine and treatment,[31] either by experience, family background or by education. The art of administration was regarded very important for the ladies of the royal household,[32] and hence was taught to them particularly.

No subject or book, was forcibly thrust upon them. Their study depended upon their own choice, interest, ambition and future aims. No duration was fixed for the study of a book or subject it extensively depended upon the girls' intelligence. The entire subject as far as possible was taught to them for the sake of learning. "Therefore, there was no mania for diploma or certificate such as now prevails".[33]

Purpose of Female Education

During that period, the aim was to develop the faculties of the students, and to equip them with necessary ingredients for their moral and mental development.[34] By education, a girl was expected to prove to be a devoted wife, an excellent future mother, expert in household work and, above all, punctuality in religious duties, the latter being the highway to lead them to the final goal, after death.

Mughal Emperors' Contribution to the Field of Girls Education

The Mughal rulers of India remarkably contributed in the field of learning and education. Under their supervision and care, their daughters and other distinguished ladies of the *harem,* received education that immortalised their names. Babar's daughter, Gulbadan Begum, was credited the authorship of Humayun Namah which includes the name of other educated and distinguished ladies.[35]

Akbar is famous for his keen interest in promoting education. He made excellent arrangements in this field and appointed matrons.[36] In the Mughal history, he founded a girl's school, for the first time in Fatehpur Sikri.[37] Shahjahan, the builder of the 'Taj', did not neglect the education of his daughters and appointed a Persian lady scholar, Sati-un-Nisa,[38] as the superintendent of Mumtaz's seraglio. She, later on, became the governess of princesses Roshan Ara and Jahanara.

Aurangzeb, too, was deeply interested in the education of the ladies of the imperial *harem*. He himself supervised his daughters' education and academic progress. He strongly believed, that to impart education was praiseworthy in the eyes of God. Therefore, he taught his princesses, all the necessary rules and other relevant doctrines of Islam. Under his strict guidance, all the ladies of the *harem* were engaged in worshipping God and reading and transcribing the Holy *Quran,* together with the performance of virtuous deeds.[39]

Besides, meritorious efforts were made by the chiefs and private individuals also to promote learning and diffuse education among the inhabitants of Hindustan.

Maktab Ceremony

In Mughal India, a child had to face some type of ceremonies, at every step, in which people were highly interested, as it provided entertainment of all concerned. That is why the first education, being an important event in a child's life, was started with noisy customs and practices. In Islam there is no indication regarding this ceremony, even though this practice was prevalent during these days. It was generally believed that a child's education must start by pronouncing God's name in an assembly, under the good wishes and blessings of elders, which would make the child wiser and prosperous.

The ceremony of starting education was called *'Bismillah Khani'* or *'Maktab'* ceremony.[40] It was observed only when a boy or a girl attained the age of four years, four months and four days[41] and usually, an hour was fixed after consulting an astrologer.[42] Two or three days prior to the ceremony, the girl had to sit in a state of *'Manjha',* i.e. a ceremony of marriage. She was made to wear yellow clothes, and *'suhagan'* women (only those whose husbands were alive) rubbed a scented powder of special make, known as *'ubatan',* over her body. This continued daily, morning and evening, till the day of *'Maktab'* ceremony arrived. During this period, music was played in the house of the girl concerned, by professional lady singers. On the eve of *'Bismillah Khani',* the guests were invited to share the general pleasure and had to bring clothes for the child as well as for the parents and the tutor.

The girl was bathed and dressed in new expensive red or white garments. Gold or silver amulets were then hung on the girl's neck, and then she was adorned with flower garlands. On this occasion, the girl's side locks were plaited, for the first time, with black silk strings.[43] Now she was presented before the tutor or a *'Mashaikh'* in the midst of the heavy gatherings of guests. A gold or silver plate, including a pen with inkstand, was placed before her. *Fatiha* was recited over the sweet dishes, prepared for this occasion, and the tutor would, then, write on the plate, with a sandalwood pen the words, *'Bismillah-i-r-r-rahman-nir-raheem',*[44] (i.e. I begin it in the name of *Allah*). Then she was ordered to lick it off accordingly. In rich families, *'Alhamd',* the first chapter of the Holy *Quran,* written on the gold or silver plate, was repeated by the girl herself.[45] The poor generally used red paper for writing the verse of the Holy *Quran.*[46] At the end, the girl was taught, to pronounce in succession, the whole of the ninety sixth chapter *'Surah Iqra'* of the Holy *Quran* by the tutor.[47] It was so, because the Prophet Mohammad, was first taught to pronounce it in *'Ghar-i-Hira'* by Jebrail, the greatest among angels. At last she would salute the guests, the friends, the elders, and all the participants and, then, sweets were distributed among them. After this ceremony, the girl would begin her lessons starting from the alphabets of the Holy *Quran.*[48]

On this ceremony, dinner was served liberally to the guests. The poor and needy were also fed. Muslims of the time believed that the prayers and blessings of the poor were certain meditations at the throne of God and would produce benefits of the child, in whose favour they were invoked.

It was customary to make presents to sisters and servants by the child's parents.[49] All the guests carrying gifts were recompensed with presents of greater value, before departure.[50]

When the girl commenced her education in *'maktab',* the teacher wrote on *'Idi',* generally a verse relating to *Id,* or a verse of blessing related to the girl, on coloured paper known as 'zarfishani'. She herself was made to recite this to her parents who made valuable presents to the teacher[51] as a reward. It was also customary for the parents to entertain the teacher with delicious food and offer him a suitable sum whenever their daughter had to begin a new lesson.[52]

Khatam Quran Ceremony

During the Mughal age, on having finished the Holy *Quran,* a day was celebrated with the same pomp and enthusiasm. This ceremony was called *'Khatam Quran'* or ceremony of finishing Holy *Quran.*[53] When Aurangzeb's most accomplished daughter, Zeb-un-Nisa, finished the Holy *Quran* and memorised it by heart, Aurangzeb celebrated the day with great rejoicings, and the public offices of the state remain closed for two days.[54] In course, the tutor was presented expensive gifts.[55] All the guests were entertained with different types of amusements in the big assembly of visitors. And at the end of the ceremony the elders congratulated the princess for success and advised her to keep in memory the important lessons given by them.

References

1. Ajnul lim Manbasat Ibn Hajar, Al-Nikah (Risalah) Arabic Ms. O.P.L. p. 5; also Maulana Zafruddin, *Islam Ka Nizam iffat wa Asmat* (Urdu) Pub. by Nadwatul Mussannefeen, (Delhi 1962), p. 125.
2. S.M. Jaffar, *Education in Muslim India,* Reprint, 1973, Delhi. p. 32; J.N. Sarkar, *Studies in Mughal India,* 2nd edn. 1919, p. 300, F. Steinggass, *A Comprehensive Persian English Dictionary.* Routledge and Kegan Paul Ltd. (Broadway 68-74, Carter Lane, London) p. 443; also refer to John T. Plates, *A Dictionary of Urdu Classical Hindi and English,* Vol. I (London), p. 446.
3. S.M. Jaffar, *Education in Muslim India,* p. 192.
4. *Ibid.*
5. Abul Fazl, *Ain-i-Akbari* (Bloch), pp. 288-289.
6. S.M. Jaffar, *Education in Muslim India,* p. 20.
7. B.K. Sahay, *Education and Learning Under the Great Mughals,* p. 53; F.n. 30.
8. Fryer, p. 112.
9. *Ibid;* also Shobaul, *Hindustan in Miniature,* Vol. IV, pp. 214-18; *Imperial Gazetteer of India,* Vol. IV, p. 480; see also for Takhti R.R. Diwakar *Bihar through the ages,* p. 543.
10. *Massir-ul-Umara,* Vol. I. Tr., p. 256.
11. Achutananda Das, *Haribams,* pub. by Radha Raman Pustakalaya, Cuttack, fourth canto, p. 577; also T.C. Das Gupta, *Aspects of Bengali Society* (Calcutta University, 1935), pp. 168-169.
12. *Qanun-i-Islam* (Herklots), p. 47.
13. M.L. Bhagi, *Medieval Indian Culture and Thought* (Pub. in 1965), p. 158; also *An Advanced History of India* by Majumdar, Raychaudhuri and Dutta, Part II (1951), p. 578.
14. S.M. Jaffar, *Some Cultural Aspects of Muslim Role in India,* p. 85; also M.L. Bhagi, *Medieval Indian Culture and Thought,* p. 360.
15. R.R. Diwakar, *Bihar through the Ages,* p. 543.
16. *Ibid.*
17. Makhdum Maneri, *Maadan-ul-Maani,* Pers. Text Pub. by Shah Md. Muqqabbil Hussain, Sherul Akhbar (Razbeyapur 1884 A.D.)

p. 43. also Pt. I as quoted in *Calcutta Review,* Dec. 1940, p. 315.
18. *Maadan-ul-Maani,* p. 42; also Pt. I *Cal. Review* Dec. 1940. p. 315; also R. Diwakar Bihar *Through the Ages,* p. 543.
19. S.M. Jaffar, *Education in Muslim India,* pp. 191-192; also Yusuf Hussain, *Glimpses of Medieval Indian Culture,* p. 93.
20. M.L. Bhagi, *Medieval Indian Culture and thought,* p. 361.
21. N.N. Law, *Promotion of Learning in India During Mohammadan Rule* (1973) p. 205; This book also has a picture of a Mughal princess having her lesson by an old Maulvee, Fig. I from the collection of Mr. G.C. Manuk *Bar-at-law* bankipore, also S.M. Jaffar, *Some Cultural Aspects of Muslim Rule in India,* p. 85; Edward Garrett, *Mughal Rule in India,* 2nd Indian reprint, 1962, p. 169; Dr. P.N. Ojha, *Some Aspects of North Indian Social Life,* 1961, p. 109; also *An advance Hist of India,* by Majumdar, Raychaudhary and Dutta, p. 579; P.N. Chopra, *Some Aspects of Society and Culture during the Mughal Age,* 2nd edition, 1963, p. 161.
22. *Storia* Vol. II, pp. 330-331.
23. See Zeb-un-Nisa, of the same chapter.
24. *Ain,* Vol. I. Tr. (Bloch) p. 289; also *Muntakhab-ut-Twarikh* Vol. II. Per. Text. pp. 306-307; also Tr. (Lowe) p. 316 S.M. Jaffar *Education in Muslim India,* p. 21; also G.M.D. Sufi, *Al-Minhaj* pub. by Sheikh Md. Ashraf (Kashmiri Bazar, Lahore, Ist edn. August 1941), p. 8.
25. Sarkar, *Studies in Mughal India,* (Cal. 1919), p. 301.
26. *Storia* Vol. II, p. 331; also Yusuf Hussain, *Glimpses of Indian Culture* (1962), p. 93.
27. These Persian books in form of poetry has narrated Persian Kings and Saints' life and deeds with many moral lesssons. This book also comprised few interesting love affairs, affording a pastime for readers.
28. Sarkar, *Studies in Mughal India,* p. 301; *Diwan-i-Zeb-un-Nisa,* ed. by Magan Lal, p. 8; also for Zeb-un-Nisa's proficiency in these subjects see *Maasiri-Alamgiri,* Tr. p. 322; N. N. Law, *Promotion of Learning,* p. 204; S. M. Jaffar, *Education in Muslim India,* p. 297; *Bazm-i-Taimuria,* p. 456.
29. Zeb-un-Nisa could write correctly various kinds of hands such as Nastaliq, Naskh, and Shikastah.
30. See Zeb-un-Nisa, in the same chapter.
31. For Hamidah Bano's proficiency in this field see *Tazkirat-ul-Waqlyat* (Jauhar) p. 84; For Nur Jahan's knowledge of medicine consult *Tuzuk* Tr. (R and B) Vol. II, pp. 213-214; Jahan-ara's tutoress Sati-un-Nisa had profound knowledge of medicine and treatment. *Maasir-ul-Umara,* Vol. I, Tr. by Beveridge, p. 261.

32. Nur Jahan and Mumtaz Mahal were expert administrators of their age.
33. S.M. Jaffar, *Education in Muslim India,* p. 23.
34. *Ibid.* pp. 27-28.
35. Gulbarg, Bega Begum, Dildar Begum and Ayishaa Sultan Khanam were some educated ladies during the age of Babur and Humayun. *Humayun Namah,* Persian ed. by Mrs. Bev. pp. 38-53 and 90; also Tr. (Bev) pp. 131-150, 194.
36. Monserrage, p. 203.
37. S.M. Jaffar, *Education in Muslim India,* p. 190; N. N. Law, Promotion of learning, p. 202; also F. E. Keay's *Indian Education in ancient and later times* (London, 1938) 2nd edition p. 80; also Haveli, *A hand book to Agra and the Taj* (Long Man's Green Co. London, 1904) p. 116. Here the writer has given a plan of girl's school established by Akbar which was quoted later on by N. N. Law. p. 202.
38. *N.N. Law Promotion of Learning,* p. 204; Sarkar, *Studies in Mughal India,* pp. 20-21.
39. *Maasir-i-Alamgiri,* Tr. (J.N. Sarkar) p. 318; also Elliot and Dowson, *India as Told by Its Own Historians,* Vol. VII p. 162.
40. *Qanun-i-Islam,* p. 43; K.M. Ashraf, *Life and Conditions,* p. 249; L.M. Smiths Append to *Chahar Darwesh,* p. 253; Keay *Ancient Indian Education,* p. 130. *Bihar Through the Ages,* p. 543; N. N. Law, *Promotion of Learning,* pp. 128-141; *Behisti Zewar,* (Urdu) Vol. VI, p 17; also *Masnavi Mir Hassan,* p. 35; S.K. Banerjee *Humayun Badshah,* p. 3.
41. For Prince's education in this age refer to *Bezm-i-Taimuria* Vol. I (First edn. 1973) p. 32; *Akbar Namah* Vol. I, Tr. (Bev.) p. 519; also *Akbar Nama,* Vol. III, Tr. pp. 105-106; Badaoni *Muntakhab-ut-Twarikh,* Vol. II, Tr. (Lowe) p. 173; for girls education in the same age consult, *Qanun-i-islam,* p. 43; S.M. Jaffar, *Education in Muslim India,* p. 151; *Behisti Zewar,* Vol. VI, p. 17; Hugh's *Dictionary of Islam,* p. 51; M.L. Bhagi, *Medieval Indian Culture and Thought.* p. 357; while Manucci refers that princesses started their education at the age of five, *Storia,* Vol. II, pp. 346-347.
42. Abul Fazl, *Akbar Namah,* Vol. I, Tr. (Bev.) (1972) p. 519; also K.M. Ashraf, *Life and Conditions...* Journal A.S.B. Art. No. 4. 1935, p. 249.
43. Herklot's *Qanun-i-Islam,* p. 43.
44. *Ibid.,* p. 44.
45. *Ibid.,* also Ashraf Ali Thanvi, *Behisti Zewar* (Urdu), Vol. VI, p. 18.
46. Herklot's *Qanun-i-Islam,* p. 43; also Ashraf Ali Thanvi, *Behishti Zewar* (Urdu) Vol. VI, p. 18.
47. *Ibid.,* also R.R. Diwakar, *Bihar Through the Ages,* p. 543.

48. K.M. Ashraf, *Life and Conditions* (Herklot's) p. 249; *Qanun-i-Islam,* p. 44; R. R. Diwakar *Bihar through the Ages,* p. 543.
49. Ashraf Ali, *Behishti Zewar* (Urdu) Vol. VI, p. 18.
50. Herklot's *Qanun-i-Islam,* p. 44.
51. S.M. Jaffar, *Education in Muslim India,* pp. 190-191; N.N. Law, *Promotion of Learning,* p. 200; also Herklot's *Qanun-i-Islam,* p. 52.
52. N.N. Law, *Promotion of Learning,* pp. 200-201; S. M. Jaffar, *Education in Muslim India,* p. 191; also Herklot's *Qanun-i-Islam,* p. 52.
53. *Qanun-i-Islam,* p. 51; S.M. Jaffar, *Education in Muslim India,* p. 191; N. N. Law, *Promotion of Learning,* p. 200; *Behishti Zewar,* Vol. VI, p. 18.
54. Sarkar, *Studies in Aurangzeb's Reign* (Cal. 1919), p. 130; also Sarkar, *Studies in Mughal India* (Cal. 1919), *Tarikh-i-Hind* (Urdu), p. 670.
55. *Qanun-i-Islam* (Herklot's) p. 51; N. N. Law, *Promotion of Learning,* p. 200; S.M. Jaffar, *Education in Muslim India,* p. 191.

4

Purdah, Divorce, Widowhood

Segregation of women is enforced by Islam. Women according to the Holy *Quran* should be confined to homes and if forced to go outside of her home, they should strictly observe *purdah.*[1] Further, their dress and conduct should not of attract the male passers-by. Thus complete seclusion came to be a rule for all Muslim ladies of the world.

In India among the Hindus, however, the *purdah* system existed long before the advent of the Muslims. S.M. Jaffar writes, "Seclusion of women could be traced back to all ancient communities and it was particularly so among the aristocracy during the palmy days to Hindu civilization".[2]

In ancient India ladies were truly excluded from mixing with males and they observed *purdah* by moving lapel of their saris or other head dress slightly over their face when passing by a stranger.

Thus undoubtedly *purdah* is an ancient indigenous institution and has been existing in India from time immemorial. Truly with the advent of Turks in India strict *purdah* system became very common, and new plans about the *purdah* was introduced in this land from Persia.

In Mughal India, *purdah* was mainly observed by classes of Muslim ladies with slight differences. Hamilton writes, "The Mohammedan women always go veiled when they appear abroad."[3] Ladies of the upper class society strictly observed *purdah* none could notice the toes of their feet. In fact *purdah* came to be considered as a dimension of respectability among higher classes. Della Valle remarks, 'For these unless they be dishonest or poor never come abroad'.[4] Caveri writes "The Mohammedan women do not appear in public except only the vulgar sort, and the leud ones.'[5] No Muslim could tolerate his wife noticeable in public at any cost. Once when a soldier was travelling with his wife and daughter, the tax collector on the way tried to search the cart by force, where the ladies were sitting. The soldier became so furious that he removed the head of the tax collector and also wounded his several attendants. He also felt himself dishonoured as his wife and daughter seen by the tax collector and so he killed them too.[6]

It was regarded dishonour if a Muslim lady of high family discarded *purdah* to save her life even temporarily. Manucci writes, "Among the Mohammedans it was a great dishonour for a family when a wife is compelled to uncover herself'.[7] Amir Khan felt much degraded and decided to divorce his wife when she had failed to observe *purdah* in an effort to save her life by leaping from the back of the elephant who had run amuck.[8]

Purdah was so strictly observed that even doctors, being males, could not see and touch a woman patient. Manucci writes that the Mohammedans are very touchy in subject of allowing their women to be noticed and even touched by hand.[9] A curious procedure was adopted by doctors for diagnosing the malady as best as they could, without seeing her face or feeling her pulse. A handkerchief was rubbed all over the body of the female patient and then it was put into a jar of water. The doctor afterwards judged the course of illness by its smell and prescribed the medicine[10] accordingly.

In case of illness of a woman of a royal harem the physician was taken to the patient covering his eyes with a coarse cloth, so that he might not see the retired ladies. The physician remained outside the door behind the screen and the patient presented only that part of the hand un-wrapped so that pulse could be felt. He, thus, diagnosed the disease by feeling the patient's pulse from behind a curtain.[11]

But like Razia Sultan, Empress Nurjahan also defied the *purdah* convention, and showed her extraordinary personality in the public. On state occasions, she appeared in public and always insisted to see personally the things and the people whose conditions and whose affairs she was called upon to regulate and rule.[12] However, face was covered upto the lips.

Whenever, the honourable ladies of the higher section moved about, they were carried in 'dolis' with men in attendance. The ladies of middle class also strictly observed *purdah* and always appeared abroad in *'chadar'*[13] and *'burqas'* or long garments covering their heads[14] and bodies down to their ankles.[15]

But no such strict *purdah* system was observed among the people of lower classes like Peasants and working class women, working in fields. They moved about freely without any veil or *'burqas'* and observed only *'ghunghat'*,[16] like their Hindu sisters, and hid their faces from men while appearing in public. Thus to some extent they followed this *Quran*ic rule, "Women can move about and earn their living but they have to cast down their eyes and to conceal those parts of their body that are apt to excite passions and not to display their ornaments.'[17]

In Muslim society *purdah* was observed so strictly that it was considered a great dishonour even to address a respectable lady by her name in the assembly of men. Even in her own household she was forbidden to talk or laugh loudly lest other men hear her voice. Association with any male relatives other than her husband or such male relatives as are forbidden in marriage by reason of consanguinity, was prohibited. Della Valle remarks, 'the Mohammendans would not allow their wives to talk even to their relatives except in their presence".[18]

There was no such complete seclusion of Turkish women from the outside world as in India.[19] Mughal ladies could receive their male relatives from abroad more liberally than Indian Muslims. Monrique also records that on one occasion he dined with the minister Asaf Khan and met the Emperor and various members of the Imperial family. In this feast, many unveiled ladies of rank took their seats at the table.[20] Thus all these show that, the prohibition regarding *'Purdah* of the Mughals of that time was never severe.[21]

How *Purdah* was Observed ?

The first step towards the seclusion of women happened in the life of Prophet Mohammad who commanded the women to cover their face and figure while going out. Due to some departure from strict propriety by Aishah, one of his wives, Prophet Mohammad issued a command that all ladies belonging to the faithful should be compelled to wear a close veil over their face and figure whenever they went abroad.

Thereafter the Muslim ladies of Arabia and other countries began to observe *purdah* by wearing a veil when walking or riding out.

Muslim entered India with such ideas of *purdah.*

During the Turko-Afghan period the practice of strict seclusion originated in India with Amir Timur, the conqueror of India. He entered India with his women and army and issued a proclamation by saying, 'As they were now in the land of idolatory and amongst a strange people, the women of their families should be strictly concealed from the view of strangers.'[22]

Amir Timur himself invented different types of covered conveyances, suiting to each grade of female rank in society. He commanded the ladies to be confined to their own apartments and behind the *purdah,* prohibiting any social intercourse with males of their own religion except those closely related. It was a crime for any woman to willingly suffer her person to be seen by men out of the prescribed limits of consanguinity.

During the Mughal age all Mughal emperors emphasised on the enforcement of *purdah,* but Akbar made a regulation to which Badaoni refers, "And if a young woman were found running about the lanes and bazars of the town and while so doing either did not veil herself or allowed herself to be unveiled she was to go to the quarters of the prostitutes and take up the profession."[23]

Consequently all Muslim ladies, with the exception to peasants or inferior servants had to save themselves strictly from observation. Young girls were directed by their elders to seclude themselves from the eyes of strangers. Little girls when only four years old,[24] were kept behind the *purdah* and always moved about in covered conveyances and under the guardianship of a loyal female domestic, as tenacious as the mother to preserve that little girl's reputation, unblemished, by concealing her from the gaze of man.

Child Marriage and its Impact on Medieval Indian Society

An early marriage had become almost a distinctive feature of Medieval Indian society. Both the Hindus and the Muslims were victimised to this evil practice. Their children were commonly wedded before attaining the age of puberty, mostly at the age of seven, eight and nine.[25]

Muslim law fixes no particular age for marriage of Muslim girls. Prophet Mohammad commanded to perform three things at the earliest—Prayer *(Namaz),* funeral *(janaza)* and the *Nikah* of daughters.[26] He advised the believers, "All young men who have arrived at the age of puberty should marry, for marriage prevents sins'.[27] But there were many instances scattered in Islamic history about early marriages. Bibi Aiyshah Siddiqa the youngest wife of Prophet Mohammad, was bound with the marriage knot *(Nikah)* at the age of only six and her *Rukhsati* (departure to her husband's house) took place when she reached the age of nine.[28] Therefore the Muslims married their daughters at a tender age.

During this period, child marriage was common in Muslim society, particularly in rural areas. It was believed that a girl not married before the age of puberty caused anxiety to her parents and disgraced them in their society. In the circumstances, parents generally preferred their daughter's marriage at an early age. Carerl also states, "The Mohammedan Indians marry very young".[29] Sometimes, parents fixed the marriages of their children even before their taking birth. Purchas writes, 'These marriages are made when they be young, sometimes almost before they be".[30] In such cases the ladies having very good relations between them, promised during pregnancy that they would marry their children in case there might be a girl and a boy. In fact, when death or the sex did not prevent them, they contracted the marriages of their children at an earlier age *viz.* three, four[31] or six or seven.[32]

It was believed that early marriage would mould the girl more easily in her husband's house according to their standards and that the married children living in the same house could develop an attachment for each other in maintaining conjugal happiness.

In urban areas, Muslim girls were married when they reached the age of twelve or thirteen. So Terry refers, 'They marry for the most part at the age of twelve or thirteen.[33] But if the parents of a girl could easily secure a suitable match, they preferred to marry her even her at an earlier age. It is also noteworthy in such cases, that when the marriages of the girls were finalised, they were mostly left in their parental home after *Nikah* ceremony till the marriageable age. And as such the actual marriage ceremony and Rukhsati were performed when the bride and the bridegroom had attained the age of puberty."[34]

During the Mughal age the evil practice of early marriage was usually observed by Indians Muslims. In Imperial families, however, marriages were celebrated when the girls completed the age of thirteen of fourteen. Babur's daughter Gulrang's marriage took place in 1530 A.D., with Isan Timur on completion of her fifteenth year.[35] Similarly, another daughter, Gulchihra's marriage to Tukhta Bugha Khan was celebrated when she was fourteen.[36] Gulbadan Begum's marriage was also solmenised with Khizr Khwaja Khan not prior to fourteen years.[37] Arjumand Bano Begum was married to Shahjahan, when she was 19 years five moths and seven days old.[38]

Marriages of boys took place at the age of fifteen or sixteen. Jahangir was married to Man Bai, daughter of Raja Bhagwan Das, in his sixteenth year.[39] Dara was over eighteen, when he was married.[40] Aurangzeb was also married at eighteen years and seven months.[41] Prince Mohammad Sultan was married at the age of twenty.[42] Manucci also records that young princes were brought up in the palace, upto the age of 16 years and then they were to be married.[43] Some marriages were performed at earlier ages also. Babar's first marriage with Aiyshah Sultan[44] took place at the age of eleven. Bakhshi Banu Begum, daughter of Humayun and Gunwar bibi, was married to Ibrahim, when she was only ten years old.[45]

But the prevalent system of child marriage was not admirable. Abul Fazl remarks, "In the extensive country of India men are active to form this union at a tender age. and this introduces the leaven of evil".[46] These all stopped the girl's progress, prosperity, the development of her mind and physical stability.

Not only that, the girls were given in marriage at so unripe an age that they could not even know the actual meaning of it. Therefore, a little newly wedded girl often experienced feeling when confined in the environment of her husband's house\, which was not familier to her. In case she became a widow at an early age, her whole life was doomed. The purport of her life's happiness and its existence was meaningless for her.

Another evil consequence was that child marriage spoiled the health of girls who became mothers of several children at an early age.[47] Thevenot writes, "......but the women who have children so young, soon leave off child bearing and commonly do not conceive after thirty years of age, but became extremely wrinkly'...[48]

The evil results of child marriage did not escape the keen eyes of Akbar, who made laws to check this practice. Abul Fazl writes, "He abhors marriages which take place between men and women before the age of puberty. They bringforth no fruit and His Majesty thinks them even hurtful; for afterwards, when such a couple ripens into manhood, they dislike having connexion and their home is desolate".[49] As the children born of early marriages were generally weak, he forbade girls before fourteen and boys before sixteen years of age to be married.[50]

But despite the strict proclamation of Akbar's regulations, the system of child marriage, could not be stopped fully and continued subsequently too.

Child manuall still prevails in rural areas, although it is declining steadily because of the efforts made by the educated and the enlightened Muslims to discourage this system.

Unmatched Marriages

Unmatched marriages were allowed in Muslim society during the Mughal age. Among the Mughal emperors Humayun was the first of the Mughals to contract marriage with Hamida Bano Begum[51] when she was only fourteen years old, whereas Humayun himself was thirty three. Thus he was nineteen years older than this wife.

Unmatched marriages were the worst of all marriages. The Muslim girls also realised and always attempted to avoid such marriages but they could not escape from such evil practices. Emperor Akbar was opposed to such marriage and passed a law that a man could not marry a girl more than twelve years younger to him[52] and vice versa. Coming to the age of Akbar unmatched marriage was a common evil. Akbar for the first time, therefore, tried to ban this bad system by enforcing this law in the country.

Unmatched marriages were never contracted voluntarily by both the parties; in some cases some social pressures imposed on the greed given to a poor victimised girl. Therefore, poor young girls married rich old men and only the money factor played an important role in fixing such marriage.[53] Contrarily, the old wealthy women tempted young men quite junior to them in age and victimised them who never objected to it, for they wanted wealth and a prosperous life.

System of Divorce

In Mughal India, the system of divorce was prevalent in Muslim society, but wise and honourable persons always disapproved of it. Undoubtedly, it is lawful in Islam but disliked by God and allowed only under stringent conditions and as the last resort. Islam strictly emphasised that every effort should be made by both the parties to remove differences if any and at reconciliation and their conjugal disputes must be settled by means of arbiters.[54] The *Quran* says, 'And if ye fear even a breach between them (husband and wife), then send ye a judge chosen from his family, and a judge chosen from her family, that peace be maintained'.[55] But if differences become serious and all attempts at reconciliation have failed then divorce is the only remedy. Gulbarg Begum, daughter of Nizamuddin Ali Barlas was married to Mir Shah Husain but the alliance was not happy[56] and a separation took place which resulted in divorce.

Divorce is lawful in Islam because marriage is considered as a civil contract rather than a sacrament of divine origin, and so the marriage may be severed.

During the Mughal age, a man and a greater rights than a woman and could divorce his wife even against her will. During Akbar's time, the mother of Saif Khan Koka was threatened by her husband to be divorced if she would give birth to a girl again. The loyal lady, who was very faithful to her husband and never wanted to be separated from him, complained to Akbar's mother.[57] But in course of time a son was born who was named Saif Khan Koka.

During the reign of Jahangir, Asaf Jah's daughter Misri Begum was married to Jarullan, son of Asaf Khan, but out of congruity their marriage had never been consumated. Then Jahangir ordered Jarullah to divorce his wife[58] so that she could remarry and save her from mental torture.

A husband could pronounce a divorce in the state of anger as Babar's sister Khan Zada was divorced by Shaibani in anger.[59] She supported her brother against him. Once, Shahebji, the wife of Amir Khan, was going in a litter on the back of an elephant when it ran amuck. She removed her *'purdah'*, ran into a money-changers shop and saved her life. Amir Khan became so angry that he was about to divorce her, but Shahjahan rebuked him and forbade him to do so.[60]

Sometimes a man had to divorce his wife reluctantly, but because of pressure by others: He repeated the word *'Talaq'* (Divorce) thrice and divorce took legal[61] effect, as is the practice even today; with this the relationship between husband and wife ceased. During the reign of Akbar, Abdul Wasi divorced his beloved beautiful wife as Akbar wished to marry her.[62] In that age if the emperor reflected his desire to marry a married woman, her husband was bound to divorce her to save himself from the king's anger. After divorcing his wife he left the city and went to Bidar[63] to try to forget his past.

When divorce was finally decided upon, the husband had to pay his wife the *Mehar* stipulated at the time of *Nikah,* as was customary, based on the instructions of Islam. When the daughter of Ali Khan, the ruler of Kashmir, was divorced, the dower was demanded from the husband.[64] Therefore, generally heavy dowers were fixed for refraining the husband from wrongfully or causelessly divorcing the wife, and Emperor Akbar also accepted it.[65]

Divorce was effective either orally or in writing without any witness, and the written deed was known as *'Talaq Nama'* or deed of divorce. In case of divorce the father/guardian of a divorced lady demanded *'Talaq Nama'* from her husband to keep it as proof. The son-in-law of Ali Khan had to provide a deed of divorce when he divorced Ali Khan's daughter.[66]

When a divorce took legal effect, the dowry *(Jahez),* given to a bride at the time of *Rukhsati* (departure after *Nikah*) could also be demanded back by the parents or guardians of the woman and the husband had to return whatever he had received. But he had no right to take away from his divorced wife anything he had offered her[67] at the time of marriage or after it. Not only that, a husband was forced according to Islamic law to support his divorced wife during the period of probation,[68] an additional compensation, besides payment of *mehar.* Manucci writes that the husband had to pay compensation to the divorced wife for her maintenance.[69]

The wife was also entitled to ask for a separation on the grounds of ill-treatment, the withholding of due and proper means of maintenance and certain other causes. Then an agreement entered into for dissolving marriage was known as *Khula*[70] and was prevalent during the Mughal age.[71] Following this practice, *'Khula',* the wife had to give back her dower or any other additional amount proposed by the husband. But such divorce was also husband's choice to grant her a divorce.[72]

A divorced woman had to live a life of seclusion and abstain from all luxuries for three months, and this period was called *'Iddat',* which extended in case of a pregnant lady. During this period she had to avoid cosmetics, jewellery, new and fashionable dresses, betel leaf (if for the purpose of dying the lips) nor could she go out of her house, except under unavoidable circumstances, and that too, only during the day time. And marriage with another man was also prohibited. These conditions were strictly observed by the Muslim ladies of the Mughal age,[73] as they were religious injunctions.

Thus, unlike Hindu marriages, Muslim marriages could be dissolved by divorce under certain conditions but people hated it and considered it a necessary evil. The Prophet Mohammad expressed his extreme disapproval towards[74] it and stated that it is calculated to undermine the foundations of society. Therefore, he strictly prohibited the ladies to claim divorce and said, "The women who asks her husband to divorce her, without a cause, even the smell of paradise is forbidden to her."[75] In accordance with this saying, Sheikh Muin, *Qazi* of Lahore, requested a lady who applied for divorce, not to separate but to await her husband's return,[76] in case of his absence.

In fact, during the period from 1526 to 1707 A.D. divorce in practice was exceedingly rare as respectable people regarded it as the greatest blot on their reputation. The occasion for divorce was also very rare as marriage was settled after considering all existing and contingent circumstances. Another reason was the long impact of Indian culture that Muslim ladies were opposed to taking divorce and were prepared to overcome problems, however, difficult they might be. They preferred to die of family torture rather than be separated from their husbands for good.

Muslim Widows

Muslim widows enjoyed an honourable position in society throughout Mughal period. Unlike Hindus, a Muslim widow was allowed to attend and enjoy the festivities of engagement, *Nikah* and birth ceremonies, as Islam is more generous and liberal towards them and permits them to enjoy the life. The only ban on the widow, was to observe strictly the period of *'Iddat'* of four months and ten days.[77] She had to abandon all physical decorations, make-up ornaments [78] and not wear new, gaudy and silk garments[79] made of flowers or metals. The use of perfume, antimony *(surma)* and *'missi'* were also prohibited. Even during the period of *'Iddat'* she could not use scented oil for her hair and was forbidden to comb it smoothly. She had to be secluded in the house and was not permitted to move about except under unavoidable circumstances, that too during the day and covering herself with a veil.[80] In course of pregnancy pregnant, she had to follow the Islamic rules of *Iddat* only upto the birth of her child.[81]

During this age, a Muslim widow strictly observed these rules and neither used forbidden dresses nor any ornament.[82] In her *'Iddat'* she was regarded more respectfully and people had a more sympathetic attitude towards her.

Fryer, reffering to a peculiar custom observed by the Muslim widows of that age, writes, 'The widow once a moon go to the grave with her acquaintance to repeat the dole ful Dirge, after which she bestows Holy way a kind of sacramental water and entreats prayer for the soul of the departed."[83]

After completion of the period of *'iddat',* a widow could remarry if willing. Mostly all foreign travellers of the period (1526–1707 A.D.) recorded the system of remarriage prevalent among the Muslims, and it was not disapproved till the reign of Aurangzeb but after him widow remarriage lost its popularity in Muslim society as in Hindu society. (During the reign of Mohammad Shah (1719–1748 A.D.) widow remarriage was regarded undesirable especially among higher and respectable families).[84] Therefore many religious heads tried to check this prejudice as Prophet Mohammad strongly favoured the widow remarriage. In fact, Islam, unlike Hindu faith and dogma, took a more generous and frank view of natural instincts and considered widow remarriage as desirable as fresh marriage. All the wives of Prophet Mohammad, except the youngest Alshah, were previously married. Therefore, Mughal rulers never forbade their ladies to remarry rather they encouraged widow remarriage by themselves marrying widows. Consequently, during the Mughal rule, widow remarriage was widely practised by the rich and the poor alike.

In a family where there was a young widow not only the members of her husbands's family but his parents and relatives and other respectable person of society took pity on her and tried their best to adjust her in the family by remarrying her with the younger brother of the deceased, a Turkish custom. Therefore, Sultan Nigar Khanam, daughter of Yunus Khan, on her husband Awiq's death, was remarried to his brother Qasim as per the custom.[85] Manucci also refers to this custom thus, 'Since the law thus directed that the wives of a dead elder brother belonged to the living younger brother.'[86] Under this custom Aurangzeb wished to marry Rana Dil the widow of Dara[87] but this marriage did not materialize.

Some Muslim widows opposed remarriage and most of them preferred to live in retirement, embracing the memories of their late husbands. Such widows were greatly honoured not only in the family but in society too. When Aurangzeb came to know that Rana Dil did not went to remarry, he gave her more respect and always treated her with the courtesy[88] which she deserved.

Widow's position in society was better than that of the Hindu widows. A Muslim widow could enjoy property rights and had a share in the property of her diceased husband, however small. If she had a child or son's child, her right over this property was 1/8th but if childless, then 1/4th of the property, according to Islamic rule.[89]

After the observation of 'Iddat' a Muslim widow could put on jewellery, fine dresses and shoes. She could grow long hair, use scented oil, eat any type of food of her choice, drink cold water and sleep according to her will as Islam imposed no restriction in such topics, quite unlike Hinduism.[90] Consequently, a widow passed her life almost as she did in her husband's life time but with minor changes. Overall, she lived a simple life as compared to her past.

A Muslim widow was not deprived of social privileges and her presence on festive occasions was not considered inauspicious as considered among Hindus.[91] She could freely negotiate some one's marriage and could enjoy the marriage festivities. When Babar's widow Maham Begum proposed to Humayun to marry Maywajan, he as a mark of respect, agreed to this and married the women according to Maham's wish.[92]

Unfortunately, Hindu widows were not allowed by the society to participate in birth, marriage, or any other ceremony. Unlike this a Muslim widow never felt like a stranger during a wedding or any other happy event in family or society. She participated in a marriage feast with no hesitation or objection and could enjoy the gathering of the ladies of rank without discrimination.[93] Widows of royal families not only feasts and festivals but also arranged the *Jashn* as a mark of some significant event as they wished.[94] Similarly she could actively participated in the birth ceremonies of the children of her son; she also enjoyed the pleasure of picnics,[95] and the journey on expedition,[96] with other members of her family and was treated with great respect.

The death of her husband increased a widow's responsibilities in the family and so she devoted most of her time to the house and in taking care of her grand children and daughters-in-law.[97] She kept watch on the domestic problems and tried her best to solve them.

Educated widows enjoyed an honourable position in the Mughal age. They imparted learning to the inmates of the royal *harem* and the nobles families. The rich classes respected them and.appointed them as tutors of the daughters and sisters.

Muslim widows generally led a life of solitude and prayer. They kept themselves busy in performing religious duties like performing *Namaz* (Prayer), reading the *Quran,* fasting, and repeating God's name with the help of Tasbeeh (rosary) and doing good.[98] Such virtuous deeds impressed all and sundry, and she was regarded as a model of virtue by them.[99] Babar's widow Maham Begum performed pious works for the departed soul of her husband. For two and a half years, she made an allowance of food to the poor twice daily from her own estate.[100]

Muslim widows also took great interest in conducting their 'Haj' by going to Macca and therefore they had permission to go on pilgrimage[101] but not alone.

A widow in her family was treated with more respect than before by her children who believed that the paradise lay under mother's feet and always obeyed her and took care of her.[102] Great care was taken by her son to save her from being avoided by the family. He also inquired about her health from time to time. Mughal kings paid much honour to the royal widows and spoke with kindness and commiseration.[103] Knowing about the illness of his widow mother, Akbar turned from Sikandrabad to Delhi[104] for seeing her, which shows Akbar's love for his mother. Aurangzeb also had respect for widows and made good arrangements for them in their respective apartments, 'suhagpura'.[105]

Mughal emperors, their ladies and many pious persons of the time had great sympathy for the poor Muslim widows and for their maintenance they fixed allowances[106] to avoid misfortunes.

The life of a Muslim widow therefore, during the Mughal age was not miserable, because she enjoyed a respectable position in society.

References

1. *The Holy Quran* refers, 'O Prophet I speak to thy wives and to thy daughters and to the wives of the faithful that they let their wrappers fall low.' Chapt. XXII Surah XXXIII.
2. S.M. Jaffar, *Some Cultural Aspects of Muslim Rule in India,* pp. 200-201.
3. Hamilton, Vol. I, p. 163 also for purdah see Fryer, Vol. II, pp. 117-118 also Barbosa Vol. II, p. 147.
4. Della Valle, p. 411 also De Laet, p. 80.
5. Careri, Indian Travels, p. 248.
6. *Storia,* Vol. II, Tr. p. 175.
7. *Ibid.*
8. *Masir-ul-Umarah,* Vol. I, Tr. pp. 251-252.
9. *Storia,* Vol. II, Tr. p. 209.
10. *John Marshal in India* (1668-72), ed. by Sri Ahmad Khan, Oxford, 1927 p. 328.
11. *Storia,* Vol. I pp. 352, 357 also Bernier, Eng. Tr. p. 267.
12. *Introducing India* Pt. I Pub. R.A.S.B. 1947 Art No. 9, p. 92; also Powell Price, *History of Jahangir* (1955) p. 294.
13. Badaoni, Vol. I (Ranking) p. 503.
14. *Careri Travels,* p. 240.
15. J.A.S.B. Vol. I (1935) p. 342 also Hamilton, p. 97.
16. S.M. Jaffer, *Some Cultural Aspects of Muslim Rule in India,* p. 202.
17. The Holy Quran, Chapt. XXIV Verses 30–31.
18. Della Valle, p. 430.
19. Humayun Namah, Tr. (Bev.) Introduction, p. 7.
20. Manrique, p. 52.
21. H.G. Keene, *History of Hindustan* (c) 1972, p. 199.
22. *Observations,* Vol. I, p. 322.
23. Badaoni, Vol. II (Lowe) p. 405; also Pers. p. 391.
24. *Observations,* Vol. I, p. 322.
25. Mandelslo, Vol. I, pp. 51, 115; also Linschoten, *Early Travels of India* (1864) p. 197; also Purchas, p. 106; also Thevenot, *Indian Travels* (ed. Sen) pp. 72, 248; also Finch, *Early Travels in India,* ed. by Foster, pp. 16-19; also Withington, *Early Travels in India,* ed. by Foster p. 221; For other references to child marriage, see Manucci, *Storia Do Mogor,* Vol. III Tr. pp. 54, 58; also Pelsaert, p. 84.
26. *Al-Nikah,* Arabic MS. O.P.L. Patna, p. 214.
27. Hugh's *Dictionary of Islam,* p. 314.
28. Md. Aslam, *Khwateen,* (Delhi, 1951), p. 40. A reference may also be made to Aiyshah Siddiqa's child marriage in Badaoni's *Muntakh-ul-Twarikh,* Vol., II, Tr. (Lowe). p. 349.

29. *Indian Travels* (ed. Sen) p. 249; also for the references of early marriages among Muslims; refer Colliver Rice, *Persian Women and their ways* (London, 1923) p. 91; also S.M. Jaffar, *Some Cultural Aspects of Muslim Rule in India* (Peshawar, 1939) p. 168.
30. Purchas, *Pilgrimage,* p. 90.
31. *Ibid.*
32. Mrs. Meer Hassan Ali, *Observations,* p. 347.
33. *Early Travels,* ed. by Foster, pp. 320-321.
34. Manucci, *Storia Do Mogor,* Vol. III, Tr. pp. 58-59; also Mrs. Meer Hassan Ali, *Observations,* p. 347.
35. The actual year of Gulrang's birth has not revealed but she was born between 1511 and 1515 A.D. Gulbadan Begum, *Humayun Namah,* Tr. (Bev.) p. 232.
36. *Ibid.,* p. 231.
37. Gulbadan Begum, *Humayun Namah,* Tr. (Bev.) p. 31.
38. Qazwini, *Padshah Namah,* Pers. MS. (Buhar, Coll.) p. 30.
39. *Badaoni, Muntakhab-ul-Twarikh,* Vol. II Tr. (Lowe) p. 352.
40. *Qanungo,* Dara Shukoh, pp. 13-19.
41. Sarkar, *Studies in Aurangzeb's reign,* (Calcutta, 1933) pp. 1-2.
42. Sarkar, History of Aurangzeb, Vol. III, p. 44.
43. *Manucci, Storia Do Mogor,* Vol. II, Tr. p. 347.
44. *Babur Namah,* p. 21; also Gulbadan Begum, *Humayun Namah,* Tr. (Bav.), p. 209; S Lanepoole also says that Babur was betrothed to Aiyshah at the age of five and married after few years. 'Babar', pp. 55 and 193.
45. Gulbadan Begum, *Ibid.* p. 214.
46. *Akbar Namah,* Vol. III, Tr. p. 791.
47. Stavcrinus, *Voyage to East Indies* (London, 1798), Tr. by Samuel Hill, Vol. I, p. 440.
48. Thevenot, *Indian Travels* (ed. Sen), p. 117.
49. Abul Fazl, *Ain-i-Akbari,* Vol. I, Tr. (Bloch), p. 287; also for the reference of Akbar's saying with regard to child marriage see Ain Vol. III, Tr. (J&S), p. 448.
50. Badaoni, *Muntakhab-ul-Twarikh,* Vol. II, Tr. (Lowe), p. 315.
51. *Humayun Namah,* Pers. Tr. (Bev.) pp. 151-152 also *Tazkirat-ul-Wakiat* (Stewart), pp. 44-45 Fn. 2, also *Journal of the United Provinces Historical Society* Vol. VII 1934, also S.K. Banerjee, Humayun Badshah, pp. 37-38; also Badaoni, *Muntakhab-ul-Twarikh* Vol I, Tr. (Ranking) p. 560.
52. *Badaoni,* Vol. II (Lowe) p. 405.
53. *Manucci, Storia Do Mogor,* Vol. III, Tr. p. 55.
54. Mohammad bin Saleh, Almajmuah, *Al-Nikah wa Al Talaque,* Arabic MS. No. 2622, O.P.L. Patna, p. 127; also Md. Zafruddin *Islam ka Nizam iffat wa Asmat* (Urdu), p. 53.

55. *The Holy Quran,* Chapt. 5, Surah 4, Verse 35.
56. *Ain-i-Akbari,* Vol. I, Tr. (Bloch), p. 375.
57. *Humayun Namah,* Appendix A, p. 230.
58. *Maasir-ul-Umarah,* Vol. II, Part II, tr. p. 819.
59. Khafi Khan, *Muntakhab-ul-Lubab,* Vol. I, Tr. (Urdu), p. 49; also *Humayun-Namah,* Tr. (Bev.) appendix A, also S. Lanepoole, *Babur,* pp. 59-60.
60. *Maasir-ul-Umarah,* Vol. I, Tr. (Bev.) p. 251.
61. Badaoni, *Muntakhab-ul-Twarikh,* Vol. II, Tr. (Lowe) pp. 59-60.
62. *Ibid.*
63. *Ibid.,* p. 251.
64. *Ibid.* Vol. III, Tr. (Haig) p. 99.
65. *Ibid.,* Vol. II Tr. (Lowe) p. 352; also *Tabaqat-i-Akbari,* Vol. II, Tr. (B.De) p. 599.
66. *Badaoni,* Vol. III (Haig), p. 99.
67. *The Holy Quran,* Chapt. 4, Surah 4, Verses 19-20.
68. *Hugh's Dictionary of Islam,* p. 680; also Md. Zairud Din, *Islam ka Nizam Iffatwa-Asmat* (Urdu) p. 208.
69. *Storia,* Vol. III, Tr. p. 152.
70. Ma-hammad-bin-Saleh, Almaimuah, *Al-Nikah wa Al-Telaque* Arabic MS. p. 125; also Md. Zafirud Din, *Islam Ka Nizam Iffatwa-Asmat* (Urdu) p. 83.
71. Badaoni refers to a lady who filed for separation (Khula) from her husband on the ground of his absence from her, *Muntakhabaul-Twarikh,* Vol. III, Tr. p. 147.
72. *Miskhat,* Vol. III, 173, p. 47.
73. Mrs. Meer Hasan Ali, *Observations,* p. 46.
74. Mohammad bin Saleh, Ajmajmuah, *Al-Nikah wa Al-Telaque* MS. (Arabic) p. 126.
75. Mishkat, XIII C. XV also *Hugh's Dictionary of Islam,* p. 87.
76. Badaoni Vol. III Tr. (Halq), p. 47.
77. *Miskhat,* Vol. III, 188, p. 53.
78. Like Hindu widows whom Careris refers to break their glass and ivory brackets they wear on their arms, *Indian Travels,* p. 250.
79. *Miskhat,* Vol. III, 190, p. 53.
80. *Behishti Zewar* (Urdu), Vol IV, p. 34.
81. *The Holy Quran,* Surah IXV 4, II, 234.
82. *Observations,* p. 46.
83. Fryer, p. 94.
84. Maulana Syeed Abul Hassan Ali Nadvi, *Hindustani Mussalman Ek Nazar Men* (Urdu), p. 63.
85. Gulbadan, *Humayun Namah* Tr. (Bev.) p. 291; also S. Lanepoole; *Babar,* p. 114.

86. *Storia,* Vol. I, tr. p. 361.
87. *Ibid.*
88. *Ibid.*
89. *The Holy Quran,* Chapt. IV Surah IV Verse XII.
90. Withington, *Early Travels,* p. 219 also *Storia,* Vol. III p. 61 also Keshav das, *Ramchandrika Purvardha,* edited by Lala Bahgwandeen pub. by Ram Narain Lal (Allahabad) third impression ninth cento (Prakash) Chhandas 18 and 19; also *Miss Cheep Man's English Book,* Tr. (Urdu) p. 10.
91. *Miss Cheep's Man English Book,* Tr. (Urdu), p. 9.
92. Gulbadan, *Humayun Namah,* Pers. p. 27 also Tr. (Bev.), p. 112.
93. In Hindal's marriage feast many widows participated and were given respect there, see Humayun Namah, Pers. p. 33. also Tr. (Bev.) p. 122.
94. Maham Begum the widow of Babur arranged a grand feast in honour of his son Humayun, *Ibid.,* Pers. p. 28 Tr. (Bev.) p. 113.
95. *Ibid.*
96. *Ibid.* Tr. p. 129.
97. *Ibid.* Pers. p. 29 Tr. p. 115 see Chapt. IV of this work.
98. *Maasirul Umarah,* Vol. I Tr. (Bev) pp. 49-50 also H.G. Keene History of Hindustan (c) 1972, p. 189.
99. *Hindustani Mussalman Ek Nazar Men* (Urdu) pp. 62-83.
100. *Humayun Namah,* Tr. (Bev) p. 111.
101. Badaoni, Vol. II Pers. Text p. 310 also *Akbar Namah,* Vol. II Tr. (Bev.) p. 569 also *Humayun Namah,* Tr. (Bov.) APPENDIX A.P. 279.
102. Prof. Khalique Ahmad Nizami, *Tarikhi Maqalat* (Urdu), Nadwatul Mussennefeen (Delhi, 1966, First edn.) p. 49.
103. *Humayun Namah,* Tr. p. 110, Pers. p. 29.
104. *Ain-i-Akbari,* Vol. I, Tr. (Bloch) p. 352.
105. Manucci, *Storia Do Mogor,* Vol. II, Tr. p. 127, also. f.n.I.
106. *Maasir-ul-Umara* Vol. II, Tr. (Bev.) p. 525.

5

The *Devadasi* System

Ritual dancing, as part of religious services in a temple has a long history. In India the practice originated and developed during *the early medieval period,* but in countries like Mesopotamia, Egypt and Greece, the system flourished several thousand years earlier.

In India, the temple women came mostly from the low caste non-Brahmin families, although, the cases of Brahmin and other higher caste women are not unknown. Slaves were also dedicated to or purchased by the temple.

The instances of some higher caste people, including the royal families, are also available, In 1047, Bicabbarasi, the younger sister of Kunda Raja, was donated to the temple of Jagadeka Mallesvara. Kulasekhara, the Chera king, is said to have dedicated his daughter as devadasi. Some high caste Hindu women become devadasis in order to escape widowhood.

In India, even today, people dedicate girls to goddes Yellamma of *Saundatti* in Karnataka in fulfilment of their vow.

Justification for the Study

In India the whole process of social formation from the fifth-sixth centuries onwards appears to be inseparably connected with developments in the field of religion. In South India too, the process of development was similar. Religious authority in early medieval South India was as much rooted in ritual purity of the *Brahmanas* as in the institutional authorities of the temple and the monasteries. Inscriptions, which frequently refer to the washing of the feet of a religious figure, priest or pontiff, at the time of grant of land and benefices, bear testimony to the subordination of political authority to religious authority. The development becomes fairly marked when we take the study of *devadasi* system in South Indian temples.

The keynote of the religious life in early medieval South India was the various kind of activities centring round temple. At the centre of the temple network was a principal deity or deities surrounded invariably by his divine associates and human retinue. The *devadasi* was an important member of the human retinue. She had to participate in almost all the daily rituals and occasional ceremonies. Since the rousing of the deity from sleep in early morning through the various ritual services in the day, to the time when the god went to sleep, the presence of the *devadasi* was necessary. Even when the god went out for a chariot-ride, as during the processions, the *devadasis* followed the lord as faithful maids in waiting.

Songs and dance performances by *devadasis* in the temple were a source of attraction for both the lay worshippers and pilgrims, which ultimately brought more benefits in the form of grants and offerings. Temples with *devadasis* drew liberal patronage from both rulers and private individuals. We have specific evidence to suggest that the *devadasi* was sent to the king to solicit grant for the temple. Although there were quite a large number of temples which did not have devadasis at all. The temples could not afford to have them either. The presence of *devadasis* in a temple had its own significance and socio-religious purpose. The amount of sanctity attached to a *devadasi* on account of her association with the deity, brought ritual sanctity and social eminence. The sources of the modern period illustrate that even outside the temple the *devadasi* was an integral feature of the social life. Important social occasions would not be ritually auspicious and complete without the presence of *devadasi.* She was a welcome guest to every marriage *pandal* of South India, and it was the *devadasi* who prepared the *tali* (marriage badge) for the bride.

The selection of the peninsular region for a detailed study of the devadasi system is not without reasons. The system, was not so popular and widespread in Northern India as in South India. In the North the *devadasi* system could not emerge as an institution, having strong base in the society. Nor was it a common feature of the majority of temples there. This is the reason that we have only a small number of inscriptions relating to *devadasis* in Northern India.

But in South India *devadasis* were a common feature in

almost all the major brahmanical temples, particularly the saivite ones. It was a matter of prestige for the temples to employ *devadasi* in a good number. The famous Rajarajesvara temple at Thanjavur had four hundred *devadasis,* and the temple of Palakol had five hundred *devadasis* during the reign of Velanandu Codas. Three hundred dancing girls were served in temples at Chebrolu in the Guntur district and Srikakulam in the Krishna district.

Even in South India the development of the institution was not uniform everywhere. The sources make it clear that the *dasis* were concentrated in some selected pockets. On the basis of inscriptions it can be said that the institution was more popular in Chingleput, North Arcot, South Arcot, Thanjavur, Tirunelveli and Tiruchirapalli district of modern Tamil Nadu; Krishna, Guntur and Nellore regions of Andhra Pradesh, and Dharwar and Kolar in Karnataka.

The number of *devadasis* went on increasing and in the course of time, they became so numerous and widespread in South India that they emerged as a separate sub-caste, with their own traditions, rules of behaviour and etiquette, and their own *panchayat* whose decisions were binding on all members.

The period, from the ninth to the twelfth century, marked the origin, development and the maturity of the *devadasi* institution in South India. It is interesting to note how the introduction of dancing girls in temples about the eight-ninth centuries led to the growth of the *devadasi* system, with attendant developments in the fields of ritual practices, value structure and social influences.

The period, from eleventh century to twelfth century, was the high watermark of the institution. It is interesting to note that is approximately the Central part of the feudal age in India. The feudal formation was on its peak in the eleventh-twelfth centuries.

Review of Works

In modern times the first serious attempt to collect detailed information regarding *devadasis* was made by Edgar Thurston in the first decade of the present century. The second volume of his seven-volume *Castes and Tribes of Southern India* contains a survey of the *devadasi* system in the nineteenth and twentieth centuries. The survey is mainly based on the census reports and the judicial proceedings relating to *devadasi* in the different courts of South India. The work is significant in the sense that it throws light on the various aspects of the system, e.g., the particular areas of their concentration, structure of the caste sub-groups among which the system was more popular and also the superstitions and other factors responsible for its growth.

The early inscriptions refer to certain castes, such as Kaikkolan and others, from which *devadasis* were generally recruited. At the present day also the system is found most deeply entrenched in these social groups. One of the important reasons for dedicating a girl to a temple was the absence of a male heir in the family. This is as much evident from early records as from the modern census reports.

Anata Sadasiva Altekar, in his *Rashtrakautas and their Times* attempts to give an authentic and systematic account of the *devadasis* in India. On the basis of literary sources he has reached the right conclusion that the custom came into existence during or after the time of the Guptas, when the *puranas* were being written.

K.K. Pillay, in his Sucindram Temple, gives a detailed account of the *devadasis* at Sucindram.

The chief merit of the work lies in the fact that for the first time we are told about the functioning of the *devadasi* system in a particular temple for over a period of eight hundred years. Different aspects of the institution of devadasis have been mentioned in detail viz., the duties assigned to them in the temple, hierarchical divisions among them, titles of honour conferred upon them, the process of their retirement, etc. However, these facts mostly relate to the period between the seventeenth and nineteenth century.

Rajatnandan Dasgupta's work, entitled "The Institution of Devadasis in Assam" is based on literary sources and the Tejpur Copper Plates Grant of *Vanamala.* The different aspects which are briefly discussed are the castes from which *devadasis* were recruilted, centres of their concentration, dances perormed by *devadasis* and the incidence fo the practice in differebt parts of the country. Besides, the origin of the custom in Assam, has been also discussed. In Assam and other parts of the country, the development of the custom is not recognisable before nine-tenth centuries. Even a cursory study of the practice would show that the *devadasi* system developed and flourished during a particular period, the early medieval period.

Noting a point of difference between the *devadasi* system prevailing in Assam and the one flourishing in South India, Dasgupta states that in Assam a *devadasi* was dedicated to the temple for the sole purpose of dancing at the time of *arti* twice a day and that 'no mysterious or semi-religious association is made with the profession as in the case of South India'.

A Vaidehi Krishnamoorthy in her *Social And Economic Condition in Eastern Deccan*, throws welcome light on the custom in early medieval Andhra. The work is based on epigraphic records. The decription is brief but informative and constitutes a valuable addition to the subject in as much as it is the only piece which seeks to present a more or less complete picture of the *devadasi* system in a particular region of South India.

The institution of *devadasis* in Andhra has some special features. For example, the settlement of three hundred or five hundred *devadasis* in different temple establishments worked as guilds and exercised great influence on the people.

M.G.S. Narayanan's "Handmaids of God", published in his collection of articles *Aspects of Aryanization in Kerala*. Is based on both epigraphic and literary sources. He starts the discussion with a short introduction on dance referring mainly to the description of dance in Bharata's *Natyasastra* and the Silappadikaram; then he describes how the study and performance of *Bharatanatyam* spread in Kerala with the growth of the practice of dedicating girls to temples. On the basis of literary references which are corroborated by epigraphic evidence, Naraynan tries to highlight the social status of the *devadasis,* who are often depicted as the heroines of some of romantic poems in medieval Kerala.

Narayana believes that the expansion of the temple system and the growth of the *bhakti* movement brought into existence the class of temple dancing girls. This seems to bc a reasonable form in *bhakti* in which the element of self-surrender, and devotion to service is predominant. The unholy system of *devadasis,* it may be argued, is a personification of this predominant element.

In her work "Social Status of Courtesans in Early Medieval Kerala" M. Sumathy tries to analyses the system of *devadasis* in Kerala in the general background of the early medieval society of Kerala. Based on the epigraphic and literary sources, the study is espically useful in so far as it seeks to investigate a general problem in a regional setting and makes good use of regional sources, particularly *manipravala* literature. Sumathy divides her study into several subheadings and discuss various aspects of the subject, such as donations to temples by *devadasis,* management of endowments, wealth and status of their clients, their relation with ruling chiefs, their patronage by *brahmanas* and so forth.

Origin and Development

The system of *devadasis* was an integral part of the religious services in temples. The temple was an essential part of the early medieval society and economy, the understanding of the development of *devadasi* system has to be in background of the early medieval period.

The medieval temple emerged as the owner of vast landed property and the employer of a large number of religious and non-religious functionaries. The religious functionaries included the priests, dancing girl, dancing masters, drummers conch-blowers, singers, pipers and others. The non-religious functionaries included masons, potters, garland makers, tailors, washermen, etc. For example, the Rajareshvara temple of Thanjavur employed four hundred dancing girls, twelve dancing masters, sixteen musicians, seventy-two drummers, seven pipers, eleven potters, five carpenters, three barbers and others, altogether six hundred and nine servants. All these employees were allotted portions of land usually measured as *veli.* The produce of one *veli* of land was calculated at 100 *kalams* of paddy. The temple of Pidariyar in Kolar had twenty-our dancing girls, four *brahmacaris,* four *yoginis,* four *yogesvaras,* two flower-gatherers besides conch-blowers and others. These employees were paid in both cash and kind.

The deity of an early medieval temple can be compared to a feudal lord who was provided with all the amenities and pleasures of life that were needed by a feudal lord. The amenities included a big and comfortable house, a host of servants, best of food, choicest jewellery, attractive garments, and wives and concubines. The *devadasis* had therefore to be employed to give company to the god as wives and concubines.

The origin of the custom is traceable to the practice of ritual dancing which formed an integral part of the ritual service of gods and goddesses. A dance performed with the intention of moving the deity was considered to be the real form of prayer, and hence its popularity among many ancient peoples of the world. The practice of ritual dancing was also an important aspect of the peoples' life form primitive times. Trances of this custom appear to have influenced the earliest writing of the Tamil people which frequently refer to various aspects of tribal life. The Tolkappiyam, which is the earliest extent grammar of Tamil language and which was composed about the time of the third Sangam, mentions two kinds of ritual dancing-*vallilkuttu* and *kalanilaikkuttu.* Probably, *vallikkuttu* was performed in honour of *Valli,* the consort of god Murugan or the Tamil war god. This kuttu (dance) was popular among the lower classes of society. Another type of dance called *kalanitlaikkuttu* was of a higher order and popular among the nobles and chieftains. Besides these two, there was another form of ritual dance known as *atal Sustra* 60 of the *Purattinaiyial* refers to *velanveriyatal*. The chief feature of this dance was the offering of *bali* or animal sacrifice to god Murugan. In the course of such worship the devotee fell under trance and began to dance. Other in the crowd responded by joining the dancer. Generally this dance was performed with a view to ascertaining the nature of the ailment of a person and also to find a remedy. Rital dancing is prominently mentioned in other *Sangam* works also. It was inseparably connected with the primitive modes of worship. Preferences to such dance in *Kuruntogai,* the *Maduraikklanji* and the *Silappadikaram* bear proof of its prevalence among the tribals. In the worship of Murugan, Mayon and Korravai (Durga) the ritual of dancing associated with the worship of Murugan were called *Veriyatal* and *Velanatal.* The Officiating priest bore the *vel* (spear) in his hand. He acted as the symbolic representation of *Velan* which was another name of the war god and offered worship to the god Murugan. The method of inviting the god to accept the offering is described in an ode in the Kuruntogai.

The religious dance performed at the time of worshipping

Visnu was called *kundam.* This was a form of ancient worship of Lord Krsna, primarily conducted by the cowherd community. We find an example of this dance in the *Maduraikandam* of the epic Silappadikaram. When the innocent Kovalan was sentenced to death at Madurai on the charge of stealing Queen's *silambu* (anklets), there were innumerable bad omens indicated the impending calamity. The cowherd women immediately notice it and they began to pray to Lord Krisna to avert the impending danger. The form of the prayer was known as Kuravaikkuttu. Another example of Kuravaikkuttu is found in the same work. After losing her husband, Kannagi left the city of Madurai and, going along the river Vaigai, reached a hill near the village of Veduvars. She was under a Vengai tree, and the large number of Veduvars were waiting on her when Kovalan appeared in Veduvars by surprise and they decided to venerate Kannagi as a Goddess. In her honour they began to perform Kuravaikkutu accompanied by music. The Silappadikaram refers to another kind of ritual dance in connection with the worship of Aiyai (or Korravai), the goddess of victory, by the hunting community. Here we find that instead of priest, the priestess of the community worshipped the goddess. Salini, born in the family of the Maravars, danced before the goddess Aiyai with appropriate gestures and fell under trance. She was taken in procession to the temple of their guardian deity and worshipped in front of the shrine where the goddess was said to appear and approve what the damsel spoke.

The above description shows that dancing as a form of ritual service was popular among both tribal people such as the Maravars and important social groups as the *Veduvars.* The purpose of ritual dancing was to please the deity and seek some favour. The process of the absorption of tribal ideas and practices into the brahmanical system is very well described. In the first instance, Aiyai, who is a goddess of a hunting tribe called Maravar, is equated with Durga and chracterized as sitting by the side of Siva as the God's consort.

The association of the goddesses with the brahmanical god Siva was a popular way to brahmanise tribal mother goddess and find for them a suitable place in the brahmanical pantheon. It is also interesting to note that the *Silappadi karam* compares *Aiyai* or *Durga* with the flame shining in the heart of each of the three great brahmanical gods, Brahma, Visnu and Siva. It was only natural that the tribal dancing ritual would occupy an important position in the regular service of brahmanical gods and goddess. The Silappadikaram seems to be attributing all the features which characterize the lion-seated Durga of the brahmanical pantheon to a tribal mother goddess. It also appears that the tribal religious practices and tribal goddesses were accepted into the brahmanical pantheon even by the most orthodox among the *Brahmans.* This is a characteristic brahmanical way of absorbing non-brahmanical or proto-brahmanical religious ideas and practices.

The origin of the *Devadasi* has been traced from the early centuries of the Christian era, to which belong the relevant *Sangam* texts. And the process, once begun, got accelerated with the development of temples and temple economy during the early medieval and medieval periods.

The period fifth-sixth centuries A.D. is said to mark the end of the ancient and the beginning of the medieval phase in Indian history. From this period certain economic factors played a decisive role in paving the way for a new social and political structure based essentially on the land system. During the early medieval period we notice the emergence of a feudal economic order the most important feature of which was the system of large-scale land grants to all kinds of political, military and and religious functionaries, who were earlier paid cash salaries.

In South India the practice of land grants starts during the period of the Satavahanas and gained currency under the Pallavas. It is from a Pallava inscription of the third century from Andhra Pradesh that we get the first instance of sharecroppers being transferred along with the land to the beneficiaries, who were Brahmanas. By the fifth-sixth centuries the land grants had become quite frequent.

The large-scale transfer of lands of Brahmanas, religious institutions and officers of the state, coincide with some of the developments, such as decline of trade and commerce, the disappearance of coins and the decay of urban centres.

All these ultimately led to the closed economy of the villages. The situation proved favourable to the expansion of temple system. Owing to the closed economy of villages, large-scale converision of agricultural surplus into money was difficult.

The surplus had therefore, to be spent within the village or group of villages and preferaby on public works, e.g., irrigation channels, wells, tanks and places of public worship. In matter of building temples there prevailed a sense of competition among aristocrats and royal families for building large and magnificent structures. The king or chieftain wanted to surpass his ancestors and fellow kings in building temples. The Pallava king Mahendravarman records his achievement proudly in an inscription which says that he made the *ayatana* (home) for Brahma, Isvara and Visnu without the use of traditional material like brick, timber. metal of mortar, and calls himself *vicitra-citta* (curious or inventive minded). In Orissan sources it is recorded that the Ganga king Narsimhadeva I, who built the majestic temple of Konark, aimed at building a temple which would outdo the great temple at Puri. Numerous landowning *samantas,* princes and kings of the period wanted to acquire *punya* (merit) and fame by building temples and donating land and villages for their maintenance. Inscriptions show that in villages and mofussil towns temple constructions were entirely financed by land revenue in kind.

Another development which coincides with large-scale land transfers was the growth of the *bhakti* cult which ultimately led to the popularity of temple building activites. The *bhakti* movement provided opportunity to the worshippers of all castes-whether he be *Vellala Pulaiya,* Washerman, or a Panar to serve the god and aspire for liberation. Service to gods could be rendered by constructing and renovating temples, cleaning their premises, making garlands of flowers, lighting temple lamps, singing in praise of the deity and dancing for their entertainment. All this presupposed the existence of temples, and proved natural impetus to the construction of temples on a large-scale.

The preachings of Nayanar saints were also popularising the temple system to a large extent. Triumular was a great champion of the temple cult. By advising people to follow right conduct *(carya)* he encouraged them to build new temples, for *carya* consisted, besides other things, in the construction of temples and cleaning their premises.

Thus, all these factor combined to create favorable atmosphere for the spread of temple building activities on a large scale. Traditionally, the first systematic movement to construct brahmanical temples, especially the *Saiva* temples, was started in the third century of the Christian era by a pre-Pallava king Koccenkanam. He is said to have built seventy-eight temples. Between A.D. 450 and 600 the *Chalukya* kings of Karnataka built as many as seventy temples at Aihole in the Bijapur district. However, in Tamilnadu, the large-scale construction of temples started with the rise of the *Pallavas* of *Simhavisnu* line in the seventh century.

Large-scale transfer of *devadana* lands to temples supplemented by recurring levies in cash and kind, together with the periodic interests charged on fixed sums of money deposited with the temple added to their wealth and magnificence. The temple had grown as one of the wealthiest institution of the time on which depended a large number of persons belonging to different professions.

The growth in the economic resources of the temple led to a corresponding increase in the rituals and festivals of the temple. The temple naturally required a large number of servants to manage its vast property and observe its rituals. The number of priests increased with the multiplication of rituals. In the early *Pallava* period, when gifts in cash and kind were made to the temple on a limited scale, it was not possible for it to engage many persons for its maintenance. Nor was it necessary owing to the comparatively less complex routine and mode of worship of the deity. During the reign of the *Pallava* king Paramesvaravarman I the Siva temple at Kuram was managed by only four persons who offered daily worship to the deity, watered the *mandapam* every day and recited passages from the *Mahabharata.* But the number of the functionaries in the temple rapidly increased during the next century. The Muktesvara temple at Kanchi, which was built by the queen of Nandivarman Pallavamalla (A.D. 731-96), had fifty-four employees of whom as many as thirty-two were dancing girls.

By the ninth century the process of worship and offering had become complex. The worship offered was sumptuous; scented water for the bath, costly clothes and rich *naivedya* were provided for the god. Besides, some other items were included under the term *anagabhoga* and *rangabhoga* of the deity for which provisions were made in several Rastrakuta and Cola records. Both these terms *angabhoga* and *rangabhoga* refer to dance and drama performed by the dancing women in the *ranga-mandapa* or *natyamandapa* of the temple (which were built for that purpose), for the amusement and enjoyment of the deity. During the twelfth-thirteenth centuries a number of inscriptions mention *angabhoga, rangabhoga, devabhoga* and *kamabhoga* of the deity. In 1235, we hear at Chabrolu (in Guntur district) that Jaya, the famous General of Klakatiya Ganpatideva, erected two-storeyed houses for sixteen *devadasis* and provided for the *angarangabhoga* of the deity. Chagi Pota's Amaravati inscription mentions that during the reign of Dora, in the year 1240, the merchants made a grant for the *angarangobhoga* of the deity at Chintplle. A record, dated in the year 1209, mentions that at Pedda Konduru king Kota provided for the *kamabhoga* of the god Bhimesvara. Dancing girls of the temple were given land grants for the purpose.

The number of new items relating to the worship and celebrations in the temple went on increasing during the tenth-eleventh centuries. The process can be illustrated by reference to the *Pidariyar* temple of Kolar. The number of priestly and non-priestly functionaries increased with the multiplication of these rituals. The earlier donations merely provided for the offerings of *naivedya* to the deity, without specifying the hours when these offerings were to be repeated; sacrificial rites or other rites do not figure in these records. All these appear later in the grants of the tenth-eleventh centuries. A charter of 1071 refers to such elaborate rituals as the *ardhayama,* the *navahoma* the *madapattiyam,* the matirusandi, the seven days festival of the god. Astradeva, and the blood rites performed in honour of the goddess. All categories of temple servants, including the twenty-four dancing girls and a dancing master, were allotted their allowance in rice and money in the year 1071. The increase in the income was utilised to meet the expenses of the new cults and ritual services instituted in the temple. The inscription states that temple employed 24 dancing-girls to perform dances in honour of the god; a dancing master was also appointed for the proper training of these dancing-girls. An inscription of the time of the *Rastrakuta* king Krsna III shows that temple dancing and become hereditary occupation favouring thereby the formation of *devadasi* caste. The inscription also shows that by this time it had also become customary for dancing-girls to dance in front of the deity during procession festival. A record in the eighteenth year of *Kannaradeva,* from *Sidhalingamadam* in south Arcot, mentions the grant of land in Kodiyur by the assembly of Sirringur to a dancing women and the dependants, for dancing before the deity during processions.

Reasons for Development

During the post-*Sangam* period, the multiplication of Jain monasteries and growth of monastic landlordism seriously undermined the popularity of the saiva and *vaisnava* sects. Till about the fifth century, harmony and tolerance characterised the relations between the different religious sects. The distinctions between the orthodox religion and the other sects were not sharp.

But very soon, the phase of harmony was over. A great change was witnessed in the Tamil country. The people became afraid that the heretics would engulf the whole of Tamil land. Followers of Siva and Visnu became active. They began to preach *bhakti* for Siva and Visnu on the one hand, and hatred for the Buddhists and Jains on the other. This became the chief characteristics of the new age, which attained its peak in the seventh century. Parties of devotees under the leadership of one gifted saint or another traversed the country, singing, dancing and debating all the way.

In the early medieval period the multiplication of Jain monasteries and growth of monastic landlordism seriously undermined the popularity of the *saiva* and *vaisnava* sects. The extent of sectarian propagation, depended on the ability of the particular sect to draw upon official and private patronage. In this respect, the Jains seem to have been more fortunate. Royal and private charters registering land grants and control over local tolls raised the Jain pontiff almost to the position of a landlord. These resources now enabled them to organise the fourfold charity of food, medicine, education and residence on a large-scale and thereby consolidate the social basis of the sect in the locality. The charity, however, was meant for the Jain believers only. Members of non-Jain sects were carefully excluded from the enjoyment of such benefaction. Thus, the *Yasastilaka* emphasises that all charity practised in respect of non-Jains lead only to evil consequences.

The development, therefore, was materially disadavatageous to the non-Jain sects.

In the above circumstances, it is natural that the protagonists of the new-brahmanical movement would like to explore all the possibilities for a wider social basis. With religious structures spread all over India, the king and priests would naturally desire that their particular temples should prove to be better and greater attraction. Hence the panels of erotic sculptures in Khajuraho, Konark, Bhubaneshwara, Aihole, Badami, Belur, Halebid, Bagali, Pattadakal, Belgamve, Hangal and other places. The same motive would also explain the association of beautiful unmarried women with various entertainment services in the temple. The accompanying illustrations and charts would suggest that the practice of emloying dancing girls was most widespread among the *saivas* and after them the *vaisnavas.*

The association of dancing girls with the temple was materially beneficial to the state and the temple. For, like the tourists of today, the pilgrims, in the historical period, meant money and foreign exchange.

A large number of pilgrims helped to enrich the coffers of the temple as well as those of the state. The Muslim historians have noted the economic benefits of the sun temple of Multan, which fetched a big sum from the pilgrims. It is to be mentioned here that in the seventh century. Huen-Tsang had seen several dancing girls in the same temple. The *Prabandhachintamani* informs us that king Siddharaja of Gujarat (1094-1143) collected tax from pilgrim visiting Somnath, which Mahmud of Gazni destroyed in the year 1026, had five hundred *devadasis,* who provided music before the deity throughout the day and night.

The institution of *devadasis* helped enrich the coffers of the temples. The numerous inscriptional references to donations made by *devadasis* to different temples would suggest that the dancing girls of the god helped their bit to finance the god's expenses.

Temples with *devadasis* drew liberal patronage both from royal houses and private individuals. There is an instance of Vijayanagar period that a *devadasi* named Aramavalatta

Nachchiyar, attached to the temple of Agnesvara at Madam, personally interviewed Deva Raya II on behalf of a temple and secured from him a copper plate grant embodying a *sarvamanya* gift of a village. And in return for her services, the *rudra-maheshvaras* of the temple granted her one padakku of grain every day and two *panams* of money per month.

The interaction between the *brahmana* patriliny and the strong tie of matriliny and matriarchal families in South Indian society, was also instrumental in the development and popularity of the *devadasis* system in South India. In the beginning of the Christian era, the nature of family had society changed considerably under the influence of brahmana partriliny and *sanskritization.* The elite groups, which submitted to the northern patriarchal tradition, adopted the patrilineal and patrilocal family as the normal feature of social organization.

However, the vast majority of non-elite families, which were less affected by the *brahmana* law givers, continued with the matrilineal tradition, some temporarily reverting to matriliny, until a male heir was obtained, and others practising is as an accepted norm of social conduct.

In the absence of a male heir in the family some women would temporarily revert to the system of descent through daughter *(marumakkathayyam).* The daughter would be dedicated to the temple as a *basavi,* among whom, descent is always in the female line.

The above mentioned inscriptions illustrate the tendency of certain families, which had not yet broken away from the matriarchal tradition, to temporarily revert to the system of descent through daughters in the absence of a male heir in the family. And such families, in their own way, and for their own purpose, gave succour to the development of the *devadasi* system.

In the *Prabhāvakacarita* of Prabhācandrācārya we find references to dancing girls and their status in society. But this does not refer to *devadāsis.* It says that king Ama of Kanauj spent one night in a dancing girl's house in his enemy's camp and before he left that place, he gave one of his bracelets to that woman as a reward—probably for keeping his presence a secret—if not for dancing.

Not only literary but epigraphic references to *devadāsis* are also found.

In Silāhāra Cave inscription of the middle of first century A.D. we find that there are two caves of Rāmagadh called Sītābeṇga and Jōgīmārā. In the first cave inscription we find some verses in praise of poetry. And the second one says that there was a *devadāsi.* Sutankā who was loved by Devadinna, a native of Vārāṇasī and a banker by profession. It appears that the Jōgīmārā cave was excavated originally by Devadinna for gratifying his amorous propensities.

The Bayana Inscription of Citralekhā of V.S. 1012 refers to the prevalence of the custom of *devadāsis.* It says, "After the construction of the temple a few girls were appointed there as *devadāsis.*

The Ratnāgirī copper-plate inscription of the *Somavanśī* king Karṇa who flourished in Orissa about the beginning of the twelfth century A.D. records the grant of a village made by the *Somavaṇsi* king in favour of *Rāni* (concubine) Karpūraśri, who was the daughter of *Mahāri* Māhūṇadevī and *pautrī* (grand-daughter) of Udayamatī. Here Mahāri has been translated as a *devadāsi.*

Since however, *devadāsīs* are generally known to have been attached to Brāhmanical temples and not to Buddhist monasteries, the expression *Satoṇapura mahāvihāra* has been interpreted as a stereotyped geographical name of the area around the Buddhist monasteries at Satoṇapura. Therefore, it is suggested that Karpūraśrī, a concubine of king Karṇa, hailēd from the neighbourhood of Saloṇapura monastery but was not attached to it.

Further D.C. Sircar says that some proof has been found to show that *devadāsīs* were maintained in the early medieval period not only in the Brahmanical temples but also in the Buddhist shrines at least in East India. Thus, it is possible that this *devadāsi* was attached to Buddhist shrine.

From the sculpture of 10th and 11th centuries A.D., we do find reference to dancing girls and *devadāsīs.*

In the temples of Khajuraho, women are shown in "numerous beautiful dance poses". A woman in the Lakṣmaṇa temple is shown standing with her back to the audience, but she had twisted the upper half of her body in such a way that above her waist, the body is clearly facing the audience.

At Khajuraho again, on the outer walls of the Lakṣmaṇa and Viśwanātha temples, men are shown either sitting or standing with bowls in hand and women with jugs are shown in the act of pouring out the contents of the jugs. Sometimes the position is reversed and men holding pots are serving the liquid to women (*Viśwanātha temple*) one of women is asking for it with her hand outstretched.

It is possible that it refers to the tradition of *devadāsīs* and now they were not to sing and dance for the deity but to give pleasure to priests or devotees coming to the temples.

Such *Surāsundarīs* are depicted in sculpture at the Khajuraho temples as well as at Bhubaneśwar.

There is a standing female figure from the *devi* temple, Jagat *c.* 10th century A.D. This is the figure of a *nāyikā* with arms raised and hands interlocked in the Torana pose. Another figure is of a *nāyikā* from the Lingarāja temple, Bhubaneśwar, Kalinga *c.* 1000 A.D. In medieval art, a *nāyikā* was considered a damsel of the gods, often a dancer and invariably carved in amorous moods and poses. She stood for the ideal of female loveliness of the time. The *nāyikā* here stands in *Tribhanga* pose (triple bends of the body) a celestial beauty.

The contemporary Sanskrit literature reveals the immoralities among the people of this time. It is known from the *Rāmcharita* of poet *Sāndhyākarra* Nandi (11th and 12th centuries A.D.) that the Sena kings introduced the custom of engaging young Brahmana widows as *devadāsīs* in the service of temples.

6

Amusements

Games, sports and amusements have been closely interwoven with human life and nature since the very beginning. And, therefore, in every age women, like men, have relaxed by several games and amusements. But Mughals imposed various restrictions on games played by Muslim women who remained confined to their homes in compliance with their master's will. Recreation was an urgent need for those secluded Muslim ladies who were generally confined within the fourwalls of their houses and deprived of outdoor activities. However, Muslim ladies had to be satisfied with the types of games, sports and amusements provided for them. The women, in general, shared the resources in common with their family members, but the ladies in the harem had their own limited separate arrangements.

As far as the entertainment of the ladies of the *harem* in concerned various means of amusements were within the fourwalls of the *harem.* Beautiful gardens of fruits and scented flowers, running water flowing in channels into stolny reservers, jasper and marble, containing many fishes and rooms ornamented with large mirrors, entertained them the best. As Manucci records, "They have permission to enjoy the pleasure of comedy and dance, to listen to tales and stories of love, to recline upon beds of flowers, to walk about in gardens, to listen to the murmur of the running water, to hear singing and other similar pastures."[1]

A Muslim girl, when mere a child, had some pretty and graceful games to enjoy. She joined, of course, her little brothers, cousins, friends, in various pastimes and her first toys were generally tiny clay models. Musical instruments were provided her to play with. The swing *(Jhula)* was an invariable part of the fitting and a taste for this exercise, continued till her youth.[2] During this period, playing with dolls *(Guriyan)* was a great fun for the little Muslim girls and their mothers, aunts and other elderly ladies of the families inspired them. As Bibi Aisha, the youngest wife of the Prophet Mohammad loved this play much in her childhood. Muslim women of the Mughal age also allowed their daughters to play with dolls and other similar play materials. Sometimes they made the dolls themselves with the help of rags, thread and other things. The girls also celebrated marriages of dolls with many picturesque ceremonies, imitating the real rites performed on the occasion of betrothal *(mangni)* and marriage in presence of the elderly ladies. Generally such marriages were negotiated with those of cousins or playmates in which the elderly ladies also participated in making the function a success.

However, when grown-up, the girls chose other games suiting their age in accordance with customs in vogue.

There were a number of amusements pastimes which mughal ladies was greatly insisted.

Indoor Games

Ganjfah or playing cards, chess, *chaupar, chandal mandal, pachisi,* music and dancing parties were very popular among the ladies of aristocrats and commoners alike. Besides these, ball playing, pigeon flying, kite flying, falconry, story telling, smoking *huqqa,* swinging, display of fireworks and Chiragh Afruzi (illumination) were also liked by the Muslim ladies.

Ganjfah* or Playing Cards or *Tash

Playing cards was a favourite diversion of Muslim ladies, during that period. Gulbadan in her *'Humayun Nama'* states, "Twelve players had each twenty cards and twenty cards and Shahrukhis who ever lost, lost those twenty Shahrukhis which would make five misqals. Each player gave the winner his twenty Shahrukhis to add to his own."[3] Royal ladies were very fond of it in the palace and the *harem* and they often played it with members[4] of their family. Ladies of commoners also amused themselves by playing cards.[5]

In the reign of Akbar, it became widely popular and Akbar himself made certain improvements in it.[6] Abul Fazl[7] informs us that this game consisted of twelve suits of twelve cards each, making a total of one hundred and forty four, with different kinds of kings and their attendants. Subsequently, Manucci,[8] John Marshall,[9] Mandelslo,[10] Deleat,[11] Ovinston,[12] Terry,[13] Fryer[14] and Sir Thomas Roe[15] even today found this game very famous in India. Its popularity continues even today.

Shatranj or Chess

It appears to have been popular in India from ancient times. During the Mughal age this was played by Muslim women also. It was played on a board, divided into sixty four squares, eight on each of the four sides. Each player had, at his disposal, small army of sixteen men, from the king down to a foot soldier. The game could be played two-handed and four handed.[16] Akbar played the game of living chess with slave girls as pieces moving on the chequered pavement of the Pachisi court at Fatehpur Sikri,[17] Manucci,[18] Mandelslo[19] and Ovington[20] refer its popularity among aristocrats and commoners alike.

Chaupar

Chaupar has remained throughout the ages as one of the most popular diversions of people. The inmates of the *harems* presumably enjoyed it. In the 17th century *chaupar* became the pet game of the ladies of the royal household. Zeb-un-Nisa,[21] the eldest bachelor daughter of Aurangzeb, was very fond of playing it with her girl friends in her free time.

In this game two parallel lines of equal length were drawn with two others bisecting them at right angles making a rectangle, each divided into four equal spaces of three lines on its (four) adjoining sides.

It was generally played by four players, two lines competing against the other two. Each had at her command four pieces of the same shape, but different in colour from those of her companion. Three dice were used with dots marked one to six. To start with each player was required to put two of her pieces in the 6th and 7th and 8th spaces of the right line were occupied by the other two pieces. The left row was left vacant. Each moved her pieces according to her throw till She Arrived at the Row to the Left of the Place of her Start. She would then move to the blank space in the middle when she threw the exact number needed to carry each of her pieces to the blank square, she was not arrived[22] ('rasida'). If any of the four players had placed her four pieces into the blank square, even then she continued to throw for her companion in her turn to get her out too.[23]

This game was equally popular among their Hindu sisters.[24]

Chandal Mandal

It was improved game of Chaupar invented before Emperor

Akbar.[25] The figure or board for playing it contained sixteen parallellograms arranged in a circular form around a centre. Each parallellogram was divided into twenty four fields, every eight of which made a row. The number of pieces was sixty four, and four dice were used, of which the four longer sides were marked with one, two, ten and twelve points respectively. The number of players was sixteen but it might be played by fifteen or even less players, the figure being lessened accordingly. Each player received four pieces which were placed in the middle.[26] In this game the pieces were moved as in *Chaupar* and moving to the right passed through the entire circle. Betting was allowed. The first player who was out received the "stipulated amount" from the other 15, the second from the other 14 and so on. It could be played in twelve different ways.[27]

This was a favourite game of Muslim ladies during the Mughal age and they indulged in it whenever possible.

Pachisi and *Chausar*

These games were also prevalent among Muslim ladies.[28] These were very ancient Indian games, but similar to *Chaupar*. The distinction consisted not in the rules of the game or in the way of playing but in minor and negligible respects.[29]

Music and Dance Parties

Music and dancing parties entertained the ladies of the royalty and commoners greatly. Not only at marriages, birth ceremonies and festivals but also whenever free, they were entertained by professional singing and dancing girls. Slave girls and maid servants, and dancing and singing girls were employed inside the *harem* for this purpose[30] and entertained their mistresses. In fact the favourite pastime of the ladies of the *harem* was watching dances, performed usually by dancing girls, a necessary constituent of the *harem*.

Among other indoor games popular with Muslim women was playing ball. During the latter half of the 17th century this game became favourite with the ladies of the royal *harem.* Manucci writes, "During entertainments, such as balls and such like, there are dancing women who have the same privilege."[31] This ball game is also referred to in 'Sursagar'[32] and *'Bihari' Ratnakar*[33] showing its popularity with the Hindu ladies also. This game had many players. To begin with, one player threw the ball at another to strike her. If she was able to do so, the player who was struck with the ball, was stated to be killed or out of the game. Then other players attempted to capture the fallen ball.

Pigeon Flying or *Ishq Bazi*

Pigeon flying was an old pastime of the Muslim men, but the leisured class women were also equally fond of it.[34] A large number of pigeons were brought from foreign countries particularly from Iran and Turan, and reared in Muslim homes.[35] Different owners ordered their flock of pigeons fly all together. These pigeons were encouraged to attack the flock of some one else. They were trained to fight in the air by the owners whistling at them and or waving a cloth fastened at the end of a stick and rushing and making signal from terraced roofs. When the owners whistled and signalled, the pigeons assembled and retired to their houses. But in the confusion a few lost their way and were carried away along with their enemies. The owners flew their flocks over and over again and were delighted if any owner won pigeons in this way. Manucci says, "Every owner is overjoyed at seeing his own pigeons the most dexterous in misleading their opponents."[36] Pigeons were also taught to perform *"Charkh"* and *"Bazi"* which greatly entertained the audience. *Charkh* is a lusty movement ending with the pigeon throwing itself over in a full circle. If this circular turn be not completely carried out, the moment is called "Katf" (shoulderly) and is held in no esteem.[37]

"Bazi" is the same as "Mulallaq Zahan" lying on the back with foot upwards and quickly turning round. It is known in Hindi as "Kata".[38]

During the Mughal age pigeons were also used for carrying messages[39] (letters), from one place to another. Akbar was very fond of pigeon flying and gave it the romantic name of *"Ishq Bazi"*[40], i.e., love play.

Kite Flying or *Patang Bazi*

The game was played with great zeal both by boys and Muslim girls.[41] Great expertise was exhibited in the endeavour of each player to keep his kite uppermost. The kite was square in shape without tail and the cord was strengthened with starch and covered with powdered glass to assist in the interesting contest of cutting the thread of the kite of an adversary.[42]

Falconry

Playing with birds was a popular pastime of the Muslim women, especially of the royal *harem.* There is a miniature painting of the notable queen Chand Bibi on horseback hunting with a falcon in her hand[43] showing the fondness of Muslim ladies of it.

Story Telling

'Qissa Kahani' i.e., Story telling[44] was one of the chief recreations, the domestic old ladies being the performers. The stories had charm for young and old alike, and some of the older women had an unlimited repertory. Educated Muslim women, relaxed by reading different kinds of novels, short stories and other literary books, many verse in form. Gulistan, Bostan and Diwans of various Persian poets were the favourites with these conversant in Persian.[45] Besides reading, they rested by listening to tales and loved stories.[46] It was usual to listen to stories of adventures, heroes and lovers before going to bed at night. Mrs. Meer Hassan Ali refers such Muslim women whose business was to entertain mistress by telling stories and fables while she was composing herself to sleep. These stories mostly partook of the romantic cast, which characterized the well remembered Aribian Nights recreations, one story begetting another to the end of collection. The story was stopped when the mistress was fairly asleep.[47] The fable of Amir Hamza containing 360 tales was also preferred and Akbar in his female apartment often recited them like a story teller.[48]

Smoking *Huqqah* (pipe) or *Hubble Bubble*

Smoking of *'Huqqah'* was an innocent amusement of Muslim ladies to make themselves more lively. The *huqqa* was almost in general use with females.[49] Lady guests were also entertained with huqqah. It was common practice with the lady host to present it to her favoured guest.[50]

The pipe of the huqqa was usually presented to the lady sitting at her right who after taking a puff or two, used to hand it over to the next at her right, and so on.

Swinging of *Jhula Jhulna*

Swinging was one of the favourite pastimes of Muslim women during the Mughal age.[51] Ladies had their swings fixed in beautiful gardens inside the *harem.* In the families of the nobility they had their own private arrangements in which their ladies used to amuse themselves. Sitting on the seat, they apparently felt deeply relaxed with regular backward and forward sway.[52] This was used at any pleasant hour but mid-days, evening and summers were preferred.

Display of Fire Works

The display of fire works was an exciting entertainment of Muslim royal ladies.[53] It was in vogue among the commoners. Ladies of royal *harem,* were especially fond of it.[54]

Chiragh Afrozi or Illumination

During the end of the 17th century women of the Mughal *harem* sometimes entertained themselves by illuminating the interior of their residence.[55] For illumination large torches made with wax or oil were lighted. Manucci, referring the heavy expenses of the royal office in this typical recreation, says. "Their amusement at night is generally to have large torches lighted on which they will spend more than one hundred and fifty thousand rupees."[56] During the reign of Shahjahan in 1050 A.H. Alam Ara, with other ladies, enjoyed the illumination in Kashmir sitting on a boat.[57]

Outdoor Games

Hunting, polo or *Chaugan* and excursion were popular among Muslim ladies.

Hunting or Chase

Hunting was the most adventurous outdoor recreation for the Muslim ladies of the royal *harem*. It was common in Mughal India for ladies to accompany their masters in hunting expeditions. Only a few Muslim ladies were expert in hunting while others entertained themselves only with the sight of hunting.[58] Among Mughal ladies the only personality was Nurjahan[59] who was also an excellent shot and whose expertise was praised by an expert hunter like Jahangir. In 1617 A.D. Nurjahan and other women went with the Emperor; she killed four tigers about which Jahangir writes, "On the 7th as the huntsman had marked down four tigers, two watches and three gharis had passed. I went out to hunt them with my ladies. When the tigers came in sight Nurjahan Begum submitted that if I order her she herself would like to kill the tiger with the gun. I said, 'Let it be so.' She shot two tigers with four shots. In the twinkling of an eye she deprived of life the bodies of these four tigers. Until now such shooting was never seen, that too from the top of an elephant and inside of a hawdah (amari) six shots should be made and not one miss, so that the four beasts found no opportunity to spring and move. As a regard for her good shooting I gave her a pair of bracelets (pahunchi) of diamond worth 1,00,000 rupees and scattered 1,000 asharfis (over her)".[60]

On another occasion when the huntsmen reported the arrival of a tiger, Jahangir asked them to surround the beast and reached there with his hunting party and the ladies of *harem.* Jehangir himself mentions in his Tuzk-i-Jahangiri "As I had vowed that I would not injure any living thing with my own hand, I told Nurjahan to shoot him. An elephant is not at ease when it smells tiger and is continually in movement and to hit with a gun from a litter (Amari) is a very difficult matter, in so much that Mirza Rustan, who after me, is unequalled in shooting, has several times missed three or four shots from an elephant. Yet Nurjahan Begum so hit the tiger with one shot that it was immediately killed".[61] This might have been an exception but Muslim ladies went for hunting with their husbands in their own parks and with their own hunting parties.

Besides the tiger hunt, deer hunting was very popular among the ladies of the royalty as it was very pleasing and less dangerous. The ladies of Jahangir's *harem* often enjoyed the sight of deer hunting both in the usual manner and in the form of *'Qamarghan.'*[62]

On one occasion when Jahangir hunted at Samongagar with his ladies, 84 live deer out of 641 were set free after putting silver rings in their noses.[63] The flesh of killed antelopes was distributed to the *Begams* also. *'Paristaran-i-harem sera'* (ladies of royalty) also enjoyed hunting the blue bull (nilgao) in the company of the emperor.[64]

Fishing was another favourite outdoor recreation for ladies.[65] Nurjahan put golden rings in the nostrils of the fishes and would then leave them into the water to dance, which amused her very much.[66]

Besides, ladies of royal families and nobles enjoyed witnessing the animal fighting through the golden window of the *harem.*[67]

Chaugan or Polo

Chaugan or polo was strenuous game quite old in its origin. It dates back to the Sasaniyan dynasty of persia. This was adopted by the Abbasdes, the Mongol Kings of Persia and the Turks in India.[68] It was first introduced into India by the Turkis *Sultans*.

During the Mughal age this game became the favourite outdoor recreation of emperors and noblemen. Few ladies played this dangerous sport as it required skilled horsemanship and accurate aiming while in motion. Expert female riders participated of royal household sometimes in it despite strict seclusion.[69] But Chaugan was not popular among the Muslim ladies of the commoners.

The game was played on horse back involving not more than ten players. These ten players were divided in two parties, each having five players. But many more were kept on the waiting list, two of whom replaced another two in field after every twenty minutes. This was played in two ways.[70] The first way was to get hold of the ball from the centre to the goal with the crooked end of the Chaugan stick, known as roll. In the other method the game was conducted to and fro where the players forcibly hit the ball with Chaugan stick towards their rivals' goal known as Ballah in India.

Being very fond of this game Akbar liked to play it in the night with the help of an illuminated ball[71] which caused must astonishment even to clever players in his reign. The ball for polo as made of Palas wood as it was very light and burnt for a long time. For adding splendour to it, Akbar had knobs of gold and silver fixed at the tops of the Chaugan sticks.[72] If it broke, whoever, among the players, got the pieces, kept it.

On festivals, especially on Ids, people enjoyed the display of Chaugan.[73]

Excursions or Picnics

During the Mughal age excursions or picnics greatly attracted the ladies confined to the fourwalls. From time to time the men took their ladies to some pleasure spot for a change. Mughal emperors were very fond of excursions and literally allowed their ladies to participate in them. Ladies belonging to the leisured class had enough facility to enjoy such trips quite freely and to visit meadows gardens and buildings and to enjoy the sight in the open air.

Whenever emperors and noblemen planned for an excursion, all preparations were made under the supervision of their ladies. On the fixed day, they set out as per the programme. Reaching the excursion spot, tents and pavillions were pitched for the emperor and his ladies. Many dainty dishes were cooked and they enjoyed in eating together. All of them spent the day in roaming on horse-back and the[74] evening passed pleasantly in amusement and sociable talk. When Babar's son Alwar died after a short illness, both he and his wife Dildar Begum became wild with grief. After a few days Babur proposed to take his ladies out for a change. Gulbadan writes thus, "As her (Dildar's) lamentation passed due bounds' his Majesty said to my lady and the begums, 'Come let us make an excursion to Dholpur."[75] After finalising this plan Gulbadan informs us that they went on the proposed excursion by boat.

For excursions, the royal women preferred the spring season,[76] the best season to visit the countryside. During the reign of Humayun his women expressed their desire, more than once, to go for a trip to see *Riwaj* growing on the hills (Daman-i-Koh). Humayun took them with him.[77] On their way they enjoyed by talking, telling stories hearing songs,[78] as all were in a picnic mood.

On another occasion the women of the royal *harem,* mounting on horsebacks, went on an excursion with Humayun to enjoy the sight of a beautiful waterfall above farza situated between Laghman (Lamghan) and Balkh.[79] Humayun visited the orange gardens of mountain passes (Tangayna) from time to time. Once he took all his three wives, Bega Begum, Hamidah Banu Begum and Mah Chuchak Begum, accompanied with other ladies of the royal *harem* and his brother Mirza Hindal, to the mountain passes to see and eat the oranges.[80] Humayun was so fond of princes that on court days, Sunday and Tuesday, he used to visit the other side of the river with his ladies and engaged the party.[81]

Akbar and Jahangir also continued usage during their respective reigns, for the recreation of their ladies. In 1581 A.D. Akbar approached the Bagh-i-Safa (a garden) with his ladies when on way to India from Kabul.[82] In 1591 A.D. (999 A.H.) Akbar went on an excursion to Kashmir accompanied by his ladies.[83]

As regards pleasure trips, the reign of Jahangir was the ney day for the women of the royal *harem,* as the Emperor took great interest in taking his ladies on excursions.

Shahr-ara-garden, situated in Kabul, made by Babur's aunt Shar Banu, was a pleasant picnic spot and preferred by Emperor Humayun. Jahangir, in his reign, adorned this garden with streams and named it 'Jahan ara garden' or garden of world adorning.[84]Jahangir often visited it with his ladies.[85] In Kabul,

Jahangir once, with the ladies of his *harem* visted the *julgah* (plain) or Safid Sang, a very bright and enjoyable place.[86]

In 1613 A.D. Jahangir and his women spent one evening in walking across the melon beeds made Khwaja Jahan in the neighbourhood of the city.[87]

In 1615 A.D. on the night of *Shab-i-barat,* Jahangir visited Ana Sagar Tank with the ladies of the *harem.* Jahangir ordered for the illumination of the consecrating to the memory of his ancestors and passed most of that night in merry making on the bank of the tank alongwith his ladies.[88]

In 1617 A.D. the ladies of the royal *harem* of Jahangir visited the courts and buildings on the Shakkar tank founded by former rulers of Malwa, and greatly enjoyed pleasantness, greenness and open spaces of the surroundings; they returned to their destination in the evening.[89]

Nur Afshan garden situated on the opposite side of the Jumna was a favourite picnic spot for Jahangir. In 1621 A.D. he and his ladies went there by boat and were recreated by his beloved consort Nurjahan Begum who also made great offerings to them.[90]

Nurjahan enjoyed the pleasure spots of Kashmir with her husband Jahangir. Once she visited a beautiful garden having a tank. Many fishes were caught and she ordered them to be released after putting rings in their nostrils.[91]

The reign of Shahjahan was also not free from ladies excursions. Jahan Ara, the most affectionate daughter of Shahjahan, once went on an excursion to Kashmir alongwith the emperor.[92] There she visited many pleasant gardens with tanks and buildings.[93]

In 1050 A.H. Shahjahan took many of his ladies to Bagh-i-Safa and stayed there for three days,[94] enjoying natural beauty.

Alam Ara, the daughter of Shahjahan went on an excursion to Kashmir, she visited various picnic spots there and also enjoyed the pleasure of boating.[95]

During the later half of the 17th century the royal ladies lived in seclusion. But they were not strictly confined within homes. They could also go on pleasure trips after seeking prior permission from the emperor, though rarely.

In 1662, when Aurangzeb recovered from illness, his sister Roshan Ara with other women went on an excursion with him to Kashmir and Lahore.[96] Aurangzeb started his long journey from

Delhi after taking the joint decision of astrologers.[97] On the way he halted the *'Shahi Bagh'* in Aghrabad,[98] spending six days there land enjoying the company of his ladies.

Upto the reign of Jahangir, excursions were liberally allowed to ladies. The emperors themselves participated in such trips alongwith the begums and the ladies of the *harem.* The reign of Shahjahan was a turning point regarding excursions because of his political and personal difficulties. No doubt Aurangzeb alongwith his ladies participated in many an excursion in the early part of the reign but in later part, excursion trips for ladies became rare.

Expedition

The Mughal emperors carried their women even at the risk of their lives during battles. It was common to keep their ladies with them both in peace and war. In peace, their ladies enjoyed the company of their men in hunting and excursions. In battle marched with them on military expeditions. All Mughal emperors indulged in this strange practice. Careri thus observed, "The Moghals will march at their ease carrying their women, abundance of provisions and tents, so that their army looks like a moving city."[99]

The first Mughal emperor Babur took his wife, Maham Begum and daughter Gulbadan Begum on the expedition from Agra to Dholpur in 1526 A.D.[100]

Humayun also took his queens and many ladies of his *harem* to Hausa.[101]

When fighting against Sher Khan, Hindal took his mother Dildar Begum and his own sister Gulchehra Begum, Afghani Aghacha, Gulnar Aghacha, Narqul Aghacha and many noblemen and their wives and families.[102]

In 1542 A.D. Humayun, marching against Maldeo, took his wife Hamidah Banu Begum, Fakhrun Nisa, mother-in-law of Akbar's wet nurse Maham Anga and other women.[103]

During the reign of Akbar the women of the *harem* with other great women and female slaves and servants enjoyed the company of the king on the way to the battlefield. In 1574 A.D. Akbar went by boat to the eastern provinces with a few ladies of his *harem,* while the army and the camp travelled by land.[104] In 1599 A.D. when Akbar went on an expedition to the Deccan, 'many ladies accompanied him.'[105]

Jahangir also carried ladies on military expeditions. In one such expedition, the daughter of Shahryar and her Atka (servant) were sitting in Nurjahan's Amari when this Atka was wounded by the enemy's (Rajput) arrow.[106]

Shahjahan, on an expedition towards Burhanpur, stayed in the fort of Asir for three days with his ladies.[107] On another expedition against Raja Bhim, Shahjahan was accompanied by his women.[108]

In 1678 A.D. in a battle against the Rana of Chittor and the Raja of Marwar, Aurangzeb's favourite wife Udaipuri was with him.[109] In the royal march to the Deccan in 1681 A.D., the ladies of the emperor Aurangzeb accompanied him, all except Begum Sahib, who being old, desired to remain in Agra.[110]

In 1684 A.D. Jani Begum, daughter of Dara and wife of Mohammad Azam was in the expedition against the Deccan.[111]

In the 28th year of emperor Aurangzeb's reign, his wife Udaipuri Mahal was in Aurangabad or Ahmadnagar with Aurangzeb.[112] In the siege of Satara in 1698-99 A.D. Aurangzeb's camp was at Islampuri; Zinat-un-Nisa, the king's daughter with other ladies of the *harem* was present.[113]

Women in the family could also participate in military expeditions. Humayun's wife Chand Bibi was seven months pregnant when she went on an expedition to Chausa.[114] On another expedition Hamidah Bano Begum[115] was with child when she went with Humayun. Shahjahan's beloved wife Arjumand Bano Begum also went on an expedition when she was expecting Murad.[116]

Not only ladies but their children too accompanied the emperor on military expeditions.[117]

On an expedition the ladies were the last to go after the baggage was despatched, but they always reached first, adopting a shorter route.[118]

Elaborate arrangements were made many days before the arrival of the ladies at the place. Tents, pavillions and numerous requisites were despatched beforehand so that they found everything in order. The advance party was called *'Pesh Khima'*[119] (advance tent).

In the reign of Akbar each *'pesh khima'* needed 100 elephants. 500 camels, 400 carts and 100 bearers[120] for its transportation. While in the reign of Aurangzeb 70 elephants, 200 camels, 100 mules and 100 porters were needed. Artillery and well-equipped boats to cross rivers, when required, were also sent. Bulky things were carried by elephants, smaller tents by camels, the baggage and kitchen pots by mules, and light and expensive things such as the emperor's procelain, painted quilt beds and rich kargah (sara parda) upon the heads of porters.[121]

An eligible place for encampment was selected by Mir Manzil or Mir Saman (Quarter Master), where officers and men appointed in the *Farrash Khana* (Excellent dwelling place) made arrangements.[122]

For the ladies, a site was assigned on the field near *'Shahi Khima'* (imperial quarters). Abul Fazl informs us that during Akbar's campaigns, the royal tents were pitched in the open. The imperial seraglio, the audience hall and the *'Naqar Khana'* (a turret on the top of which the band plays) occupied 1530 yards. To the right, left and behind was an open space of 360 yards to the 'left centre' were the tents of Hamidah Bano Begum (queen mother), Gulbadan and other senior women. Adjoining the royal tents there were tents of Begum, Princesses and other prominent ladies and the principal lady attendants of the *harem.*[123] These tents were enclosed on every side by rich *'quanat'* or folding screens. Tents were also pitched for *'Urdu Begls'* (armed women), female servants and other ladies of low degree. During the reign of Aurangzeb too, all the tents were arranged according to the ranks of the women concerned.[124]

These tents were dyed red,[125] a prerogative of the royal household. In the reign of Akbar the female quarters were situated within the *Gulal-bar.* According to Abul Fazl, "The Gulalbar is a grand wooden enclosure, the invention of His Majesty, the doors of which are made very strong and secured with locks and keys[126] where watchmen were stationed." When the king reached the halting place and passed through the doors of the tents, queens and ladies who had already reached there, congratulated him by saying, *'Manzil Mubarak'*[127] (Happy to the journey) and then retired to the rooms allotted to them. Their rooms were furnished with beautiful comfortable carpets and embroidered masnads.[128] These women spent their time in resting, talking, eating the daintiest food and chewing *pan* (betel) and all arrangements were made by the king.[129]

On the day of battle women were ordered to mount elephants and were carefully guarded by the escorts posted at some distance behind the centre where stood the king and other chiefs.[130]

Sometimes ladies also participated in war, from their howdas. Jahangir's queen Nurjahan has been the best example of this. Jani Begum, wife of Mohammad Azam used the bow and arrow bravely from the top of her elephant[131] during the war near Bijapur in 1684 A.D.

Sometimes ladies were captured by adversaries. Humayun's wife Bega Begum, well known as Haji Begum, was captured by Sher Shah's party,[132] in the war of Chausa. Manucci says that after the time of Timur, no queen was made a prisoner, except Humayun's wife who was captured by Sher Shah and sent back.

Sometimes the loss of several women and children created a terrible void in the royal household by such battles. In the battle of Chausa Ayisha Sultan Begum (daughter of Sultan Husain Mirza), Bachaka (a servant in Babur's household), Bega Jan Kuka, and Aqiqa Begum (Bega Begum's daughter), and Chand Bibi and Shad Bibi (Humayun's two wives of low degree) were lost.[133]

Thus the risk of heavy loss on military expedition sometimes forced Mughal emperors to think that 'Now again it is difficult to convey ladies with us[134] but they never forsook the practice of their forefathers'. Thus ladies on military expeditions were sometimes happy with the conquest of the Emperor, but sometimes it proved a curse for them.

Acrobats, Jugglers and Mountebanks

Acrobatics, jugglery and other feats have been common features of public recreation from very early times in India, and during the Mughal age they were invariably conducted skillfully and courageously.

Jugglers, mountebanks, conjurers, dancers and magicians of different classes were found all over India and earned their livelihood by displaying their dexterity and agility and thus provided significant source of amusement to the royalty, nobility and commoners alike. Their feats were so popular that whenever they performed, Muslim ladies generally managed to see it from their houses, behind a screen or *Jharokha.*

These were generally performed with dexterity and even the closest attention could not reveal 'how it was done'. Abul Fazl remarks that 'cunning jugglers and conjurers performed such extraordinary feats that not the vulgar alone but the acutest minds are deceived into a belief in their miraculous power'.[135]

Memoirs of Babar contain many references to diverse tricks performed by male and female professional performers. Babur was once surprised to see an acrobat, who arranged rings one on the forehead, two on the knees, two on fingers and two on the toes and set them in movement with one jerk.[136]

Jahangir's Mernoirs refer to Karnatic jugglers "who had no rivals of equals. He played with ten balls, each of which was equal to an orange and one to a citron, and one to a Surkh (The seed of Abrus pre-catorius), in such a way that notwithstanding some were small and some were large he never missed one'.[137]

On another occasion, Jahangir with Nurjahan and other begums enjoyed the magic shows from Bengal.[138] They surprised the audience by growing trees, from seeds which bore fruits[139] and were eaten by the Emperor and the noblemen, within a few minutes. Every one was surprised to see birds singing on these trees.

Next day these 'Bazigars' cooked meat without fire and 100 persons ate it.

One *'Bazigar'* exhibited his magic by throwing a cord in the air, and told the audience that he was going on a journey to paradise, to kill his opponent. He left his wife there, climbed on the rope and vanished.

A little later, drops of blood and scattered limbs fell down one by one. Seeing this, his wife began crying over the supposed death of her husband. She begged permission for *Sati* from the Emperor and gathered the remains and then committed *Sati.* After a while her husband reappeared and demanded his wife. Knowing about her *sati* he began to cry and tried to commit self-immolation. In the meantime his wife appeared and said, 'why are you going to burn, I am alive.' The *Bazigar* told the emperor that the blood shed and limbs were his opponent's. Audience were surprised to see it.[140]

Abul Fazl also refers to the wonderful feats of *Bazigars.* They would cut a man into pieces and then restore him to his natural state, and sometimes one would carry an enormous stone on his back.[141]

Nats and *Natwars* were the rope dancers, who walked on stretched tight ropes, at some height. 'They also played on *Tala* and *Duhul'.*[142] Thus sometimes their feats involved music and dancing.

Norris was impressed much by a girl of ten years who displayed dangerous and happy feats on ropes and bamboos.[143]

Thevenot has described the wonderful feats of agility of body of a girl of thirteen or fourteen years of age, who performed for two hours. He states, "This amongst other feats of agility which she did, appeared to me extremely difficult".[144]

Besides these jugglers and acrobats, monkeys and apes also entertained the people at public places by dancing and performing tricks at the order of their master.[145]

Snake charmers kept snakes in baskets and at the sound of their flutes, the snakes danced before the audience. As Ovington, states thus, "He that carries it about plays upon a pipe when he exposes them, at the noise of which the snake will hiss, spread his head and throw it about."[146]

Bhands[147] (jokers, jesters, clowns and buffoons) entertained the people by their antics, tricks, caricatures and witty remarks. For amusement Mughal kings and their nobles employed such persons in their courts. Dara Sukoh had appointed a number of baffoons.[148]

Besides, *Bahrupias*[149] changed different gulses and displayed their mimicry by moving from door to door and thus entertained people.

On festive occasions, like marriage and birth ceremonies, not only professional musicians but mimics[150] were also invited by wealthy families of both Hindus and Muslims, to recreate the audiences.

All festivals and inspiration originated from the male side, but the women made them the occasion of merry making. Festivals attract children greatly and women have been directly responsible for pleasing their men as well as children. Therefore, in every age women have devoted their times in celebrating festivals elaborately.

Feasts

Muslim ladies of the Mughal period were very fond of arranging feasts which provided them an occasion to meet many other ladies to examine and exhibit to one another their jewellery and fine apparels, and spend their hours in joy and mirth in addition to pleasing numerous people attached to the court.

Ladies of the loyal *harem* felt greatly ecstatic both in arranging and attending a *Jashan,* as they were rarely permitted[151] to visit the houses of other ladies. Hence this was the best way to meet one another. Therefore, every important occasion, such as birth, circumscision of a prince or a marriage or recovery from illness and accession of an emperor, was marked by grand receptions generally organised under the supervision of queens, princesses and other exalted ladies of the family.

On the return of Humayun from the Bihar campaign, his mother Maham Begum organised splendid banquet to celebrate his grand success in the east. She ordered the illumination of the entire market not known in India before. The soldiers and the rich people were especially commanded to decorate their houses and their shops accordingly which gave the thoroughfares of Agra, a beautiful countenance. A special jewelled throne with four steps was made in the banquet hall for the Emperor. It was furnished with golden embroidered pillows, cushions and hangings. The state canopy used on this occasion was lined with European brocade inside and Portuguese velvet outside on gilded and ornamental poles. Maham Begum herself had made a tentlining and a *Qanat* and a *Sar-i-Qanat* of Gujrati cloth of gold. An ewer for rose water, sprinkler, candle stands and drinking vessels, all of jewelled gold were also provided there, without which no feast was complete. As it was usual to pour rose water frequently over the party for a refreshing and cooling effect, rose water sprinklers were always present. Thus, "with all her stores of plenishing, she made an excellent and splendid feast"[152] and entertained all her guests as best as she could. At the closing of the party she followed the popular custom of her age, *Dasturi-i-raftan,* or parting the gift.[153] In this way festivities continued for many days and ended with the bestowal of *Khilats* and horses on many noblemen.[154]

After the death of Maham Begum, Babar's sister Khanzada Begum arranged the feast of the *'Khanah-i-Tilism',* and the ceremonies related to the marriage of Hindal, who was married when Maham was alive, were delayed as the organizer was changed.

For the Mystic feast one large and one small octagonal room were furnished with rich Persian carpets having gold and pearl fringes. In the forecourt of the house a jewelled throne, presented by Maham Begum, was put and a gold embroidered *'divan'* was laid in front of it, on which Humayun and Khanzada Begum sat together.

A number of lady guests from India, Kabul and other countries, attended the feast with gifts. In this feast, besides other things, they were offered various kinds of fruits, dainty wines and betel, all served in jewelled gold and silver utensils. Vocal and instrumental music was played for the recreation of the guests. Thus, all the guests enjoyed this grand feast and departed with gifts.[155]

For Hindal's wedding feast Khanzada Begum arranged a most splendid and entertaining *'Jashan'.* Gulbadan writes, "She arranged a reception such as had not been made for any other child of my royal father. She designed all and carried it all out".[156] As Hindal's bride Sultanam Begum was under her supervision since the age of two, she presented everything she had gathered for the bride and the bridegroom at the feast.

Dildar Begum, another wife of Babur, also took interest in arranging feasts.[157] In 1541 A.D. she organised agrand feast at which Hamidah Bano, with other ladies of the court, was present.

When Humayun expressed his desire to marry Hamidah and was refused by Hindal, he got angry and went away. Dildar Begum fetched his majesty and gave a party.'[158] After arranging a compromise between Hindal and Humayun, she arranged a grand nuptial banquet[159] in honour of the marriage of Humayun with Hamidah Banu Begum. When Hamidah Banu Begum came from Qandhar, Akbar's circumscision feast was arranged and all the Begums attended and enjoyed the feast. Gulbadan refers, "In Bega Begum's garden and Begums and ladies made their decorations quite wonderful in a new fashion."[160]

During the reign of Akbar this usage was continued and guests were entertained in great banquets. Murad's marriage reception was arranged by Mariam (Hamidah Banu) in her palace.[161]

Akbar's wet nurse, Maham Anaga, prepared a delightful banquet on the auspicious occasion of her elder son's marriage. Abul Fazl states, "Every day there was a new arrangement of the festival, and all and sundry partook of excellence and joy".[162]

Nurjahan, the most distinguished lady of her age and the queen of Jahangir, never lagged behind anything. She frequently organised feasts during Jahangir's reign. She feasted Jahangir, his Amirs and courtiers in one of her palaces situated in the midst of large tanks. Jahangir himself says, 'A grand entertainment took place and the drinkers of cups took more cups than they could carry'.[163] Manucci also refers to a feast given by Nurjahan in honour of Jahangir.[164]

Nurjahan, the step mother of Shahjahan, on another occasion, held a great feast in honour of his conquest, and offered him honourable dresses with other costly things. The children and ladies were honoured with dresses and gold jewellery, and then the servants were taken care of. The estimated cost came to about 300,000/- rupees.[165]

The completion of the high house and the royal garden at Nursarai built by Nurjahan, was a great achievement, and so she had organised a grand *'Jashan'* and 'by way of offering, with great pains, produced all kinds of delicate and rare things".[166]

In 1621 A.D. at Nur Afshan garden which was established by Nurjahan, she arranged a great feast to celebrate the commencement of the 16th year of jahangir's reign and presented great gifts,[167] in the shape of jewels, jewelled ornaments and all kinds of precious goods to the Emperor and other guests. The presents given to Jahangir alone, were worth rupees one lakh.

Among Mughals, the recovery from illness of an emperor, prince or princess was always celebrated by grand receptions. In 1021 A.H. when Jahangir recovered from illness, Nurjahan organised the *Jashn* of *'Ghuli-i-Sehat'.* All weighing ceremonies on Jahangir's birthdays, both lunar and solar, were always organised by Nurjahan but on this occasion she had paid greater attention than ever and offered valuable gifts to him besides distributing alms among the poor. This grand Jashn cost about two lakh rupees exclusive of the offerings.[168]

During the reign of Shahjahan, the clothes of Jahanara caught fire on 4th Feb. 1644 A.D. and she was seriously burnt. She recovered after 8 months and 8 days. On this occasion Shahjahan celebrated great *Jashn* of *'Ghusl-i-Sehat',* and festivities continued for 8 days.[169] All nobles and their *Begums* enjoyed this feast with heart and soul.

In the reign of Shahjahan and Aurangzeb, arrangements of banquets by ladies continued, and Roshan Ara,[170] Jahan Ara[171] and Zeb-un-Nisa[172] displayed great interest in it.

Even the ladies of noblemen also followed the footprints of the queens and princesses and arranged the feasts from time to time and entertained guests. The wife of Zafar Khan was a liberal lady and she often entertained her guests. Once, she invited Aurangzeb[173] and gave a reception in his honour.

The women of the commoners also used to organise feasts and entertained their kinsmen and friends in their houses on significant occasions such as birth, circumscision, marriage etc. according to their means.

Festivals

'Islam has little or no scope for social festivals unlike Hinduism'. However, a few anniversaries of some of the very significant events were observed from the early history of Islam. In India, in the new environments, other festivals were added and celebrated with great zeal but these do not exist in Islamic countries where Islam originated. Of these the more important ones so observed by the Muslims are as follows :

Nawroz or New Year's Day

Nawroz, the new year's day, according to the Persian calender, was one of the most celebrated festivals of the Persians. This festival, falling usually on 21st of March, is of great antiquity and its history dated back to the time of Jamshid or "the seven ringed cup" who is stated to have fixed the Persian calendar ordaining that new year should start on the first day of the Persian month of Farwarddin when the sun enters Aries.

Emperor Humayun was the first emperor who prohibited its observance professedly under religious compulsion and influence. Akbar reintroduced it, but was afterwards eliminated by the orthodox religious Aurangzeb in 1677 A.D. He, to protect the faith, changed it to the *Nishat-Afroz-Jashan* which started in Ramzan and continued till Idul Fitr.[174] Being a spring festival it was usually celebrated in big gardens and river embankments. In 1546 A.D. the ladies of Humayun's *harem* celebrated it happily by walking on the hill, Gulbadan says, "On the first day of New Year, *'Nawroz'* they went out to the Hill of the Seven Brothers and there passed many days in ease and enjoyment and happiness."[175]

Nawroz was celebrated gorgeously by the Mughal Kings as a court festival. Under them not only the upper class but the people in general decorated their houses and celebrated it delightfully.

Nawroz was celebrated for six days and the first and last days were regarded most auspicious.[176] Alms were distributed and gifts were exchanged.[177] Akbar ordered the festivities of

Nawroz to continue for nineteen days.[178] Thevenot refers to its nine day celebration in the reign of Jahangir.[179]

On this occasion the Mughal Court was lavishly decorated and illuminated. Tents were erected, their inner sides decorated by fringes of velvet, embroidered with gold, pearls and other precious stones.[180] People wearing richer and finer green[181] dresses flocked "from the neighbouring cities and villages to the court[182] and there they were welcomed "with large free supply of wine and free banquet".[183] Hindus also freely participated in the festivities of *Nawroz.*[184]

Women were also permitted to visit the palace and see its magnificent annoinments. Special enclosures were arranged for ladies of the *harem* from where they could view everything without being noticed[185] by others. Singing, dancing, games and amusements were the order of the day, and thus women were entertained, thanks to this festival.

Inside the palatial building of Nurjahan, she used to celebrate *Nawroz* with great enthusiasm and pleasure. The walls of her apartments were painted with auspicious colour for the day as suggested by her astrologers. Even the curtain, carpets and the outfits of *Begums* and slaves, the trappings of the elephants, horses and camels had the same colour. On the day of Nawroz, Jahangir would come to the Mahal and sit with the Nurjahan on the throne. Nurjahan showered money over the head of Jahangir. Both queen and the emperor used to witness the procession of *Nawroz* from the balcony. In various parts of the city free banquets were served by the order of Nurjahan.[186]

On the day of *Nawroz* ladies exchanged dainty dishes alongwith eggs and other gifts.[187] People visited one anoher's houses, and exchanged greetings. The women of the nobles visited their queens and princesses and greeted them and received robes of honour and promotion in rank, besides other gifts. When they retired, their hands were filled with *'Kichri'*, a mixture of gold and silver coins with various kinds of precious stones and pearls, large and small.[188] The festival was celebrated by the court rather than the common folk. It ended with the Mughals and appears no more in India.

Id-ul-Fitr

It was the most popular religious festival. It is celebrated by all orthodox and unorthodox Muslim enthusistically. It began as soon as the month's fast of Ramzan was over, on the first day of *Shawwal,* the tenth month of the Muslim calender. Id-ul-Fitr also called *Id-I-Ramzan,* Idu's *Saghir* or *Choti Id* or *Idus Sadaqa* (least of Alms), closed with the breaking of the fast and observance of the festival at length.

Id-ul-Fitr was one of the greatest festivals for people when they generally remembered all their departed friends and relatives towards the closing of Ramzan. According to the custom, some Muslim women lamented bitterly in memory of their deceased husbands and children as Terry states.

"There are many foolish women who often in the years, so long as they survive, moisten the graves of their husbands or children with affectionate tears."[189]

The sight of the new moon preceding Id-ul-Fitr, was proclaimed by the firing of artillery guns, blowing of trumpets,[190] feasting and Jubilee. Muslim ladies visited the houses of friends and relatives for congratulating them.[191] As this was a thanks giving day amongst the devout persons, they passed this night in 'Praying very devotedly'.[192]

On the day of the festival, early in the morning, all Muslims, irrespective of age and sex took their bath and dressed themselves in their best attire, 'the poor in clean white clothes'.[193] Scents and antimony were used by all the Muslims before Id-ul Fitr's two *Rakats Namaz* (prayer).[194] Men generally went to pray in the *Idgah,* in special mosque built outside the city for this purpose, while ladies offered their prayer in their respective homes. Once at the pleading of Akbarabadi Mahal, Shahjahan performed his Id prayer in the mosque newly constructed by the Begum.[195]

Before Id prayers *Sad-qa-Fitr* (alms) were distributed to the beggars and poors[196] as prescribed by Muslim Law, by every person, man and woman, old or young, to purify the fast.[197] At the close of the service, men saluted and embraced one another and mutually congratulated and then returned to their homes and spent the rest of the day in feasting and merriment.

In some parts of India, when men returned from Idgah, their women sprinkled coloured water over their heads to protect them from the evil eyes.[198]

During that period, in every Muslim house from the Emperor's to the meanest of his subjects, it was an Indian custom to eat *Sheer Khurma,* Sweet food and vermicelli on the day of Id,[199] duly prepared by Muslim ladies with such care as if it was an injunction of Islam.

Muslim ladies, from the royal household down to the peasant class, dressed themselves in their best clothes. They were very careful to adorn themselves with their finest jewellery and different cosmetics. Now in full make-up they paid and received the visits of their lady friends and relatives. They were welcomed,[200] embraced and congratulated[201] by other women. After feasting, every lady departed to her homes the same day.[202]

It was usual to make presents, best known as *Idi,* on the day of this solemn festival. The Emperor bestowed gifts on princes, princesses, nobles, rajas, amirs and *'Qazi'* the one who recited the Id prayer.[203] Haji Koka, one of Akbar's foster sister, was gifted land and money by the Emperor Jahangir on the day of Id.[204]

On the day of Id, *Begum Sahib* was offered one lakh of gold coins by Aurangzeb, and her annual pension (formerly twleve lakhs of rupees) was increased by five lakhs of rupees. Pur Hunar Banu Begum and Gauhar Ara Begum also got one lakh rupees[205] each on this occasion. New fabrics and other gifts were distributed by wealthy men and women to their dependents and the poor as well.

Muslim ladies sent food to their friends and relaives with good wishes.[206]

To mark the auspicious occasion, palaces as well as houses of the commoners were lavishly decorated and lighted with lamps.[207] Different kinds of amusements were provided in the assembly of men, whereas the court poets recited special composed praises[208] in the palace.

Id-ul-Zuha

Id-ul-Zuha, Id Qurban, Baqarah Id or Idul Kabir (the great Id) was one of the great festivals of the Muslim year and both the educated and the illiterate shared it equally. It was celebrated on the 10th day of *'Zil-Hijjah'* the twelfth month of the Muslim year. In India, it was generally considered as a substitute for the sacrifice celebrated by pilgrims in the valley of Mina near Mecca.

Like Id-ul-Fitr, on the morning of Baqarah Id, all Muslims with no distinction of sex and age, took their bath, and men visited

Idgah for prayer[209] in their best attire. Ladies offered their prayers in their houses.

After returning from Idgah, men sacrificed,[210] according to their means, a goat, sheep, camel, or cow, perfect in all respect and not below one year of age, in commemoration of Prophet Ibrahim, who was prepared to sacrifice his second son Ismael[211] and who miraculously escaped and sacrificed instead *dumba* (a kind of sheep, with a thick tall). The Holy *Quran* says, 'It is not their meat nor their blood that reaches God, it is your piety that you may glorify God for his guidance and proclaim the good news, to all who do right'.

Kings, princes, and noblemen, sometimes, sacrificed the animals with their own hands.[212] Shahjahan was very particular about this festival.[213] The rich sent gifts animals to the poor as to enable the meanest of the people to offer sacrifice.[214] The flesh of the animal was then divided[215] into three equal parts, one third for the relations and the other one third for the poor, and the remaining one third was kept for the family. Fryer refers to a unique custom of the sacrificed animal's blood, and says 'And (they) sprinkle their (animals) blood on the sides of their doors.'[216] The permissible dates for this sacrifice were 10th, 11th and 12th Zil-Hijjah,[217] i.e., three days time was allowed for the sacrifice.

On the day Muslim ladies made different dainty dishes of sacrificed meat, every lady displaying her own particular taste in the prepared meat which was eaten by the family, friends and relatives, delightfully. Mandelslo refers to it thus, "...In memory of the sacrifice of Abraham, at which they kill the goats which they eat at the entertainments they make among themselves that day."[218]

Ladies dressed in their most costly jewels and apparel received and paid visits.

On this joyful day delightful gifts were distributed both by commoners and Emperors.[219] On Id-ul-Zoha Aurangzeb presented five thousand Mohars to Purhunar Banu Begum, his sister and other five thousand to Gauhara Begum.[220] On this occasion gifts were presented to teachers by the pupil's family, in the form of money and *Khilat* (dress).[221]

Thus, people passed their Baqr-Id festival happily with different kinds of recreations.[222]

This festival is still celebrated with no change.

Shab-i-Barat

It was an important Indian Muslim Festival celebrated all over the country with great zeal. It was performed on the 14th night in the month of *Sha'ban*, of the Islamic Calender. Shab-i Barat, also known as *Lailatul Barat,*[223] being a night of forgiveness of crimes and record of all good and evil was to be spent in prayer and vigil[224] according to the Prophet Mohammad. Md. Salih Kamboh says that this is considered as a sacred and blissful night (for forgiveness of sins). Prayers are accepted (By God) and life and livelihood (of individuals) are decided on this very night. The pious people had great regard for the night, and spent it in prayers.[225] Therefore, generally people spent that night in the performance of *Namaz.*[226]

Muslim ladies normally began preparing for it several days before the festival. They took great care and pride in cleaning their houses on the eve of this festival, believing it to be a night of prayer and every house was visited by angels as instructed by God Himself.

As Thevenot refers to it thus, "They call it the feast of Choubret and believe that on that day the good angels examine the souls of the departed and write down all the good that they have done in their life time, and the bad angels sum up all their evil actions the same day".[227] On this occasion, all people of religious faith made it a night of strict devotion and prayers, read the *Quran* and prayed for the souls of their departed friends and relatives, as the Holy prophet did.[228] A fast was observed on this solemn festival.

Muslim ladies prepared a variety of special dishes, typical custom not found abroad. They made *'Halwa'* and *'Chapati'* (bread) besides stew, curds and other varieties of sweet meats.[229] These special dishes were exchanged with friends and relatives.[230] The trays of delicious presents prepared by the ladies for their friends were the result of many days' previous labour. The Muslim ladies rivalled each other in their exhibition of novelty and good taste, both in the eatables and the manner of displaying them.

On this occasion friends were also invited to one another's house, and thus enjoyed the reception.[231] During the reign of Jahangir, Nurjahan in her palace at Mandu, arranged a grand feast and invited Jahangir and his courtiers. Jahangir himself records thus, "I ordered them to give the people cups and all kinds of intoxicating drinks according to the desire of each". And all sorts of roasted meats *(Kabab)* and fruits by way of relish, were ordered to served to everyone.[232]

On this occasion, alms were distributed to the poor and needy.[233] Among Mughal emperors, Shahjahan was the first to celebrate this festival in a puritanic way and spent the night in prayer, and every year he distributed ten thousand rupees in alms.[234] He also gifted learned men[235] from the gold used for weighing him.

The people, generally enjoyed this festival and entertained themselves by illumination and display of fireworks. At night, palaces, huts, mosques, roads, tanks and shops were illuminated by commoners as well as kings. Jahangir and Shahjahan were keenly interested in it, and sometimes spent this night with their ladies in viewing illuminations, "on the banks of the tanks".[236] Lamps of different colours were also lighted.[237] Mandelslo remarks, 'The windows of all the houses that stand in the Maidan were beset with lamps before which were placed vessels of glass, filled with waters of several colours which made a very delightful prospect". He also refers to the peculiar fashion of lighting wheels at Ahmadabad. According to him, "some had fastened lamps to certain wheels which hung on though the wheels turned about perpetually with great violence.'[238]

There was a great display of fireworks in the evening involving handsome money. Emperor Jahangir witnessed the illumination and display of fireworks from boats on the river Yamuna.[239] Various inventions were made by the commoners[240] in the competitive display of fireworks. Muslim women greatly enjoyed the wonderful sight of these illuminations and display of fireworks sitting in their homes behind a screen or window. It was copied perhaps from the Hindu festival Shivratri, Diwali or Mahanadi, a south Indian Hindu festival[241] and so Mashaikh, Mir Murtaz of Aurangzeb's reign opposed this custom.[242]

In a family where death occurred in the previous year, *halwa, chapati* and other dishes were cooked by the ladies of the house one day before Shab-i-Barat, i.e., on the 13th *Shaban*. This food was portioned out in the name of that departed soul and *fatiha* was recited over the dishes. This Indian custom was called, *'Arfa'* or *'Arafa'*. The delicious dishes prepared on this occasion were sent to friends and relatives, and the poor and the needy were fed.[243] The whole night was spent in similar manner, but prior to day break the Muslims would visit the grave yards and illuminate the graves of their relatives with candles and *'agarbatti'* and recited *'Fatiha'* for the departed souls. Prophet Mohammad himself supported reciting *fatiha* for departed souls, but was disapproved of illumination on graves.

Shab-i-Barat is still performed nowadays in the same spirit and fashion as the Mughal period.

Muharram

It is the first month of the Islamic Calendar very significant for the Muslims. The first ten days of Muharram were observed as more of mourning by the Muslims in commemoration of the martyrdom of Hazrat Islam Husain, the second son of Bibi Fatimah, the Holy Prophet's daughter, who was married to Hazrat Ali, the fourth orthodox Caliph. During the Mughal age these days of remorse were strictly observed by the Shia Muslims because a number of distinguished Mughal queens belonged to Shia Sect.

In commencing this remarkable event, every comfort, luxury or even convenience was rigidly avoided. The expressions of grief, manifested by the Muslim women for greater, deeper and more lasting than that of men. On the very first day of Muharram, they would loosen their hair from its usual confinement and allowed it to flow. Mourning clothes were put on and the very zealous mortified themselves in clothes with no change during the ten days of Muharram.[244] The different kinds of ornaments which gave them great delight, were also entirely taken off. They rested on common mats spread on the floor. Throughout Muharram[245] their food was limited to simple and composed of boiled rice, barley, bread, boiled peas and pulse. Betel, a common luxury of Muslim ladies, was abandoned for ten days. In Golconda, a Shia state, drinking of wine as well as meat eating, cutting of hair and the sale and purchase of betel was not allowed for fifty days starting from 1st Muharram to 20th *Safar*, the 2nd month of the Islamic Calendar.[246] The first ten days of Muharram were held sacred not only by the Muslims, Shia and Sunni, but also by the Hindu people.[247] Orthodox and religious minded Muslims spent this duration in reading the account of the martydom of the protagonists of Karbala, in fast[248] and offering prayers for their spiritual benefit.[249] Muslim women assembled and chanted *Marsiya*[250] (funeral eulogies) in the language of the country; the ladies were so deeply moved that they burst into violent tears and sobbings.

Muslim as well as Hindu women often made oaths to be performed at the Muharram. For example, the Queen mother of Abdullah Qutub Shah of Golconda had taken an oath for the return of her son, when the *Sultan* was still a boy and was taken into the forest by his favourite elephant Manmurat. The prince returned after abcut a week, on the fifth of Muharram, and the queen maintained her vow.[251]

During the Mughal period the miniature models of the mausoleum of the martyrs of Karbala, known as *Ta'Ziyas* (introduced by Amir Timur) were very famous. *Ta'ziyas* are found in no other Islamic country and Indian Muslims perhaps copied it from the Hindus Jagannath Car and the celebration of Krishnalila.[252] Some Muslim women set up *Ta'Ziyas* in their female apartments and assembled in the evening round the *Ta'Ziyas.*[253]

In the evening of the tenth of Muharram *Ta'Ziya* processions[254] were taken out with light, alam (banners) poles and the silver plate representing Husain's hand, swords, clubs and staves and then, at last, all the necessary "Properties" were buried at the Karbalas. The effigie of Yazid, (Killer of Imam Hussain) and his men were burnt on the last night. Monserrate remarks thus, "The people jump over these and afterwards scatter the glowing ashes with feet." Meanwhile they chant 'Hsson Hossen' with wild and savage cries.'[255] Although Aurangzeb forbade Muharram Processions, the usage carrying the *Ta'Ziya* was never stopped completely.[256]

The tenth day of Muharram was called *Ashura* and was observed by the Sunnis also as commemorating the day on which Adam and Eve, God's throne, heaven and hell, the pen luck, life and death were brought into being.[257] People fasted[258] on the *'Ashura'* day and applied collyrium to their eyes.[259] This is observed by some men and women even now.

In remembrance of the privation of the sufferers at Karbala, many Muslim people set up *Sabil* (houses for water by the roadside) and distributed milk,' *sherbat* and perfumed water to all persons who accepted it.[260] Women prepared food, which was also offered to bless the soul of Hazrat Imam Husain,[261] the martyr. Some also made charity of money and clothes. Emperor Shahjahan every year distributed ten thousand rupees as alms.[262] Men approached their deceased parents' or friends' graves "newly white washed and decorated for the occasion", with flowers and food, which was distributed among the poor, after 'Fatiha'.[263]

In the Mughal age, for official celebrations of Muharram festival, pavillions were erected and adorned with embroidered tapestry. Costly carpets were spread and lamps were lighted. The professional dancing girls entertained the viewers "by their extravagant dances, habits and head tire."[264] *Sherbat* and *betel* were distributed to the visitors and sometimes jugglers, athletes and other showmen displayed their skill and prowess.[265] In Aurangzeb's reign "Muharram celebration was reduced"[266] to a greater extent, partly due to the impact of Mir Murtaza, the famous Mashaikh who was against it, and partly due to the competition between two groups of men in procession.[267]

Barah Wafat or *Fatiha Doaz Dahum*

Barah Wafat[268] (Fatiha Doaz Dahum), associated with the birth and death anniversary of the Holy Prophet, falls on the 12th day of Rabi-ul-Auwal every third month of the Islamic calendar. During this period it was celebrated with great solemnity. Being a sacred month of the first twelve days of *Rabi-i,* especially the 12th, made the occasion for *'Milad-un-Nabi',* the celebration of the Prophet's birth day. In palaces as well as private houses and mosques, Muslims celebrated it by conducting a meeting of the pious, scholars, Mashaikh and the reciters of the Holy *Quran (Haffiz).* In this religious meeting not only friends and relatives but people in general gathered to hear sermons related to the Prophet's birth, life and teachings, portions of the Holy *Quran,* Traditions and other related works appreciating the Prophet Mohammad. At the end of the meeting salted and sweet dishes[269] were served to all.

Akbar held a *Majlis-i-Urs* on this occasion every year, and people were entertained there suitably.[270]

Shahjahan was very particular about this festival and every year, held Majlis-i-Milad, and distributed twelve thousand rupees, and sometimes more, to the pious accomplished reciters of the *Quran* and the needy of who attended the meeting.[271]

Aurangzeb followed his father Shahjahan and began to celebrate the festival of Barah Wafat and Majlis-i-Milad in his court in the orthodox Islamic manner.[272]

In some parts of India *Barah Wafat* parades were also taken out.[273] Even on this pious occasion, general merry-making, illuminations, music, dance and fireworks were the order of the day.[274] During the reign of Abdullah Qutub Shah of Golconda, musicians and dancers from Hindustan and Iran displayed their art before curious audiences. Perfumes were used by all and sundry, and betels distributed in lakhs.[275]

On the eve of this festival women maintained extraordinary purity while preparing salty as well as sweet dishes for the purpose of *Fatiha Doaz Dahum.*[276] Since the occasion was regarded very holy, alms were distributed and the poor were fed. Some people fed the poor daily from 1st to the 12th of the month of Rabi-ul-Awwai.[277]

Id-Gulabi or *Ab-i-Pashan*

This festival was celebrated by the Mughal Kings with great elegance at the beginning of the rainy season also known as *Id Trukan.*[278] The princes and the nobles would participate in it by sprinkling rose water over the emperor and on one another. 'Jewelled golden or silver flasks consisting of rose water, jujube tree flower juice and the aroma of orange flowers were presented to the emperor.'[279] Jahangir mentions in his memoirs that in the 9th year of his reign *'Majlis-i-Gulab Pashi'* was held.[280] Shahjahan[281] and Aurangzeb[282] also celebrated this festival enthusiastically. Ladies of Mughal *harem* and the nobility also enjoyed this festival.[283] But this festival was not popular among the masses.

A few other annual celebrations, not true festivals but regarded as festivals, were also observed in the Mughal period. They included the recital of the *fatiha* prayer, fasting, and alms giving. Of these *Shab-i-Miraj, Gyarahvin, Akhiri Chahar Shambah, Terah Tezi, Chahallum, Knwajakhizr ka Bera,* and *fatiha* of Bibi Fatima are important.

Shab-i-Miraj

Shab-i-Miraj or *Lailatul Miraj* was the night of the Prophet Mohammad's ascent or racturnal journey to heaven on a super natural horse, *'Burraq'.* It is said to have taken place in the twelfth year of the Prophet's mission on the night preceding the 27th day of the month of *Rajab.*[284] Muslim people commemorated this event by setting up all night prayer.[285] Alms were distributed, and a fast was observed[286] on the following day (the 27th).

Emperor Akbar was never approved of this, though his courtier

Faizi, in his last days, wrote some couplets praising the Prophet and his ascent.[287] Shahjahan celebrated it, and distributed ten thousand rupees among the poor, needy, pious and acomplished[288] every year.

Shias celebrated this festival with great rejoicings and illuminations not because of *Shab-i-Miraj* but because it was the birth anniversary of Ali,[289] which by chance, fell on the same day.

Gyarahvin

Gyarahvin or the eleventh day of the fourth month *Rabi-us-Sani* was observed as a festival in remembrance of 'Sufi Sayyed Abdul Qadir jilani', Surnamed as 'Pir-i-Dastgir',[290] also known as Bare Pir.[291] He was famous for his truthfulness and honesty. It was his habit from the very childhood to ask for meals from God after prayer *(Namaz).* As his mother being a pious lady, guided him at every step according to the principles of Islam. He never lied throughout his life. When he was captured by a group of robbers on the way to Basra from Jilan, and asked for money, he expressly indicated the place within his rugged clothes where 40 *Ashrafis* were stiched up-expectedly. At first the robbers disbelieved him, but just to find out the truth they searched and were stunned to find the exact number of 40 *'Ashrafis'.* Out of curiosity they inquired why he told the truth. He, then, told them about the instruction of his mother not to lie even if in trouble. This incident made the robbers repent and embrace Islam. He was a true believer in God. He was an honest and sincere devotee, a man of strong character and belief, a true guide and above all a pious man who sacrificed his life for the cause of Islam based on the teachings of *Quran* and Traditions of the Holy Prophet, Mohammad.

Sunni Muslims of the Mughal age strongly believed that if Fatiha was recited on the occasion of *Gyarahvin,* in his honour, their needs would be fulfilled, they would live long and the earnings of their livelihood would multiply.[292]

Fatiha was recited over sweet and salted dishes, and their friends and relatives were invited to share the food[293] and they also went from door to door exchanging[294] the dishes.

During the reign of Akbar, Shahbaz and Amir distributed hundred Ashrafis, every Thursday evening in honour of renowned Abdul Qadir Jilani.[295]

Gyarahvin was also called *Gyarahvin Shariff* and it is observed even today.

Akhiri Chahar Shamba

The last Wednesday of *'Safar'*, the second month, was observed as a festival in comemoration of Mohammad in view of the fact that on this day, the Holy Prophet felt some mitigation of the fever, which in the next month proved fatal to him. On this occasion Muslim ladies prepared sweet cakes for the purpose of fatiha. People and children went for picnics in the gardens and passed the day in prayer and merrymaking,[296] regarding it an auspicious occasion.

In some parts of India, it was customary to write seven *salam*s or greetings we with saffron water, ink or rose water. Then they themselves washed off the writing and drank the melt content in the hope that they might be preserved from calamity and enjoy peace and joy on the day of resurrection.

As for *Shias*, they regarded it unlucky', and called it *Charshamba-i-Suri'*, the Wednesday of the Trumpet.[297]

Terah Tezi

Terah Tezi, fell on the thirteenth day of *'Safar'* when the Prophet after thirteen day's illness showed symptoms of improvement. Jahangir, for the first time, gave it the name of *'Terah Tezi'.*[298]

On this day, most Muslims took their bath. No reason existed for ceremonial bathing on this day, but a new custom was introduced by Muslim ladies.[299] *Fatiha* was recited over the food for the Prophet's soul. Food was also exchanged among friends and relatives, and the poor were fed.[300]

Women of this period regarded this month inauspicious and distributed cooked food to the poor, to be saved from the evils that might prevail.[301]

Khwaja Khizr Ka Bera

This festival was celebrated in honour of Khwaja Khizr, a Prophet who discovered the source of the water of immortal life and was supposed to be the patron of water. On the last Thursday of the Bengali month of *Bhadon*, people prepared a *'Bera'* and took it to the bank of river at night celebrating many ceremonies.[302] There they would light lamps and tapers and offer oblutions, while the swimmers would push the *'Bera'* into the middle of the river as an offering to Khwaja Khizr. This festival was observed with great merrymaking also participated by children and women. *'Dalia'* cooked for the occasion was distributed, and the poor and the needy were fed.[303]

The Muslims believe even today that Khwaja Khizr is alive and that shows the right path to bring back the lost man from the wilderness. But this festival is no longer celebrated.

Fatiha of *Bibi* or *Kandur*

'Fatiha' of *Bibi* Fatima Zohra (daughter of the Prophet Mohammad) was one of the festivities connected with marriage. It originated with the reaching of the Mughals in India due to the impact of Hindu culture. It was celebrated a day before the marriage ceremony. This *Kanduri* was first introduced by Jagat Gusain, 3rd wife of Jahangir, also known as Jodha Bai, to degrade her co-wife Nurjahan.[304] On the day of *fatiha,* food was prepared carefully and purity and then lady friends and relatives were invited. The food was covered with a clean cover till *fatiha* was recited. After *fatiha* the guests were feasted but re-married ladies had no permission to have the food; like the men,[305] whether married or bachelors.

Once Jodha Bai celebrated this festival and invited ladies of Omrah including Nurjahan. When the *fatiha* recital was over the prepared food was completed, she cordially invited all those present to participate in the feast. Being a peculiar type of festival, meant for those married only once, Nurjahan remained seated and was stunned. On being insulted which was obviously done deliberately. Jahangir was complained by Nurjahan about the serious incidence. Jahangir called for Jodha Bai and inquired about her gesture. Jodha Bai explained to the emperor that it was no fault of her, because the festival meant for the ladies who were married only once and could take the food prepared in honour of Bibi Fatima Zohra.[306]

Fairs

Besides feasts and festivals, fairs also provided opportunities of recreation to the Muslim ladies during the Mughal age. On the occasion of *'Nawroz'* a special kind of fair was organised inside the *harem,* known as 'Mina Bazar'. It formed an important means of enjoyment for the ladies of royal families besides the women of the Umra.

Khushroz or Mina Bazar

Mughal emperors were very fond of providing opportunities to their ladies for recreation and pleasure. Therefore, Emperor Humayun, for the first time, in the history of India, founded the custom of *'fancy bazar'* which subsequently, was known as *'Khushroz'*. After the mystic feast a *bazar* for women was held by him on boats,[307] in such a fashion that the female visitors not only enjoyed the *bazar* but were surprised to see its decoration and praised the inventions of Humayun's creative mind.[308]

His son and successor, Akbar introduced this fair in quite a new fashion and named it a new as *'Khushroz'* (joyful day fair) or a gala day because such days provided enjoyment to those concerned. In fact, in its original form it was a great social event though limited to the ladies of the nobility.[309] Abul Fazl informs us that on the third feast day of every month this fancy market was held. As it was for the entertainment of the *Begums* and the ladies of the *harem* together with the wives of nobles, it was normally managed inside the *harem,* "within the *Mahal*".[310] During the reign of Akbar this fair was organised in Fatehpur Sikri, which extended from the gate of Jodha Bai's palace to the courtyard and garden of Maryam Mahal.

As for the fort of Agra it was held near the courtyard of Mina Masjid,[311] whereas in Shahjahan's period it was held on the gallery of the *harem* itself inside the Red Fort.

The most wonderful feature of Mina Bazar was that the wives of Omrah, Rajas and other High Officials opened their stalls in the market, erected according to the emperor's set design. But Hamilton writes, "The ladies obeyed and took their booths as they thought fit".[312] These ladies desired to bring rich items generally used by the queens and princesses from all parts of the country. Sometimes these lady shopkeepers had to manage special articles asked for by the emperor and ladies.[313] On the market day the ladies acted as shopkeepers by performing the duties of grocers, goldsmiths, jewellers and mercers and the like. Court ladies of less standing who had enough wit, were also permitted to be shopkeepers.[314]

The *bazar* was open to all the women of nobles, irrespective of their caste or creed. The beautiful daughters of aristocrats never missed the chance to accompany their mothers on such visits, to come across the *Begums* closely. Hindu queens and ladies of rank also took interest in visiting this *bazar*[315] for enjoyment and pleasure. On the day of Mina *Bazar*, the emperor with his queens, princesses and other ladies of the *harem* would pay a visit[316] not only to purchase things of their choice but also for enjoyment and fun.

They moved from stall to stall where these "bewitching females"[317] demonstrated their finest goods and told their cost too. Here the emperor usually tried to act as a broker on behalf of his women, and haggled, exchanging happy and witty remarks. Sometmes the emperor and the seller bargained over small amount just for fun. In this fair the wittiest and the fairest seller was always greatly favoured;[318] she could please the kings and his ladies with her witty remarks. Finally, the amount was settled with the consent of both the parties, and the princesses and *Begums,* often paid "double the original[319] value of the things they purchased", generally in the form of 'gold' *(Asharfis).* The sellers, too, accepted the amount happily.[320] In this fair, apart from ready money, payment orders on papers in the shape of 'vouchers' were also accepted by shopkeepers, which were cashed afterwards. For this purpose, Akbar employed a separate treasurer and accountant so that the sellers could be paid immediately.[321]

During the meeting "the fortress remained shut, with no man inside but the king",[322] and lady guards were deployed at the gates of the fancy *bazar*[323] to check unauthorized entry. Mina Bazar, a purely social function, was the channel through which the secrets of the king, the character of the people and the qualification of each office and workshops were supposed to become manifest.[324] "All the pretty women of the town"[325] who visted the fair with their mothers or other elderly ladies of the family, sometimes received the concentration of the emperor and the *Begums*. In a similar fancy *bazar*, Jahangir saw Nurjahan and "took a fancy for her"[326] Muslim ladies of the aristocrats often consulted the emperor for the marriages of their sons or daughters,[327] and sometimes he introduced the parties to each other and recommended if necessary.[328] In the course of such meetings important affairs of the *harem* were also transacted.[329]

The *Mina Bazar* lasted for four or five days, but Manucci refers to its eight day celebration during the period of Shahjahan. He writes, "In those eight days the king visited the stalls twice every day, seated on a small throne carried by several Tartar women, surrounded by several matrons, who walked with their sticks of enamelled gold in their hands, and many eunuchs, all brokers for the subsequent bargaining".[330] He was so much inclined towards the fancy *bazar* that he ordered it to be organised on every festival *(Jashn)* though not always.[331] It invariably followed the *Nawroz* celebrations.[332]

Jahangir, during his reign, held the fancy *bazar* at night and arranged for lighting lamps in front of the shops for handsome look.[333]

In *'Khushroz'* all sorts of festivities and amusements were the practice of the day.[334] There was "a set of women musicians" who entertained the assembled ladies. At the end of the fair, all ladies departed to their respective homes after enjoying feasts and dance of *kanchinies.*[335] Thus, these gala days spent with great festivity, dancing, music, acting and other amusements.

After the fancy *bazar* of women, *bazars* for the *men* were held[336] (started during the reign of Akbar), where merchants from different parts sold their commodities.

The system of Mina *Bazar* was regularly observed by Akbar, Jahangir and Shahjahan respectively. The orthodox Muslim courtiers were always against these fairs.[337] and "honourable women" refrained from visiting[338] it from the time of Shahjahan. But the majority of ladies never discarded the fair and visited it punctually. Manucci reports that out of curiosity he tried to estimate the number of lady visitors in Mina Bazar and there were more than thirty thousand.[339]

The system of Mina *Bazar* came to an end after Shahjahan and was never heard of in the reign of Aurangzeb.

Urs/Fairs

Women during the Mughal age started visiting *'urs'* held at the tombs of the degnified *sufi*s who had already performed many miracles. After their death, their actions attracted the people, irrespective of caste and creed, and the mass drawn towards the death anniversary of the so-called *sufi*/saint. Consequent upon the celebration of these they took the form of a fair popularly as 'urs' or 'Chehri'.[340]

The *'Urs', 'Chehri'* was a centre of all round activities. For example, the pious and the devout took it as a visiting place to pay their sincere homages to the departed soul of the deceased. But the ladies mostly visited the 'Urs' and devotedly prayed at the grave asking the saint to pray to God on their behalf for the accomplishment of their cherished desire. They took a vow to attend regularly if their desire was fulfilled, which might be a child's birth, wealth, recovery from illness or something else.[341] In fact, it was a conspicuous place where people came to fulfil their ends. Dr. P.N. Ojha has rightly recorded, "Important Moslem Pilgrimages were mostly confined to the graves *(Dargahs)* of eminent saints and divines. The 'Urs' or anniversaries of these saints were celebrated with befitting zeal and joy, and fairs were also held on such occasions in which both the Hindus and the Moslems amicably participated".[342] He further admits, "Visits to the tombs of saints were also becoming more and more popular, and most of the visitors were females."[343]

But participants from all sections of society visited the place either attaining religious merits or to ask a favour or for merry-making.

Now the most significant places of 'Urs' being celebrated in the Mughal period and afterwards deserve special mentiion:

(i) Of them the *'urs'* being celebrated at Ajmershareef is the oldest one where lies the shrine of Khwaja Muinuddin Chishti. His mission throughout life was the highest form of devotion to God and his ultimate target was to serve the human beings. He performed uncounted miracles and his miraculous fables are still on lips of thousands of people. He died in or about 1236 A.D.

The *'urs'* at Ajmer[344] commenced from 1st to 6th *Rajab* every year; it was attended by thousands of people from all parts of the country, including the kings,[345] nobles and leading men. Akbar had great respect and devotion for his shrine. He distributed gifts, alms and devotional offerings to the residents of Ajmer[346] every year. When he was blessed with a son, Salim, he accompanied by his wife Maryam Makani to perform a pilgrimage to the tomb of Khwaja[347] and covered on foot, a distance of 200 miles from Agra. Jahangir following his father, also once travelled, on foot to the *Dargah* of Khwaja Muinuddin Chishti.[348]

Mughal queens and princesses were greatly fascinated to visit this tomb. In the year 1582 A.D. while returning from Mecca after performing *Haj* (pilgrimage) Gulbadan Begum visited the shrine at Ajmer accompanied by many other royal ladies including Salima

Sultan Begum, Haji Begum, Gulazar Begum, Sultan Begum, Umm Kulsum Khanam, Gulnar Agha, Bibi Safia, Bibi Sarw Sahi, Shaham Agha and Salima Khanam.[349]

During the period of Jahangir, Nurjahan with other ladies also visited the tomb of Khwaja Muinuddin Chishti.[350]

Shahjahan's daughter, Jahan Ara, was a great devotee of the Khwaja. At the age of 26, she authored a book entitled *'Munis-ul-Arwah'* describing the lives of Khwaja Muinuddin Chishti and his disciples. Since she had great respect for the saint, she offered the first copy of the book,[351] and this is still preserved in Ajmershareef. She also got built a beautiful *"Dalan"* in the *"Dargah"* duly decorated with gold and precious stones.

Once when she was seriously burnt, and the best medical treatment failed to recover her, Shahjahan made a vow to pay a visit to the shrine of Khwaja Muinuddin Chishti and distributed alms of Rs. 5,00,000 on her recovery.[352]

The *'urs'* of Ajmer is still observed with the same devotion and spirit.[353]

(ii) The sacred mausoleum of Sheikh Farid-uddin Ganj-i-Shakar located at Ajodhan, also called *Pattan* of Shaikh Farid or *Pak Pattan,* was a famous pilgrimage for people. Though, Shaikh Farid never abstained from practising devotion and austerities and ultimately became a leading *sufi* of the time (1175-1280 A.D.). He belonged to the age devoid of Mughals, but on the establishment of their power in India, they also began visiting the shrine with due respect alongwith their ladies. Emperor Akbar[354] also visited this shrine in the year 978 A.H.

(iii) The *'Dargah'* of Shaikh Nizamuddin Auliya lies in Delhi since 1324 A.D. and is regarded a significant place of pilgrimage. The saint had witnessed the establishment and ruin of seven sultans of Delhi. Despite their calls he never attended their royal courts. Being a man of purely religious nature he had the credit of reforming innumerable people of his time. After his death 'Urs' was held every year at his shrine on 7th Jamadus-Sani.[355] Jugglers and players participated in the *Hauz-i-Shamsi*.[356] Referring to the jugglers in such pilgrimages, Pelsaert states, "The roads and open places were full, too, of jugglers, dancers, players, and such rabble, the noise was deafening and the crowd made it even more difficult to view, or find room to move".[357]

(iv) On the shrine of Shaikh Ahmad Sarhindi, a man of dynamic personality, 'Urs' was celebrated every year, in Sarhind and several people, from far and near attended[358] it enthusiastically.

(v) Chehri Ghazi Mian was observed every year in Bahraich, where according to Abul Fazl, "The common people of Muhammadan faith greatly revered this place putting themselves in bonds and bearing gilded banners".[359]

A great victor, Salar Masud Ghazi, son of the sister of Mahmud Ghaznavi, was the commander-in-chief of latter's soldiers. He visited India one or two years before Mahmud Ghaznavi's death and stationing at Satrakh, fought many battles with Hindu kings but finally, he died fighting and was buried in Bahraich (in the *'suba'* of Oudh), a large town on the banks of the river Sarju.[360]

After the death of Salar Masud Ghazi, his soldiers were scattered in different parts of India and fought against *Rajas.*[361] The places where they fought battles and died, are called 'Ganj-i-Shahidan'. In memory of these soldiers fairs have been held every year in different parts of India, as Kara Manikpur, Ghazipur, Siwan (Bihar), Maner. The fairs known as *"Ghazi Miyan ka Mela,"*[362] were attended by men, women, and children with great enthusiasm and delight.

(vi) The tomb of Shaikh Yahiya Maneri, at Maner, situated (17 k.m. from Patna) at the confluence of the river Ganges and Sone was significant place for pilgrims.

Shaikh Yahiya Maneri, in whose respect and memory *'Urs'* has been held every year, in the month of *Rajab,* was a renowned *sufi* of his time. His forefather was Taj Faqiyah, an Arab, who conquered Maner in 576 A.H.[363] Mughal emperors had much respect for Shaikh Yahiya Maneri, and often visited his shrine.

Babur, while returning victorious from the battle of Ghaghra in 1529 A.D. stationed in Maner, paid his homage to the saint and distributed alms.[364]

Emperor Akbar also once sent Mir Ghiyasuddin Ali Naquib with a large amount, to distribute it there and ask for inspiration.[365]

'Urs' in Maner is now held as usual with great zeal in which men, women and children of all sects and creed take part.

(vii) In Biharshareef the shrine of Shaikh Sharfuddin Maneri,[366] son of Shaikh Yahiya Maneri, was an important place of pilgrimage. He was a great saint famous, for his piety. Every year *'Urs'* was celebrated with mirth and zeal where people of both sexes flocked from different parts of the province.

(viii) Phulwarishareef was also a popular centre of *'Urs'* where lies the shrine of Shah Makhdum, brother of Sharfuddin Maneri.

(ix) *'Urs'* celebrated on the shrine of Pir Shah Madar, who was buried in Makan Pur, 224 Kms from Agra, was a popular centre where numerous people from all quarters assembled.[367]

During this period in honour of all the above Muslim saints, anniversaries were celebrated and fairs were held. Fairs were celebrated every year with great enthusiasm on the campus of the shrine, with many shops mostly of flower garlands, sweets *(Naqul),* essence, stationeries, toys and utensils, etc. Pelsaert provides a clear picture of the stalls of such fairs (pilgrimages) in these lines, "Next there are the confectioners, who used to line the whole road in great numbers with stalls of sweet stuffs, and sold great quantities, together with the hawkers of toys (like pedlars of our fairs), for no one would return without having bought something for the children."[368]

Although Prophet Mohammad prohibited women to visit graves, they participated in fairs with great interest, and their number was increasing day by day so much so that Firoz Tughlaque and Sikandar Lodi tried to check it by banning it.[369] But during the Mughal age the number of lady visitors was not curtailed,[370] and they visited the shrines to ask for the fulfilment of their wishes.

As for the fulfilment of the oaths they had made in regard to the cherished wish, the ladies would embroider the *chadar,* as to cover the tomb of the saint. These *chadars* were offered alongwith burning of essence, flowery garlands, sweets (duly recited with *fatiha*) and *Chiraghi* (offer of an amount of money according to one's status) which were collected by the *Khadim* or *Mujawir* (Carguide).

Many such ladies seeking a favour for the life of one of their families, would promise to visit the shrines, again making oaths as usual, and depart to their respective homes generally late in the evening.[371]

The shrine was illuminated throughout the night and presented a beautiful scenario. The night was booked for *'qawwall',* (singing of religious songs[372]) and special Persian verses dealt with the good deeds, miracles and other attributes of the saint for whom the *Urs* was held. Now a days the language of *'Qawwall'* has changed into Urdu but *ghazals* (a sort of special verse composed on fixed syllable) have been retained, and are recited by a few *qawwals.*[373]

Since the visitors belonged to remote places, it was impossible for the ladies of distant places to return to their homes the same day and hence arrangements were made for their stay in a close secluded place, from where they could enjoy the *'qawwali'*.[374] These lady visitors belonging to families both of high and low, departed the next day.

References

1. Manucci, *Storia Do Mogar,* Vol. II, Tr. pp. 352, 353, 483.
2. Amir Khusrau treats swining a bad play for a good Indian girl. *Hasht Behisht,* Matba Institute, Aligarh College (1918), p. 30.
3. *Mishkat,* Vol. III, 166, pp. 44-45; also Sayyed Sulaiman Nadvi, *Sirat-un-Nabi* (Urdu) Vol. IV, p. 524.
4. Gulbadan Begum, *Humayun Namah,* Persian, p. 77; also Tr. Bev. p. 178; also Babur Namah, Persian, p. 584.
5. Gulbadan refers card playing by Dildar Begum, Gulchehra and herself, with Humayun. *Humayun Namah,* Persian, p. 77, Tr. (Bev) p. 178; Mrs. Meer Hasan Ali refers its popularity among Muslim ladies, *Observations,* p. 82.
6. *Ibid,* p. 156; also for its popularity in Bengal see Radha Ballav Pal, *A Glimpse of zenana life in Bengal* (Cal. 1904) p. 62.
7. Abul Fazl, *Ain-i-Akbari,* Vol. I, Pers. p. 222; also Tr. (Bloch) pp. 318-20.
8. *Ibid,* p. 319.
9. Manucci, *Storia Do Mogor,* Vol. II, Tr. p. 136.
10. John *Marshall in India,* p. 273.
11. Mandelslo, Vol. I, p. 65.
12. De Leat, *The empire of the Great Mughal,* p. 405.
13. Ovington, p. 267-268.
14. Terry, *A Voyage to East India,* p. 190.
15. *Travels in India in the 17th Century,* p. 77.
16. Sir Thomas Roe, *The Embassy of Sir Thomas Roe to the Court of the Moghal* p. 293.
17. Abul Fazl, *Ain-i-Akbari,* Vol. I, Pers. p. 222; Tr. (Bloch) p. 320.
18. Stanely Lane Pool, *History of India,* Vol. IV, p. 37.
19. Manucci, *Storia Do Mogor,* Vol. II, Tr. (Irvine) p. 460.
20. Mandelslo, Vol. I, p. 65.
21. Ovington, p. 159; for the reference of chess also see Maasir-i-Alamgiri, pp. 811-812; Badaoni, Muntakhab-ul-Twarikh, Vol. II, Tr. (Lowe) pp. 122 and 324; also Vol. III, Tr. pp. 408, 467; also Amir Khusrau, *Khazana-al-Futuh,* p. 43.
22. J.N. Sarkar, *Studies in Mughal India,* (Calcutta, 1919) p. 82.
23. *Ain-i-Akbari,* Vol. I, p. 219; also Tr. (Bloch) p. 315; also refer to

the diagram of Chaupar. PL. XVII, Figure No. 17, facing page, 314; also Mathur p. 222; Kaumudi, p. 26.

23. *Ain.* Vol. I, p. 219 Tr. (Bloch) p. 316; also for a reference to this game see Akbar Namah, Vol. II, pp. 368-391; Tr. p. 534; also Badaoni, Vol. I, Tr. (Lowe) p. 349; K.M. Ashraf, *Lif and Conditions of the People of Hindustan,* p. 297.
25. Malik Md. Jaisi refers this game played by Padmavati with Ratan Sen, vide *Padmavat* Tr. by Agrawala, p. 303; Doha 312; Nichint 27/23; also *see* Macauliffe, 348; for Mira Bai's playing this game with her most favourite god Girdhar Gopal.
26. Abul Fazl, *Ain-i-Akbari,* Vol. I, Pers. p. 220; Tr. (Bloch) p. 316.
26. *Ain.* Vol. I, Pers. 220, Tr. (Bloch) p. 317; also for reference see the diagram pt. XVII, Figure No. 18. facing page 314; of *Ain* (Bloch).
28. Abul Fazl, *Ain-i-Akbari,* Vol. I, Pers. p. 220; Tr. (Bloch) pp. 317-318; K.M. Ashraf, p. 296.
29. *Observations,* Vol. II, p. 85.
30. K.M. Ashraf, p. 295; for reference of Pachisi see *Journals and Proceedings of the Asiatic Society of Bengal.* New series 1906; Vol. II, No. 4 (N.S.) pp. 117-19. also fig. 1, p. 117; for Chausar see pp. 119-21; also Fig. 2, p. 119.
31. Bernier (Constable) pp. 273-274; also Thevenot, p. 71; also *Storia,* Vol. II, p. 308. For details see Chap. VI.
32. Manucci, *Storia,* Vol. II, p. 341.
33. *Sursagar,* Dashamskandh pp. 535-536-537; also Dr. Hargulal, *Sursagar Men Lok Jiwan,* Hindi Sahitya Sansar, p. 146.
34. Bihari Ratnakar, Granthkar Prakashan, addition, Doha, 419, p. 203.
35. Kaumudi, pp. 26-27.
36. *Ain.* Vol. I, Tr. (Bloch) p. 310; Manucci refers that Muslims were very keen on breeding pigeons on large numbers. *Storia,* Vol. I, p. 107; Hamilton also refers the store of pigeons, Hamilton, p. 76; *Maasir-ul-Umara* refers that Mirza cin Qulu of Jahangir's time had kept a number of pigeons. Vol. I, Tr. p. 435.
37. Manucci, *Storia,* Vol. I, p. 107.
38. Abul Fazl, *Ain-i-Akbari,* Vol. I, Pers. p. 217; also Tr. (Bloch) p. 312.
39. *Ibid.*
40. Manucci, *Storia,* Vol. II, p. 467.
41. Ain. Vol. I Pers. p. 215; Tr. (Bloch) p. 310; for Akbar's fondness of pigeon flying also see Monserrate, pp. 197-297.
42. Kaumudi pp. 26-27 for girls kite flying refer to painting No. 537, I.A.E. lent by the Central Asian Antiquities Museum. (Treasury wala collection).

43. *Quanun-i-islam,* p. 336; *Observations,* Vol. II, pp. 14-15; also refer to *Bihari Ratnakar,* New ed. 1955; Doha 57, p. 30; also Doha 373, p. 193; also *Bihar Through the Ages,* p. 534.
44. R.N. Saletore, *Sex in Indian Harem life,* p. 158.
45. Humayun Namah, p. 86; also Tr. (Bev), p. 189; also introduction p. 7.
46. *Storia,* Vol. II, Tr. p. 331.
47. *Ibid.* p. 352.
48. *Observations,* Vol. II, p. 81-82.
49. *Maasir-ul-Umara,* Vol. I, p. 454.
50. Kaumudi, p. 42; *Observations,* Vol. I, p. 306 for huqqah also refer to *Diwani-i-Faizi,* M.S. No. 367, p. 141.
51. Fryer refers 'They invite us with a hubble bubble a long reed as brown as a nut with use, inserted the body of a cocoe shell filled with water and a Nasty Bole, just pressing the water they ran tobacco into it, uncut out of which we may suck as long as we please' p. 8; also for reference see Grose al. p. 146; *Storia* Vol. I, p. 177; *Observations,* Vol. I, p. 304.
52. *Bihari Ratnakar* refers swinging of the heroine, Doha, 99, p. 46; also Doha 686, p. 273.
53. For reference of Jhula or Hindola see *Ghanannd Granthavall,* ed. by Vishav Prasad Mishra. Doha, 382 p. 418, also Doha 516, p. 450; Doha 517, p. 450; Doha 688, p. 494; Doha 1024, p. 578.
54. Kaumudi, p. 55; also painting.
55. *Storia* Vol. II, p. 341.
56. *Ibid.*
57. Lahori, *Badshah Namah,* Vol. II, p. 208.
58. Gulbadan refers, 'There was hunting eighth times while he (Humayun) was in Iraq and each time trouble was taken for him also Hamidah Banu Begum used to enjoy the sight, from a distance in either a camel or a horse litter.' *Humayun Namah* English Tr. (Bev) p. 169; also p. 197 for ladies presence in hunting; also *Tuzuk* Vol. I, Tr. p. 375.
59. *Tuzuk-i-Jahangiri,* Tr. Vol. II, pp. 74 and 105; also *Introducing India Part I,* pub. by R.A.S.B. 1947. Art. No. 9, p. 92; also Beni Prasad, History of Jahangir (Allahabad 1940, 3rd edn.) p. 157.
60. Tuzuk, Tr. Vol. I, p. 375; also Elliot and Dowson, *History of India* (IInd ed. 1952) p. 133; also for Nurjahan's hunting sitting on the back of elephant refer to Powell Price, *A History of Jahangir,* (1955) p. 294; also *Waqiat-i-Jahangiri* (Elliot and Dowson) Vol. VI, p. 366.
61. Tuzuk, Vol. I, Tr. p. 105; Due to successful tiger hunting a poet

recited this couplet in praise of her skill which runs thus: Though Nurjahan be in form of woman, in the ranks of men she's a tiger slayer.

62. Tuzuk, Vol. I, Tr. p. 105, pp. 129-130 and 206.
63. *Ibid.* p. 204; also *Iqbal Namah-i-Jahangiri* (Urdu), pp. 65-66.
64. *Iqbal Nama-i-Jahangiri,* (Urdu), p. 241.
65. *Muntakhab-ul-Lubab,* (Calcutta, 1874), p. 99.
66. Bernier, Tr. (Urdu), p. 439.
67. Pelsaert, p. 3; also De-falt, pp. 39-40; Storia, Vol. I, p. 178; Manrique Vol. II, pp. 161-162; also Fryer, 'Travels in India in 17th century, p. 20; Early Travels, p. 184; also Finch, Early Travels, p. 183; Petar Mundy, Vol. II, pp. 50 and 120.
68. K.M. Ashraf, p. 187, A. Ansari, *A Social life of the Mughal emperors,* p. 171.
69. Humayun Namah, Persian p. 43; also Tr. (Bev) p. 120; refers chaugan liked and played by Shad and Mihr Angez.
70. *Ain.* Vol. I, pp. 214-215, Tr. (Bloch), p. 309-310; For reference of polo also see *Akbar Namah,* Vol. II, p. 236; also Tr. p. 357, K.M. Ashraf, p. 287; Mathur, p. 278; Kaumudi, pp. 5. 6; Badaoni Vol. I, Tr. p. 489; also Vol. II, p. 70; Tr. p. 69; Monserrate, p. 197; Stochonkine PIXXI (d); also refers to *Sursagar* Dashamskandha, Pada 243 and 4166; *Bhushan Granthavali,* by Braj Ratan das, 2nd ed. 1950, Allahabad, p. 99 Pada 23.
71. *Ibid.* p. 310; *Akbar Namah,* Vol. II, p. 272; also Tr. (Bev) p. 405 and F.N.I. Badaoni Vol II, p. 84; also Tr. (Lowe) p. 86; *Tabqat-i-Akbari,* by Nizamuddin Ahmad, Vol. II, (Tr. by Bede) R.A.S.B. Calcutta 1936, p. 315.
72. Ain. Vol. I, Pers. pp. 214-215; also Tr. (Bloch), p. 310.
73. *Akbar Nama,* Vol. III, p. 414, Tr. (Bev), pp. 614-615; for a reference of chaughan see Amir Khusrau's *Khazana-al-Futuh,* p. 97; also for a picture of the players busy in playing chaugan see *Ain-i-Akbari,* Vol. I, Pers. Text. opposite p. 153.
74. *Humayun Namah* Persian, pp. 86-87; also Tr. (Bev), pp. 189-190-191; Gulbadan also refers Hamidah Banu Begum on excursion in Iraq with the sister of Shah (Shahzada Sultanam) and other ladies and wives of Khans, Sultans and Amirs. Persian p. 69; Tr. (Bev), pp. 170-171.
75. *Humayun Namah,* Tr. (Bev), pp. 103-104; also Pers. p. 20.
76. *Ibid.* Introduction p. 43.
77. Riwaj was a shrub two or three feet high in appearance like beetroot but much larger. Its flowers were red and white in colour and taste was sub-acid with little sweetness. Humayun Namah, Tr. (Bev), p. 188; F.N. 2; For mention of name Riwaj see *Taqbat-i-Akbari,* Vol. II, Lucknow, p. 215; also Tuzuk, Tr. p. 47.

78. Gulbadan refers, 'It was a moon lit night we talked and told stories, and Mir and Khanish Aghach and Zarif the reciter and Saru-sahi and Shaham Agha softly-softly'. *Humayun Naman,* Pers. p. 86; Tr. p. 189.
79. *Ibid.* Pers. p. 87; Tr. p. 191.
80. *Humayun Namah,* Pers. p. 93; Tr. (Bev), pp. 196-197.
81. *Ibid,* Tr. p. 129.
82. *Akbar Namah,* Pers. Vol. III, p. 370; also Tr. p. 543.
83. *Ibid.* p. 537; to 540, also Tr. (Bev), pp. 817-821.
84. *Iqbal Nama,* (Urdu) refers that Jahanara garden was made on the side of Shahr-ara-garden, pp. 34-36.
85. *Tuzuk,* Tr. Vol. I, pp. 106-107.
86. *Ibid,* p. 110.
87. *Ibid,* p. 241.
88. *Tuzuk,* Tr. Vol. I, p. 298.
89. *Ibid,* p. 384; 390; for Jahangir's entertainment with ladies on the bank of the river Narmada.
90. *Ibid,* Vol. II, pp. 199-200.
91. Bernier Tr. (Urdu), p. 439.
92. Lahori, *Badshah Nama,* Vol. II, p. 195; also Bernier, *Travels* Tr. (Urdu), p. 384; also Manucci, *Storia,* Vol. II, Tr. p. 66.
93. Lahori, *Badshah Namah,* Vol. II, p. 195.
94. *Ibid,* p. 195.
95. *Ibid,* p. 208.
96. Bernier (constable) p. 351; also Tr. (Urdu), pp. 383-384. Bernier mentions the year 1664 A.D. while Manucci, 1662 A.D. Storia, Vol. II, Tr. p. 66.
97. Manucci, *Ibid.*
98. *Ibid.* p. 67.
99. *Travels.* p. 184; for military expedition also refer to *Storia,* Vol. II Tr. p. 390.
100. Gulbadan, Humayun Namah, Pers. pp. 19–40; also Tr. (Bev), pp. 102-117.
101. *Ibid,* Pers. pp. 71-72; also Tr. pp. 136-137.
102. *Humayun Namah,* p. 77; also Tr. p. 143.
103. *Humayun Namah,* p. 56; Tr. (Bev), pp. 154-155.
104. *Akbar Namah,* Vol. III, Pers. Text. p. 83; also Tr. (H. Bev), p. 116.
105. *Ibid,* p. 768; also Tr. p. 1140; Manserrate, refers ladies accompanied expedition with Akbar, p. 79.
106. *Iqbal Nama-i-Jahangiri,* (Urdu), p. 234; During the reign of Jahangir a royal maid servant Aqa Aqayan always attended royal journey and expeditions. Jahangir himself writes, "In no journey or expedition had she of her own will remained absent from

attendance on me." *Tuzuk,* Vol. II, Tr. (R&B), p. 110.

107. *Iqbal Nama-i-Jahangiri,* (Urdu), p. 191.
108. *Ibid,* p. 191.
109. Robert Orme, Historical Fragments of the Mughal Empire, ed. with an introduction by J.P. Guha (second re-print 1978, Delhi), pp. 58-59.
110. Manucci, *Storia Do Mogor,* Vol. II, Tr. pp. 255-256.
111. Khafi Khan, Vol. II, 317.
112. Shah Nawaz Khan, *Maasir-ul-Umara,* Vol. II, part. II, p. 616.
113. Zahiruddin Faruqi, *Aurangazeb and his Times,* p. 136.
114. Gulbadan's *Humayun Namah* Pers. p. 72; also Tr. (Bev), pp. 136-137.
115. *Ibid,* p. 59; also Tr. (Bev), p. 157.
116. *Iqbal Nama-i-Jahangiri* (Urdu), p. 211.
117. *Humayun Namah,* Pers. p. 72.
118. Manucci, Storia Do Mogor, Vol. II, p. 74.
119. Bernier (constable), p. 359; also Tr. (Urdu), p 391; also *Storia,* Vol. II, Tr. p. 67; Shah Nawaz Khan refers it 'Peshkhima' *Maasir-ul-Umara,* Vol. I, Tr. p. 526.
120. Abul Fazl, *Ain-i-Akbari,* Vol. I, Pers. Text p. 51; also Tr. (Bloch) p. 49.
121. Bernier (constable), p. 359; also Tr. (Urdu), p. 391; *also Storia,* Vol. II, p. 68.
122. *Ain,* Vol. I, Pers. p. 51. Tr. (Bloch) p. 49; also Bernier (constable), p. 359; also (Urdu) pp. 391-392.
123. *Ain.* Vol. I, *Ibid.* Tr. (Bloch), p. 49-50.
124. *Bernier, (Constable),* p. 359; also Tr. (Urdu), p. 393.
125. *Bernier, Travels,* p. 359; also Tr. (Urdu), p. 393.
126. Ain, Vol. I, Pers. p. 50. Tr. (Bloch), p. 47.
127. *Ibid.*
128. Bernier, p. 359; also (Urdu) pp. 393-394.
129. *Ibid.* pp. 364-365; also (Urdu) p. 395.
130. *The Army of the Indian Mughals,* its Organisation and Administration by William Irvine, (New Delhi, 1962), p. 200.
131. Khafi Khan, *Muntakhab-ul-Lubab,* Vol. II, p. 317.
132. Gulbadan, *Humayun Namah,* Tr. (Bev) Introduction, p. 30 also *Maasir-ul-Umara,* Vol. II, Part II, p. 729; also Mutamid Khan, *Iqbal Nama-i-Jahangirl,* Pers. Text p. 56.
133. *Humayun Namah,* Pers. pp. 71-72; also Tr. (Bev) pp. 136-137.
134. *Ibid.* p. 77 tr. (Bev) p. 143.
135. *Ain.* Vol. II, Pers. p. 58; also Tr. p. 119.
136. *Tuzuk-i-Baburi,* pp. 633-634.
137. *Tuzuk-i-Jahangiri,* Vol. I, Tr. p. 143.
138. *Tarikh-i-Hind* (Urdu). P. 546; also Major David Price Memoirs of

Jahangir, p. 99.

139. Bernier also refers this show. Travels, Tr. (Urdu), p. 519.
140. *Memoirs of Jahangir* by Major David Price, p 99; also *Tarikh-i-Hind* by Sadique, pp. 546-547-548.
141. *Ain* Vol. I, Pers. p. 143; also Vol. III, p. 258; Badaoni also refers to it. Vol. II, p. 367; Tr. (Lowe), p. 379; for some remarkable feasts see Peter Mundy Vol. II, p. 254; Terry, *A Voyage to East India,* pp. 190-191; John Marshall in India, p. 354; For Jugglers also refer to Monserrate, p. 198; Pelsaert, p. 72.
142. Ain, Vol. III, Tr. p. 258; also Vol. II, Pers. p. 143.
143. Norris *Embassy to Aurangzeb,* 1959, pp. 166-167.
144. Travels of Thevenot, p. 109; also for a photo of Juggler's feat see opposite, p. 107.
145. Della Valle. p. 460; Terry, *Early Travels,* pp. 312-313; De Laet, p. 82; also Babar Namah (Bev), p. 492; also *Memoirs of Babur,* Tr. John Leyden and W. Elskine, Vol. II, p. 23; also De Laet, pp. 82-83.
146. Ovington, p. 154; Terry, *A Voyage to East India,* p. 190; also Terry, early Travels, pp. 312-313; Della Valle, p. 405; De Leat, p. 82; also Dubois. *Hindu Manners, Customs and Ceremonies,* p. 74.
147. Ain Vol. III, Tr. p. 257; also vol. II, Pers. p. 143; for a reference to some jesters see. Badaoni, Vol. III, Tr. pp. 325, 365.
148. *Storia,* Vol. I, Tr. pp. 213-217.
149. Ain. Vol. III, p. 258; also Vol. II, Pers. p. 143.
150. S.C. Mishra, Muslim Communities in Gujarat, pub. by Asia Publishing House (1964), p. 82.
151. *Tavernier,* Vol. II, 392.
152. *Humayun Namah,* pp. 28-29; also Tr. (Bev), p. 113.
153. S.M. Jaffar, *Some Cultural Aspects of Muslim Rule in India,* p. 186.
154. *Humayun Namah,* pp. 28-29; also Tr. p. 114.
155. *Ibid.,* pp. 41 to 45; also Tr. (Bev), pp. 118 to 126.
156. *Ibid.,* Persian, pp. 45-46; Tr. (Bev) pp. 126 to 129.
157. *Tazkirah-Tul-Waqiat* (Jauhar) pp 30-31; *Humayun Namah,* Pers. p. 53; Tr. (Bev). p. 150.
158. *Humayun Namah,* Persian, p. 53; Tr. p. 150.
159. *Tazkira-al-Waqiat* (Jauhar) p. 31.
160. *Humayun Namah,* Persian, p. 77; Tr. (Bev) p. 179; *Tabqat-i-Akbari,* Tr. (E.D.) Vol. II, p. 3.
161. *Akbar Namah,* Vol. III, p. 519; Tr. (Bev) p. 791.
162. *Ibid.* Vol. II, p. 133; also Tr. (Bev), p. 205.
163. *Tuzuk,* Tr. Vol. I, p. 1385.
164. *Storia,* Vol. I, p. 158-159.

165. *Ibid,* p. 397; also see *Iqbal Nama-i-Jahangiri,* Pers. Text (1865) pub. by A.S.B., p. 105.
166. *Ibid.* Vol. II, p. 192.
167. *Storia,* Vol. I, pp. 199-200.
168. *Tuzuk,* Tr. Vol. II, pp. 214-215; also *Iqbal Nama* (Urdu), p. 171; also *Storia,* Vol. I, p. 163.
169. Lahori, *Badshah Nama,* Vol. II, pp. 395-396; for this feast also see *Maasir-ul-Umara,* Vol. I, Tr. p. 564.
170. *Storia,* Vol. I, Tr. p. 359.
171. *Qazwini,* p. 291; *Maasir-i-Alamgiri,* pp. 31-32.
172. Aurangzeb's youngest son Kam Baksh's marriage reception was held in the palace of *Zeb-un-Nisa. Maasir-i-Alamgiri,* p. 204; also *Maqalat-i-Shibli* ed. by Sayyed Sulaiman Nadvi, Vol. II, (1955), p. 102.
173. *Tavernier,* Vol. II, pp. 389-390.
174. *Maasir-i-Alamgiri,* Tr. p. 14; also *Qanun-i-Islam,* p. 190; *Ruqqat-i-Alamgiri,* Tr. by Jamshid H. Billimoria, Delhi, 1972, p. 5; refers the letter of Aurangzeb in which he warned his son Muazzam 'not to celebrate again'; also see Md. Kazim, Alamgir Nama, Pers. Text. pub. by A.S.B. (1868) p. 390; also Khafi Khan *Muntakhab-ul-Lubab,* Pers. Text pub. by A.S.B. (1874), Vol. II, p. 79; also Elliot & Dowson, Muntakhab-ul-Lubab, Vol. VI, p. 241.
175. *Humayun Namah,* Pers. p. 77, also Tr. (Bev), p. 179.
176. Abul Fazl, *Ain-i-Akbari,* Vol. I, Pers. Text. p. 200; also Tr. (Bloch) p. 286.
177. *Ibid.* p. 22.
178. *Ibid.* Pers. p. 200; also Tr. p. 286; also Thevenot, *Travels* (S. Sen) p. 70; F. n.20; Gulbadan mentions its 17 day festivities, Humayun Namah, p. 77; also Tr. p. 179; Jahangir refers 17 & 18 days celebration, *Tuzuk-i-Jahangirl,* Vol. I, Tr. (R&B) p. 49; also see Mandelslo Vol. I, pp. 41-42; also Hawkins, *Early Travels,* ed. By Foster, p. 117. Nizamuddin Ahmad refers 18 days, *Tabqat-i-Akbari,* Vol. II, Tr. pp. 555-560; while Monserrate refers 9 days pp. 174-175.
179. Thevenot, *Travels* (S. Sen) p. 71, while De Laet refers 18 days, p. 100.
180. Mandelslo, *op. cit.* pp. 117-118; For Nawroz also consult Akbar Namah, Pers. Vol. III, p. 379; also Md. Amin Qazwini, *Badshah Nama,* MS. No. 622; *Daftar-i-Diwani* wa Mulki Library, Hyderabad, p. 167, 169; p. 313b, 314a; also Lahori's *Badshah Nama,* Vol. I, part II, pp. 77; 256, 297, 364, 418, 473; also Vol. II, p. 8; also Thevenot, p. 70; also Roe's Embassy, pp. 143-144; also Manrique Vol. II, pp. 192-198; Peter Mundy, Vol. II, p. 238; Bernier (Constable), p. 270; also Badaoni, Vol. II, Tr. (Lowe) p.

310; Terry, *Early Travels,* p. 310; also De Laet, pp. 99, 100-101, Khwanda Mir, *Qanoon-i-Humayun,* Tr. (English) by Beni Prasad, pub. by A.S.B. (1940) pp. 69-71-73; also *Waqiat-i-Jahangir,* in Elliot & Dowson, Vol. VI, p. 316; also *Muntakhab-ul-Twarikh* by Hassan bin Muhammad al-Khaki al-Shirazi, in Elliot & Dawson, Vol. VI, p. 204; Mutamid Khan, *Iqbal Nama-i-Jahangiri* in Elliot & Dawson, Vol. VI, p. 404; also Hawkins, *Early Travels* pp. 117-119; Eryer, *Travels in India in the 17th Century,* pp. 24-25.

181. Gulbadan, Humayun Nama, Pers. p. 177; also Tr. (Bev) p. 179.
182. Khwajah Nizamuddin Ahmad, *Tabqat-i-Akbari,* Vol. II, Tr. p. 555.
183. Manserrate, p. 175; also Thevenot, p. 71.
184. *The Gazetteer of India,* Vol. II, Oct. 1973, p. 413.
185. Hawkins, *Voyages during the reigns of Henry VIII, Queen* Elizabeth and James I, p. 439; Mandelslo, Vol. I, p. 42; also Manserrate, pp. 175-176, also De Leat, pp. 100-101; Peter Mundy, Vol. II, p. 238; Hawkins, *Early Travels,* p. 118; For ladies visit to palace on the occasion of Nawroz and other festivals, See *Maasir-ul-Umarah,* Vol. I, Tr. p. 651.
186. *Hindustan Ke Mussalman Hukumrano Ke Ahad Ke Tammadduni Jalwe;* ed. by Sahabuddin Abdul Rahman (Urdu), Azamgarh, 1963, p. 468.
187. *Observations,* pp. 280-287.
188. *Storia,* Vol. II, pp. 248-249; *Tabqat-i-Akbari,* Vol. II, Tr. pp. 559-560.
189. Terry, *A voyage to East India,* pp. 271-272; also Terry. *Early Travels,* p. 318.
190. Fryer, Travels in India in 17th Century, pp. 305-306, Roe's Embassy, p. 72 Della Valle, p. 428.
191. Khafi Khan, Tr. (Urdu), Vol. III, p. 402.
192. Fryer, p. 107.
193. Pelsaert, p. 73.
194. The objective of this prayer is 'to glorify God, to celebrate His praise and to render thanks on Him for the guidance provided by Him particularly with regard to all that relate to the observance of the fast and for having enabled those upon whom fast was obligatory to observe it duly,' *Islam* by Md. Zafarullah Khan, 1962, p. 116.
195. Azhar Ansari, *Social Life of the Mughal Emperors,* p. 122.
196. *Lahori, Badshah Nama,* Vol. II, pp. 134, 221; also Vol. I, p. 372. refers that in 1040 A.H. Shahjahan distributed twenty thousand as alms;' for his distribution of alms to the poor and needy also see Qazwini, Badshah Nama M.S. p. 127.
197. *Mishkat,* Book. VI, Chap. III, p. 5.

198. *Quanun-i-Islam,* p. 212.
199. In India Sewai was the symbol of Id and so Idul Fitr was also called Sewayyon ki Id, E.D. Ross wrongly says to Id-i-Quarban, Siwayyon ki Id, *Hindu Muhammadan Feasts and Holidays* pp. 101-102; For sewai also see, Observations, Vol. I, p. 192; For reference of Sewai, also see V-hafi Khan Tr. (Urdu) Vol. 1. p. 108.
200. Muanqa or embracing in Id was an Indian origin, Most probably Muslims copied it from Hindu festival Holi, when they embraced one another as a mark of jcy. For Muanqa see *Kulliat-i-Urfi,* M.S. p. 38.
201. Kullat-i-Urfi, M.S. No. 364, p. 41.
202. *Observations,* p. 324; refers that ladies always made a visit to their friends and relatives for three days and three nights except in Id; 'when the visit was confined to one day'.
203. Lahori, Badshah Nama, Vol. I, p. 372, also Vol. II, p. 134-135, 172, Storia Vol. II p. 349 Naasir-i-Alamgiri, Tr. pp. 21-25-36 Iqbal Nama Tr. (Urdu), p. 74.
204. *Tuzuk,* Tr. Vol. I, p. 46.
205. *Massir-i-Alamgiri,* Tr. pp. 21-25 and 36.
206. Pelsaert, p. 73.
207. For decoration and illumination of palaces, see *Badshah Nama,* Lahori, Vol. II, p. 174; Massir-i-Alamgiri, Tr. p. 25; for houses refer, Terry. *A Voyage to East India,* p. 272; also Terry, *Early Travels,* p. 318.
208. K.M. Ashraf, p. 164; for a general account of Id consult *Akbar Nama,* Vol. II Pers. pp. 78, 414; also Tr. pp. 109, 614; Tuzuk, Tr. Vol. I, pp. 45-46; Miraat-al-alam, By Bakhtawar Khan Sl. No. 1,051 included in the section of the *Histories of Aurangzeb's Reign, Daftar-i-Diwani Wa Mulki Library.* Hyderabad, pp. 398, 483; 518; Qazwini, 196a, 197a, 267b, 387b, Fazil Khan, Shahjahan Nama, MS. No. 235, Asifyah library, 254b, Maasir-i-Alamgiri Pers. pp. 70. 96, 102, 127; Babur Nama Tr. (Bev) pp. 235-236; 311, 410, 584, 683, 689, T.A. Vol. II. p. 605 *Badshah Namah,* Lahori Vol. II, p. 259, Roe's Embassy, p. 72; Norris' Embassy, p. 165 Bernier p. 280 Ovinagton, p. 243 Della Valle p. 428; Travels in India in 17th century, p. 306. Letters received by East India Company, Vol. IV, p. 10; *Outline of Islamic culture,* p. 704; also *Islamic Toohar,* pp. 72-78 *Hindu Mohammadan feasts and holidays,* p. 102, *Faith, Fairs and Festivals of India,* p. 201; Hugh's Dictionary of Islam, p. 194; *Maasir-ul-Umara,* Vol. I, Tr. p. 574.
209. Abul Fazl, *Akbar Namah,* Vol. II, Tr. p. 51.
210. *Ibid.* It refers that Akbar performed the rites. For Aurangzeb's performance of prayer in Akbarabadi Mosque, Nisar and Sacrifice

see Munshi Md. Waris, *Padshah Nama.* M, S. pp. 85 and 142.

211. Hazrat Aisha states, 'That the Holy Prophet said, 'Man hath not done anything on the Idul Zuha more pleasing to God than spilling blood, for verily the animal sacrificed will come, on the day of resurrection, with its horns, its hair, and its hoofs and will make the scale of his (good) actions heavy verily its blood reacheth upon the ground. Therefore, be joyful in it'. Mishkat, Book, IV, Chap. XIII sec. 2.
212. *Tuzuk,* Vol. I, p. 189; *Peter Mundy* Vol. II, p. 196 *Storia,* Vol. II, pp. 349-350; *Maasir-i-Alamgiri,* p. 78; Fryer, p. 108; *Travels in India in the 17th Century,* p. 306; Mirat-al-alam, p. 127.
213. *Badshah Nama* (Lahori), Vol. II, pp. 95, 144, 480, 625.
214. Observations, Vol. I, p. 281. It is remarkable to note that animal like goat and sheep suffices for one person while the bigger animal as camel, cow, for seven (Maximum shares).
215. *Storia,* Vol. II, pp. 349-350.
216. Fryer, p. 108.
217. Keeping it in view once Jahangir sacrificed on 11th Zil Hijjah, 'On Thursday the 10th Zil Hijjah was the festival of the Qurban (the sacrifice of Ismail) as it prohibited to take life on that day (Thursday). I ordered that on the Friday they should kill the sacrificial animal'. Tuzuk-Tr. Vol. I, p. 189.
218. Mandelslo Vol. I, p. 42.
219. Shahjahan was very liberal in this matter, *Lahori Badshah Nama* Vol. I, Part II, p. 101.
220. *Maasir-i-Alamgiri,* p. 67.
221. *Observations,* Vol. I, p. 282.
222. Mandelslo, Vol. I, p. 42; for Idul Zuha consult Akbar Nama. Vol. II, p. 31, Tr. II, p. 51; Tuzuk, Vol. I, Tr. p. 189; *Lahoris Badshah Nama* Vol. II, pp. 95, 144, 480, 625; Petermundy Vol. II, p. 186; Terry, Early Traverils, p. 318; Fryer, p. 198 Pelsaert, pp. 73-74. For other sources see Islami Teohar, pp. 78-88; *Hindu Muhammadan Feasts and Holidays,* pp. 102-103 *Faith, Fairs and Festivals,* p. 201; *Hugh's Dictionary of Islam,* p. 192.
223. *Amal-i-Saleh,* Pers. Text. Bibliotheca Indica (Calcutta 1939) pp. 285-286; also Lahori, *Badshah Nama,* Vol. II, pp. 167, 216; The Holy Quran also gives it the name Lailatul Mubarak (the blessed night), Rahmat (Night of mercy), Faraiqa (Night of discernment) *Qanun-i-Islam,* p. 203.
224. It is believed that on this night God registers annually all the actions of mankind in *'Nama-i-Amal'* (Book of Actions) which they are to perform during the year, all the matters of life, as to who are to retain health, life, property of any other blessings and sorrows, adversity and also all the children who are to born and

to die in the coming year, is recorded in heaven.

225. *Amal-i-Sallh,* pp. 285-286.
226. Khwajah Nizamuddin, *Tabqat-i-Akbari,* Vol. II, Tr. p. 180.
227. Thevenot, *Travels,* p. 44; Here Shab-i-Barat is wrongly called Choubret.
228. Badaoni, Vol. I, Tr. (Banking), p. 488; K.M. Ashraf, p. 301; *Qanun-i-Islam,* p. 204; *Observations,* pp. 302-303; It also refers that the Shias attached great importance to this night as the anniversary of the birth of Imam Mehdi.
229. The origin of this custom is unknown. It is said that in 1st Hijri a devoted Saint Qals Qarni bit his teeth in love of Prophet Mohammad whose teeth were broken in Ghazwa-i-Ohad. For his comfort, his ladies prepared 'Halwa' for him. So in memory of this saint 'Halwa' was cooked in Shab-i-Barat. But historically this event has no proof.
230. Thevenot, p. 44; *In Literary Works see Ashaar-i-Nazir* (Urdu) ed. by Hafiz Shamsuddin Maneri, Pub. by National Press, Allahabad, IInd ed. 1952 p. 17.
231. Thevenot, p. 44.
232. *Tuzuk* Vol. I, p. 385.
233. *Travels of Thevenot,* p. 44; also Amal-i-Saleh, pp. 285-86.
234. *Badshah Nama,* (Lahori), Vol. II, pp. 127, 168, 247, 317, 343, 468, and 603; for Shahjahan's prayer and alms in this night, see Qazwini's Padshah Nama, M.S. No. 69, p. 125.
235. *Ibid.* p. 168.
236. *Tuzuk,* Vol. I, Tr. p. 298, For a reference to illumination by Jahangir refer Tuzuk, Vol. I, Tr. pp. 298, 385; also Vol. II, pp. 22-23, 94 and 95, for Shahjahan's interest in illumination, see Badshah Nama, Lahori, Vol. II, pp. 167-216 and 343; Md. Salih Comboh refers that 'The flood of light is so much that it fades out the light of the moon'. *Amal-i-Salih* pp. 285-286, also refer to Md. Arnin bin Abdul Hassan Qazurini. Padshah Nama, M.S. 69 (N. Lib) p. 125.
237. Tuzuk, Vol. II, Tr. p. 22; *Badshah Nama* Lahori, Vol. II, p. 167, Amal-i-Salih, Vol. I, pp. 285-286; Mandelslo, Vol. I, p. 40.
238. Mandelslo, Vol. I, p. 46; For a reference to illumination also see *Travels of Thevenot,* p. 44.
239. Tuzuk, Tr. Vol. II, pp. 94-95; For Shahjahan's order of display of fireworks refer to *Badshah Nama,* Lahori, Vol. II, p. 167-168 and 343.
240. Mandelslo, Vol. I, p. 46; also Ashar-i-Nazir (Urdu), pp. 19-20 Travels of Thevenot, p. 44.
241. *Ain-i-Akbari,* Vol. III, Jarrett) p. 320, K.M. Ashraf, p. 301, Glimpses of Medieval Indian Culture by Yusuf Hussain, reprinted in 1962, p. 127.

242. Khafi Khan, Vol. III, (Urdu), p. 483.
243. Qanun-i-Islam, p. 203; Observations Vol. I, p. 301; *Islami Teohar Aur Utsav* by Maulvi Mahesh Prasad, Banaras, pp. 68-72; *Ashar-i-Nazir,* pp. 17, 18, 19; *Feasts and holidays of Hindu and Mohammadans* by E.D. Ross, p. 98; For the reference to Shab-i-Barat see Qutub Mushtari aur uska *Tangidi Jayeza* (Urdu), p. 238.
244. Mrs. Meer Hasan Ali, *Observations on the Musalmans of India,* pp. 42 to 47.
245. Monserrate, p. 22; also Mrs Meer Hasan Ali, *Ibid,* p. 43-44.
246. *Journal of Indian History,* Vol. XLIV, Part I, April 1966, Serial No. 130, p. 25; also *Travels of Thevenot,* p. 149.
247. Senal Al Ghaznavi, Hadiqat-ul-Haqiqat, Pers. MS. Khuda Bakhsh, O.P.L. Patna, pp. 49-57; Travels of Thevenot, p. 149; Journal of Indian History Vol. XLIV Part I, April, 1966; Serial No. 130, p. 25; also *the Gazetteer of India* Vol. II, ed. by P.N. Chopra (C) Govt. of India, October 20th, 1973, p. 413; also Qanun-i-Islam, p. 166.
248. Monserrate refers Nine Days Fast, p. 22; for fasting also see Fryer, p. 109; Pelsaert p. 74.
249. K.M. Ashraf, p. 302; *Observations,* Vol. I, pp. 51-52; also Norris Embassy to Aurangzeb, F.N. No. 59, p. 165.
250. Pelsaert, p. 74 Monserrate, p. 22; *Qanun-i-Islam,* p. 158; *Observations,* Vol. I, pp. 51-52.
251. *Journal of Indian Hist.* Vol. XLIV Part I April 1966; serial no. 130, p. 25, For vow also consult Qanun-i-Islam, pp. 166, 181, 182 and 183; Observations, Vol. I, p. 91.
252. *Yusuf Hussan's Glimpses of Medieval Indian Culture* 1962, p. 127.
253. *Observations* Vol. I, p. 51.
254. Mandelslo Vol. I, p. 42; Fryer, p. 108; Observations Vol. I, p. 93; *Journal of Indian Hist.* Vol. XLIV Part I April, 1966 sl. no. 130 p. 25.
255. Monserrate, p. 22, Plesaert, pp. 74-75; also Mandelslo Vol. I, p. 42; *Travels of Thevenot,* p. 149; Norris *Embassy to Aurangzeb,* p. 165.
256. V.D. Mahajan, *Mughal Rule in India,* tenth ed. 1972, p. 309; also for Muharram celebration in Golconda after Aurangzeb's victory see, *Journal of Indian History,* Vol. XLIV Part, I, April, 1966, Serial No. 130, pp. 25-26.
257. Hugh's Dictionary of Islam, pp. 25, 407; *Qanun-i-Islam,* p. 151.
258. This relates that Prophet Mohammad always observed this fast and said that it was a day respected by Jews and Christians, Mishkat, VII, CVII, I; also see *Hindustani Mussulman* By Maulana Abdul Hassan Ali Nadvi, pp. 74-75, for its observation during

the Mughal period see *Norris' Embassy* p. 165.

259. *Ijaz-i-Khusravi,* by Amir Khusrau, Vol. IV, p. 328.
260. Fryer, p. 108; also *Qanun-i-Islam,* p. 168; *Observations* Vol. I, p. 23.
261. Pelsaert, p. 75; *Observations* Vol. I, p. 87; *Journal of Indian Hist.* Vol. XLIV part I April, 1966, Serial No. 130, p. 25.
262. Qazwini, *Padshah Nama* M.S. p. 126.
263. Pelsaert, p. 75; where he compares this festival to Christians, "All souls day". *Feasts and Holidays* by E.D. Ross, p. 109.
264. *Travels of Thevenot,* p. 149; also Yusuf Husain, Glipses of Medieval Indian Culture, p. 127.
265. K.M. Ashraf, p. 303.
266. Fryer, p. 108; *Muntakhab-ul-Lubab,* Vol. II, p. 214.
267. Khafi Khan, *Tr. Urdu,* Vol. III, p. 197.
268. 'Barah' means twelve and 'wafat' means death. Hugh's *Dictionary of Islam,* p. 36; *Feasts and Holidays of Hindu and Mohammadan,* p. 98; *Sehishti Zewar,* Vol. VI, p. 68.
269. *Badshah Nama,* Lahori, p. 420.
270. *Tabqat-i-Akbari,* Tr. Vol. II, p. 520.
271. *Badshah Nama,* Lahori Vol. I, pp. 102, 151, 199, 303, 335, 374, 420 and 502; Amal-i-Salih, Vol. I, p. 617 refers 20,000 money given in charity; also refer to Qazwini's *Padshah Nama,* 261, a, b, 310b, 469a.
272. B.S. Nijjar, *Punjab under the Great Mughals,* p. 130.
273. Herklot's *Qanun-i-Islam,* p. 189.
274. *Journal of Indian History* Vol. XLIV, Part I, April, 1966, Serial No. 130, p. 26; also Herklot's *Qanun-i-Islam,* p. 190.
275. *Ibid.*
276. Herklot's *Qanun-i-Islam,* pp. 188-190; also E.D. Ross. Feasts... p. 98.
277. Ghulam Hussain Salim, *Riyaz-us-Salatin, a History of Bengal.* Tr. by Abdus Salam, (1975, reprint) p. 280.
278. Md. Sahih Kambch, *Amal-i-Salih,* Vol. I, p. 374.
279. Lahori, *Badshah Nama,* Vol. I, p. 204.
280. *Tuzuk-i-Jahangiri,* Pers. Text. p. 131; also Tr. (R and B) Vol. I pp. 265, 295.
281. Lahori, *Badshah Nama,* Vol. I, p. 204, also Vol. II, p. 101, also Amal-i-Salih, p. 374.
282. *Alamgir Nama,* Pers. p. 623.
283. Painting No. 636; I.A.E. Mughal, Early 17th century.
284. It is believed that Prophet Mohammad was caught up one night from Jarusalem to Heaven, While in Heaven he held (90,000) conversations with God, but on his return his bed was found warm. In religious books of Mohammedans mention is made that

on this return from Heaven his body was quite warm and full of perspiration. *The Holy Quran* refers thus, 'Praise be to Him who carried His servant by night from the Masjidul Haram (Maccan Mosque) to the Masjidul Aqsa (Mosque of Jerusalem)' The Holy Quran, *Surah* XVIII.I. Madanulmacni refers, 'Miraj Karamat' but Pers. p. 73, *Mishkat,* Vol. IV 405 pp. 158-168.

285. Sarfi, *Maslak-ul-Akhyar,* Foll 87-B-illa, M.S. p. 92.
286. *Feasts and Holidays,* by E.D. Ross, p. 112.
287. *Badaoni,* Vol. II, Pers. pp. 316-317, also Tr. (Lowe) Vol. III, p. 326; also Vol. III, Pers. p. 306; Tr. (Haig), p. 22.
288. *Badshah Nama,* Lahori, Vol. II, pp. 127, 214, 246, 311, 342, and 387; also Qazwini, *Padshah Nama,* M.S. p. 126.
289. *Qanun-i-Islam,* p. 216; *Hindustani Mussalman,* p. 79.
290. Herklot's *Qanun-i-Islam* pp. 192-193; also Hugh's *Dictionary of Islam,* p. 478.
291. Sayyed Iqbal Ahmad, *Tarikh-i-Jaunpur,* Shiraz-ul-Hind Publishing House, Jaunpur (1963) 1st Edn. p. 147.
292. Ashraf Ali Thanwi, *'Behishti Zewar'* (Urdu) Vol. VI, pp. 376-377.
293. *Qanun-i-Islam,* pp. 192-193; also *Hindustani Mussalman,* p. 79.
294. Ashraf Ali Thanvi, *Behishti Zewar,* (Urdu) Vol. VI, p. 373.
295. Abul Fazl, *Ain-i-Akbari,* Vol. I, Tr. (Bloch), p. 440.
296. Maasirul-Umara, *Akhir Chaharshamba,* Vol. I, Tr. p. 476; also *Qanun-i-Islam,* p. 187; also E.D. Ross, *Feasts and Holidays,* p. 97.
297. *Quanun-i-Islam,* p. 187; also E.D. Ross, *Ibid.*
298. E.D. Ross, *Ibid.* p. 113.
299. *Qanun-i-Islam,* p. 186.
300. *Ibid. Feasts and Holidays,* p. 113.
301. Ashraf Ali, Thanvi, *'Behishti Zewar'* (Urdu), Vol. VI, p. 384.
302. Rai Chatraman, Chahar Gulshan, MS. 39a p. 5. It refers to celebration on the bank of river Yamuna, also E.D. Ross, *Feasts and Holidays of Hindu and Mohammadans,* p. 104.
303. *Rai Chatraman,* Ibid.
304. *'Jodha Bai'* by the daughter of Nasiruddin Haider, ed. Md. Aslam. Khwateen, (Urdu) pp. 222-223.
305. *Ibid.* also Ashraf Ali Thanvi, *Behshti Zewar,* (Urdu) Vol. VI, p. 376.
306. *Khwateen,* edited by Md. Aslam (Urdu), pp. 222-223.
307. Gulbadan Begum, *Humayun Nama,* Pers. ed. by Mrs. Bev. p. 35.
308. *Ibid.*
309. Abul Fazl, *Ain-i-Akbari,* Vol. I, Tr. (Bloch) p. 286.
310. Peter Mundy, Vol. II, 238; Thevenot refer Seraglio, *Travels,* pp. 70-71.
311. *Hindustan ke Hukumrano ke Tammadduni Jalwe* (Urdu) ed. by

Sayyed Sahabuddin, p. 227.

312. Hamilton, p. 99.
313. *Ibid.*
314. *Thevenot,* Indian Travels (S. Sen), p. 70.
315. Tod, Annals and Etiquities of Rajasthan, Vol. I pp. 401-402; also Thevenot, *Travels,* p. 70.; Bhushan, 'Granthavali', IInd edn. 1950 edt. by Braj Ratan Das, Allahabad, *Kavit Man Haran Pada* 16, p. 96.
316. Hamilton, p. 99; also Bernier Tr. (Urdu), p. 580; also Thevenot, pp. 70-71.
317. Bernier (constable), p. 272.
318. Thevenot, Indian Travels, p. 71.
319. *Ibid.*
320. Bernier Tr. (Urdu), p. 580.
321. Thevenot, Travels, p. 71; also Bernier, Tr. (Urdu), p. 580.
322. Abul Fazl, *Ain-i-Akbari,* Vol. I (Bloch), p. 287.
323. Manucci, *Storia Do Magor,* Vol. I, (1907), p. 195.
324. *Hindustan ke Hukumrano ke Tammuduni Jalwe* (Urdu), p. 227.
325. Abul Fazl, *Ain-i-Akbari,* Vol. I, Tr. (Bloch), p. 287.
326. Thomas Coryat, p. 273.
327. R.P. Tripathi, *Rise and Fall of the Mughal Empire,* 3rd edn. 1963, Allahabad, p. 369, also De Laet, p. 181.
328. Badaoni, *Muntakhab-ul-Twarikh,* Vol. II, Tr. p. 350; also Md. Hussain Azad. Darbar-i-Akbari (Urdu) pp. 154-155.
329. Badaoni, *Muntakhab-ul-Twarikh,* Vol. II, Tr. p. 350.
330. *Ibid.*
331. Manucci, *Storia Do Mogor,* Vol. I (1907), p. 195.
332. Bernier (constable) p. 273; also Tr. (Urdu), p. 580.
333. *Ibid,* p. 272.
334. *Tuzk,* Vol. II, Tr. (R&B) p. 31; also Elliot & Dowson, *Waqiat-i-Jahangiri,* Vol. VI Ist Indian edn. (1964), p. 361.
335. Badaoni, *Muntakhab-ul-Twarikh,* Vol. II (Lowe), p. 331; also see Journal of Indian History Vol. I, 1921, Art. 22, *The Mughal Government with special reference to the reign of Jahangir* by Beni Prasad, p. 111; also S. Lanepool, *Aurangzeb,* 2nd Ind. Re-print, 1964, pp. 100-101.
336. Thevenot Travels, p. 71; also S. Lanepool, *Aurangzeb,* p. 101.
337. Abul Fazl, *Ain-i-Akbari,* Vol. I, Tr. (Bloch) p. 287; also Badaoni, *op. cit.*
338. Badaoni, *Ibid.*
339. Manucci, *Storia Do Mogor,* Vol. I (Irvine), p. 188.
340. *Ibid.*
341. *Kuillat-i-Urfi,* M.S. p. 38.
342. *Chahar Gulshan,* M.S, p. 4, 39a.

343. De Laet, p. 25; aldso Pelsaert, p. 70.
344. P. N. Ojha, *North Indian Social Life,* Ist end. 1975, p. 71.
345. *Ibid.* p. 72.
346. Thomas Caryat, *Early Travels,* pp. 279-280 also F.N. p. 280.
347. For Akbar's visit see *Tabaqat-i-Akbari,* Vol. II, p. 613; also William Finch, *Early Travels,* pp. 170-171.
348. Abul Fazl, *Akbar Nama,* Tr. (Bev) Vol. III, p. 298.
349. *Tabqat-i-Akbari,* Vol. II, p. 359, also *Waqiat-i-Jahangiri,* by Elliot and Dowson, Vol. VI, p. 319; also *Tuzk,* Vol. I (R&B).
350. *Tuzk-i-Jahangiri,* Vol. I, (R&B) pp. 151-152; also see plate XX of *Indian Paintings under the Mughals* by Percy Brown showing Jahangir at the tomb of the saint.
351. Abul Fazl, *Akbar Nama,* Vol. III, Tr. (Bev.) pp. 569-570, Fn. 1.
352. *Tuzuk,* Vol. II (R&B), p. 109.
353. *Khwateen* edited by Md. Aslam (Urdu), p. 238.
354. *Ibid.* p. 248, also Shahjahan in 1046 A. H. visited the shrine of Khwaja, Khafi Khan, Vol. II, Tr. Urdu, p. 130.
355. Mrs. Indira Gandhi, the late Prime Minister of India had great respect for the saint and often visited his tomb and offered 'Chadar' there.
356. *Badaoni,* Vol. II, p. 137.
357. *Chahar Gulshan,* M.S. p. 4, 39a Sir Syed Ahmad Khan, however recorded it 17th *Rabi-us-Sani. Asar-us-Sanadeed* (Urdu) p. 193.
358. *Chahar Gulshan,* M.S. p. 4-39a.
359. Pelsaert, p. 72.
360. A.L. Shrivastava, *Medieval Indian Culture* 1st edn. 1964, p. 94.
361. *Akbar Namah,* Vol. II, Tr. (Bev), p. 182.
362. *Ibid.*
363. *Khulasah Tarih Salar Masud Ghazi,* pp. 5-12.
364. *Tarikh-i-Magadh,* edited by Maulvi Fasihuddin Baikhi, (Urdu), *Anjuman Taraqqi,* Urdu (Hindi), Delhi, 1st edn. 1944, p. 96.
365. *Ibid.* p. 99.
366. *Memoirs of Zahiruddin Mohammad Babur, Emperor of Hindustan* Tr. by Laden and William Erskine, Vol. II, p. 395; also *Akbar Nama,* Vol. III, Tr. p. 132; also *Tarikh-i-Farishta* Vol. I p. 301.
367. *Akbar Nama,* Vol. III, Tr. p. 132.
368. *Ain,* Vol. I (Bloch), p. 50.
369. *Pelsaert,* p. 72.
370. *Ibid.* p. 70.
371. Elliot & Dowson, Vol. III, p. 300, *Tarikh-i-Farishta,* Pers. Vol. I, p. 362.
372. Pelsaert writes about the secluded ladies thus, 'Under pretext of a pilgrimage, they used to come without reproach to see, and perhaps even speak to their lovers...on such occasions new passions were

aroused by the sight of a handsome youth, wo took the lady's fancy and while she saw him, he might not be able to see her', p. 72.

373. J. A. S. B., 1935, Vol. I, 302.

374. G.N. Sharma, *Social life in Medieval Rajasthan,* p. 222.

7

Costumes

Cotton Clothes

The Ain has provided a comprehensive list of the cotton clothes used in India in Akbar's reign. The names common to Ain and the contemporary Hindi writers are *Khasa, Salu, Doriya, Bafta, Panchtolia, Dupatta* and *Tansukh.*

Khasa was regarded the best and costliest cotton cloth in Akbar's time, and the upper limit of its cost was 15 gold *muhars*. *Chotar* was the next best cloth costing from Rs. 2 to 9 gold *muhars*. *Tansuk* or *Tansukh Sirisaf, Gangajala, Beherun, Asawari,* and *Bafta* came next in order of price and costed upto 5 gold *muhars. Dupatta* costed upto one gold *muhar. Chhint* was an ordinary cotton cloth and was priced at from 2 dam to one rupee a yard.

Poet Parmananda Das had mentioned *Picchora* made of *Khasa* cloth.

Vrinda has compared *Bafta* to *Khadi* cloth.

Bhikari Das and Tosha have mentioned bodices made from the *Bafta* and *Tansukh* cloths.

Tansukh seems to be famous cloth for the manufacture of *Saris* as is evident from the copious references by the contemporary poets.

Doria and *Salu* referred to in the Ain, one referred in the *Padmavat* and *Sur Sagar* respectively. *Doria* was used for the manufacture of *Saris* and *Salu* used on marriages. *Salu* is in popular usage in the Punjab at the marriages even now. It is a *Khadi Chadar* embroidered by silken yarn.

Other varieties of the cotton cloth mentioned in the Ain are *Malmal, Bahadurshahi, Garbasuti, Saila-i-Deccani, Mahrkal, Mandel, Jhina, Atan, Mahmudi, Jhola, Katancha, Fota, Goshpech, Gazina* and *Salahati.*

Silken Cloths

In ancient India silk was known as *Pattanshuka, Chin, Kausheya,* and *Dhautapatta.*

Ain, under the title *Abresham* or silken cloths, mentions at least 3 dozen varieties in use at that time.

The varieties of silken cloth common to the Ain and the contemporary Hindi literature are *Makhmal, Tafta, Lah* and *Kapurdhur*.

The list of golden cloths in the Ain also contains *makhmal* or valvet. Vrinda has used this word as golden cloth used for entirely different purposes—manufacture of shoes for the feet and of *Sehra* for the head.

Bodices were made from the Lah cloth mentioned in the Ain as mentioned by Jan Sen.

Kapurdhur has been referred in the Ain and in Hindi poetry. Abul Fazl says that Kapurdhur was woven in Tibet. It was renamed by Akbar as Kapurnur.

Tafta appears to be a cheap cloth. It is priced in the *Ain* from 4 annas to 2 rupees a yard. It was a silken cloth having two colours in both the yarns. Bihari speaks of golden *Tafta*.

The words *Resham* and *Patt* have also been used for silk in the contemporary Hindi poetry.

Golden Cloths

Jarkas, Jartari, Zarbaft or *Zarbaf* were cloths prepared from the thread of gold. Tosha has referred to *Tasa* cloth. Abul Fazl's list of golden cloths include *Tas* Gujrati, a costly cloth. Its price ranged from 1 to 35 gold *muhars.*

Jarkasi and *Jartari* have been referred to the varieties from which Sari and bodice were manufactured. The Ain has mentioned in the list of golden cloths Zarbaft. The Zarbaft from Yazd was an expensive cloth and its best quality was priced at 150 gold *muhars.* Another quality mentioned here is *Zarbaft Barsar.* Its price ranged between 3 to 70 gold *muhars*.

Flax Cloth

Like Tul, Sani was a word used in ancient India. Sur Das has used the word San or flax. During the Budhistic period yarn was made from the fibres of flax. The fibre of flax is also known as *Katan. Ain* has mentioned *Katancha* cloth in the list of cotton cloths. According to an Urdu Dictionary, *Katan* was a very superior and transparent cloth which, when placed in the moonlight, it torn to pieces.

The contemporary Hindi poets have mentioned following other varieties of cloth known to the Indians in the later medieval period:

Dukul* or *Dugul

It has been mentioned in *Harsa-Charita* of Bana. This cloth was made in northern Bengal and used for making *Dhotis, Chadars,* and Pillow-covers. Dukul was prepared from the fibres of the bark of the trees. Contemporary Hindi poetry contains frequent mention of *dukul*.

Valkal

Valkal was also manufactured from the fibre of the bark of the trees and was usually worn by the saints. Another name for this was *Druma Charma*. *Valkal* cloth was forbidden to the Buddhist monks.

Chandra* and *Chandrauta

Malik Mohammad Jayasi has mentioned two other kinds of cloths, *Chandra* and *Chandrauta.* It was also known as *Chandan Chir.* The contemporary poets have termed it as *Sandali*. Jayasi has also mentioned other varieties as *Lahar Pator* (used for the making of shirts), *Chhayal* (printed cloth of Gujrat), *Khirodak* (used for making of Phariyas), *Banspor Jhilmil* and (used for Saris), *Chikwa, Chir* and *Meghauna* (worked with gold and ornamented with pearls.

Chola

Taramandal was another sort of cloth referred by Jayasi of which *Chola* was made.

Makri Ka Tar

It was a very thin and transparent cloth made of cords as thin as the web of spider.

Heud dress

The customary dress of ladies in the 16th and 17th centuries consisted of *Dupatta* or *Orhani,* Bodice, Skirt, Sari or Trousers.

The various names for women's head dress in the later medieval period were *Orhani, Pichhauri, Dukul, Nichol, Uparaini, Dupatta* and *Anchal.* In classical literature the term used for head dress was *Uttariya.* It was a 'scarf' long narrow shawl, generally of decorated, more or less transparent muslim worn over the breast and head as veil, partly or completely hiding the face. Another Sanskrit name was *Avagunthan,* meaning 'wrapper' as a portion of the overhead scarf, drawn in front of the face. Before the Christian era, the term for *Dupatta* was *'Upavasana'.* Males too covered the upper portions of their bodies with a similar garment.

The terms *Orhani* and *Dupatta* were in vogue in the centuries preceding the Christian era. *Orhani* was used in India prior to and during the Mughal period.

In Rajput paintings terms *Orhani* and *Dupatta* are applicable to all the instances. The *Dupatta* is worn with skirt and *choli,* over the *jhaguli,* in which case it is often of the same colour and material over the *'pesvaj.'*

Vyas has referred to the blue *Pichhauri.* Tulsi Das and Sur Das have mentioned yellow ones.

Uparna or *Uparaina* was another name for the head cover of ladies. It could also be used alongwith *Sari*. Sur Das has referred to the use of white *Uparna* alongwith red *Sari* or *Chunri.* Another name for it was *Uparaini.*

Yet another name for the head cover was *Uttariya.* The poet has compared the countenance of the wearer to the moon and of the *Uttariya* worn to the moonlight.

Another name for head cover was *Chunri*. When it is mentioned alongwith Sari, it perhaps indicates head dress.

Bodice: *Choli* and *Angiya*

The common words used for bodice in the 16th and 17th centuries were *Kanchuk, Kanchuki, Angiya, Angi* and *Choli* and *Chola*.

According to Ghurye, ladies used to wear *Choli* throughout the ancient and early medieval times. Vidya Pati, Jayasi, Sur Das, Vyas and almost all the Hindi poets of the 16th and 17th centuries have referred to its use.

In the Mughal paintings of the Rajput type costumes, women living in the palaces, have been shown wearing *Choli* going below the breasts.

Upto the 18th century, short sleeve bodice was in vogue. In the Western provinces, it was the common female dress and was known as *Angiya* which was also worn full sleeve.

The 'Mughal Paintings' and the 'Rajput Paintings' of A. Coomarswami and the paintings of Lalit Kala Academy of Rajasthan, contain frequent examples of *Choli*.

Kanchuka

For bodice in the 16th and 17th centuries the word *Kanchuka* was also used.

Kanchuki

Sur Das and Tosha have mentioned red and Vyas to the blue *Kanchuki*.

8

Equality with Men

In the beginning of its rise, Islam raised the status of women in the society, at least legally equivalent to that of man. *The Quran* declared both men and women equal in the eyes of the law, the only discrimination of rank being in the quality of piety and equally rewarded for their good deeds.[1] Consequently, Muslim women exercised their skills and talents in different spheres—social, economic, educational and cultural—during the times of the Prophet and early Caliphs. But the requirement for modesty was seriously considered in every circumstance of public life—promiscuity could not be tolerated.

However, with the change in Islamic polity since the eight century A.D., the women started losing their rights and privileges due to male chauvnism in the society.

Before the foundation of the *Sultanate* in North India in the beginning of the thirteenth century A.D., Muslim society in Iran and Central Asian lands had become socially stratified in which the Muslim lady fared, more or less in the similar way as her counterpart in a non-Muslim society elsewhere. Hardly, a woman of talent and skill could compete with, and outmanoevor, the man in politics. At the time of war, when two Muslim rulers fought, the victor inflicted unbearable sufferings and miseries on the Muslims in the alien territory and women suffered more because they were carried on for cohabitation.

Women in Administration

The women in the royal household enjoyed a privileged position and, sometimes they could be able to alter the course of events. The first lady in the Sultanate of Delhi, mentioned by the contemporary historian, Minhaj-i Siraj Juzjani, was Shah Turkan, the widow of Sultan Shamsuddin Iltutmish (1210–1236 A.D., She was basically a slave girl of Turk origin, purchased by Iltutmish, probably in Delhi[2]. After the birth of her son, Prince Ruknuddin, she was raised to the status of the King's wife and bestowed the title of Shah Turkan. An ambitious lady, having intelligence and ability, she took over the reins of government in her own hands after the death of her husband. The new Sultan, her son, Sultan Rukh U'ddin Firoz Shah had become negligent of his duties, owing to his over involvement in pleasure. She issued *farmans* (royal mandates) in her own name. Her magnificient generosity towards the men of learning and piety and endowments made for the help of poor and indigent people must have brought her great repute. But her malice against the other wives, sons and daughters of her deceased husband led to her and her sons' downfal. She had some of them murdered: in particular blinding and assassination of Prince Qutbuddin (the grandson of Sultan Qutab U'ddin Aibak by his daughter, married to Iltumish) led the nobles and soldiers to revolt against her son.[3] Both of them were removed from the scene.

Like Turkan Shah, the Hindu woman of princely background could also play the role of regent, if her minor son was a king. For example, in 1278, Naika Devi, the mother of Maharaja II, the minor Chalukya ruler of Gujarat acted as a regent. Immediately after untimely death of Bhima Deo she placed her second infant son, Bhim Deo on the throne. In 1278–79, when Sultan Muiz-U'ddin Muhammad bin sam, the Ghurid ruler of Ghazna started a raiding expedition towards Gujarat, she surprised near Mount Abu and put him to route.[4]

Sultan Raziya, the daughter of Sultan Iltutmish (1236–1240 A.D.) was the other lady ruler of the Delhi Sultanate. During her early phase left her mark as remarkable one on several issues. Till her time these seem to have been different opinion around the Muslim Theologians, regarding the disqualification of a woman to become the king or the temporal leader of the kingdom. Perhaps, the door for *ijtihad* (reinterpretation of the Muslim Canon Law) in compliance with the need of changed time was still opened. For example, the leading theologist of the age who acted as the *qazi* (Judicial officer), Principal of the leading college of Delhi, *Madrassa-i-Nasiri* and *Sadr-us-Sudur* (minister for the theological affairs) since the age of Sultan Iltutmish, describes Sultan Raziya as a monarch capable of providing leadership to the Empire at a critical time when the fear of disastrous Mongol thrust in the Sultanate loomed large. According to him, she was prudent, just, benevolent, strict in providing justice and took interest in the well-being of the common people (*riyaya).* She is also credited for extending whole-hearted patronage to the men of learning and piety. As a military general, she could smash armies, but inspite of possessing the excellent qualities. She failed to rule in the male dominated society. Minhaj Juzjani attributes her fall to the male chauvinism.[5]

Amir Khusrau also refers to the good qualities of Sultan Raziya when she was accepted as *Sultan* by the well-wishers as she had incompetent-brothers that she ruled successfully for three years and then came out of *purdah* (veil) and asserted her power, with the consequence that the nobility became fearful and turned against her.[6] But his junior contemporary Isami describes her differently. According to Isami, the nobility became doubtful of her relations with the *amir-i-akhur,* Yaqut, a slave of negro race, because he took liberty with the *Sultan* openly. Then he says: "All women are in the snare of the devil, in privacy, all of them do Satan's work," that, "When the passions of a pious woman are inflamed, she concedes to an intimacy even with a dog." Or, "a woman cannot acquit herself well as a ruler, for she is essentially deficient in intellect. It is better for a woman to occupy herself with the *charkha* (Spinning wheel) since attainment of high position on her part would make her intoxicated."[7] For his account of the early Sultans of India, Isami draws on folk tradition; at times he added popular tales and anecdotes to adorn his narratives. Minhaj Juzjani and Amir Khusrau do not find Raziya characterless. If Minhaj Juzjani was an eye-witness to the happenings, Khusrau must have good information about the past from his maternal grandfather, Imad-al Mulk, the *Rawat-i-arz* (pay master general of the army) who had begun his career under Sultan Iltutmish as his slave.

The relevant evidence about the daughter who happened to be the real sister of Sultan Muiz U'ddin Bahram Shah (1240–1242 A.D.), indicates that a Muslim lady did not find it derogatory at all to seek divorce from her husband if temperamental incompatibility existed. She was first married to the son of Qazi Nasir Uddin but it was dissolved subsequently. Again, she married Aitigin, who had become the *naib-i-Mulk* (regent) after her brother's accession to the throne in 1240 A.D.[8] As for the second lady, another widow of Sultan Iltutmish, she also married a senior noble, Qutlugh Khan and with his support and his friends at the court, she compelled Sultan Ala U'ddin Masud Shah (1242–1246 A.D.) to release the sons of Sultan Iltutmish from prison prince Nasir U'ddin Mahmud (her own son) and Prince Jalal U'ddin. Advised by nobles, her son, Nasir U'ddin Mahmud was given the charge of the territorial Unit of Bahraich, while Jalal U'ddin was posted as the *Wali* (governor) of Kanauj. She also accompanied her son to Bahraich because he was still a minor, agred less than fourteen years.[9] Two years later, she plotted in league with her husband against Sultan Ala U'ddin Masur and won over the nobles at the court to support her son's claim to the throne. She secretly carried on correspondence with the nobility in Delhi and when the die was finally caste, she stealthily started with her son from Bahraich for Delhi. On her departure she publicly declared that she was taking her son to Delhi for medical treatment. They were taken in a palanquin, escorted by *sawars* (horsemen). In Delhi, nobody, except the accomplices in the plot, knew about their arrival till Sultan Ala U'ddin Masud Shah was dethoroned and her son was put on the throne instead. She further attempted to consolidate her son's position by having the daughter of Balban (later Sultan Ghiyas U'ddin Balban) married to the Sultan. By now Balban had emerged as the leader of mighty Turk nobles at the Court. Soon after, Balban successfully manipulated to undermine her and Qutlugh Khan's position at the Court.[10]

In 1253, the Sultan's mother entitled Malka-i-Jahan, her husband Qutlugh Khan and his supporters among the Turk nobles, like Izzuddin Balban Kishlu Khan and Malik Arslan Khan Sanjar Chust had Balban removed from the Court to his *iqta* of Hansi. They also had their protege, Imad-u'ddin Rehan a eunuch of Indian origin raised to the ministerial post of *Vakil-i dar,* perhaps, for using him as liaison between the Centre and the Hindu land chiefs. Balban was, however, a clever politician and did not allow them time to consolidate their power in Delhi. He, with the support of his younger brother, Saif U'ddin Aibak-ul-Sultani (later Kishli Khan) and his cousin, Sher Khan Sunqar, collected the Turk soldiers stationed in the north-western territary and invited Prince Jalal Khan, son of Iltutmish who was installed by the Mongols as their vassal entitled Sultan to rule over the territorial units of Lahore and Jalandhar. Then Balban came out with full preparation for marching against Delhi. Having been informed about Balban's strategy, Qutlugh Khan and his supporters also marched with the Sultan towards Hansi. As the two armies came face to face between Kuhram and Hansi, some of the nobles interceded to reconcile between the rival groups.

On Balban's demand, Imad U'ddin Rehan was shifted to Bahraich as its *mukta* (governor). Thereafter, Balban's daughter, the royal consort seems to have instigate her husband against his mother and step-father Qutlugh Khan. Consequently, the Malka-i Jahan and Qutlugh Khan were ordered to leave Delhi for Awadh. Qutlugh Khan was given the charge of Awadh in 1254 A.D. On their departure, their protege, Imad U'ddin Hasan Ghori, the *naib-ul Mulk* was also put imprisoned and killed by the agents of Balban.[11] Now Balban became the premier noble with the title of Ulugh Khan Azam, and the sultan a puppet, in his hands. Having secured his position at the court, Ulugh Khan Azam (former Bahauddin Balban) shifted Qutlugh Khan to Bahraich. The latter refused to obey the royal *farman* and also conquered Malik Baktum whom Ulugh Khan Azam had deputed against him.[12] Now Ulugh Khan Azam began with the Sultan against Qutlugh Khan and the Malka-i Jahan. Upon their approach, Qutlugh Khan fled towards Silmaur hills (in Haryana) and sought shelter with the hill chiefs. Both the Malka-i-Jahan and Qutlugh Khan tried to unite their supporters and make a final attempt for freeing the Sultan from the grip of their rival (Ulugh Khan Azam) Izz-Uddin Balban Kishlu Khan holding the combined charge of the territorial units of Multan and Uchh, invited them to Multan and decided to march towards Delhi. In Delhi, Qazi Shams U'ddin, the chief *qazi* and Saiyid Qutbuddin, the Shaikh-ul Islam were secretly in alliance with them. When Ulugh Khan Azam left Delhi with the troops to fight against the supporters of Qutlugh Khan and the Malka-i Jahan, the Chief *qazi* and Shaikh-ul Islam invited his rivals to Delhi, promising that the doors of the city would be opened for them but their conspircy failed because Ulugh Khan had deputed his spies in every department. They informed their master in time and the conspirators were exiled from Delhi before Malka-i Jahan and her supporters appeared before the doors of Delhi.[13] Frustrated, Qutlugh Khan and Malka-i-Jahan left for Central Asia to seek refuge with the Mongol Kings while Izz U'ddin Balban Kishlu Khan, the *muqta* of multan and Uchh became the fassal of Hulegu, the Ilkhan of Iran.[14]

As the successors of Sultan Nasir U'ddin Mahmud, Sultan Ghiyas Uddin Balban (1266–1287 A.D.) was a strict disciplinarian having conservative outlook, he did not allow the ladies to meddle in politics. But his grandson and immediate successor, Sultan Muiz

Uddin Kaiqubad was fond of ladies. During his short reign of three years, the woman acquired ascendacy at the royal court.[15]

Sultan Kaiqubad's successors, Sultan Jalal Uddin Firuz Shah (Khalji, though a veteran general, gave ears to his wife, allowing her to say in the affairs of the Empire. The nobles flattered her as she had great influence at the court. Even her daughter, married to the Sultan's nephew, Ala U'ddin, became so overbearing that her husband became disappointed with her. Unable to ignite the displeasure of Malka-i Jahan, he could not even complain to his uncle against his wife's misbehaviour towards him.[16] According to Ziya U'ddin Barani, the only solution to Ala U'ddin was either to conquer a far off territory and rule over it independently or kill his uncle. Ultimately he murdered him. Barani is critical of the role played by Malka Jahan after the murder of her husband and describes her as the silly of the silliest,[17] yet the analysis of circumstantial evidence say that she was a wise lady and could take wise decision for meeting a critical situation caused by the murder of the Sultan (1296 A.D.). As Arkali Khan, the surviving eldest son, was away in Multan, she placed her younger son Qadr Khan on the throne conferning the title of Sultan Rukn U'ddin Ibrahim Shah, because Ala U'ddin had started from Kara for Delhi, scattering gold along the way. Qadr Khan was an enterprising youngman acceptable to the high nobles at the court. However, the situation having took a turn in favour of the regicide, could not be reverted. The nobles, except few, started to defect out of greed for gold of the regicide.[18] The example of the nobles was followed by the soldiers. In such circumstances, Sultan Rukn U'ddin Ibrahim Shah had to flee away to Delhi Multan, leaving to be occupied by Ala U'ddin Khalji (1296 A.D.).

Woman in Royal Culture

With the accession of Sultan Ala U'ddin Khalji to the throne in 1296 A.D., ladies were again debarred from the politics of the *Sultanate.* But they did play a significant role in royal culture. Certain customs and ceremonies offered to the royal ladies opportunities to organize festivities on large scale. For example, the down on the cheek of the youth was indication for the mother to host a banquet and entertain the guests.[19] The sister of Alap Khan and mother of Prince Khizr Khan who had been raised to the status of the cheif wife of Sultan Ala U'ddin Khalji with the title of *Malka-i-Jahan,* annoyed the Sultan during his illness due to her over indulgence in festivities held on the marriage of her children and birth of grandsons, etc. The *Suitan* was unable to take care of property. These circumstances provided Malik Kafur, the *naib-i-Mumilikat* and the rival of *Malka-i-Jahan* and her son, Khizr Khan to capture the mind of the ailing Sultan and nominate Prince Umar Khan, born of the Princess of Deogiri, her apparent in place of Khizr Khan. On Sultan Ala U'ddin's death (1316 A.D.), Malik Kafur put Umar Khan on the throne under the title of Sultan Shinab U'ddin and operated the government on this behalf. Now Khizr Khans's mother was replaced by Shihab-U'ddin's mother as *Malka-i-Jahan.*[20] But her ascendancy did not last long. Malik Kafur was killed by the night guards in the *Qasr-i-hazar Satun* (One thousand pillared palace) and Shihab U'ddin was dethorned by Prince Mubarak Khan after six months reign. The latter assumed the title of Sultan Qutbuddin Mubarak Shah (1317–1320 A.D.).

The ladies of royal families were honoured by the members of ruling elite and the public as well. When Khusrau Khan married the widow of Sultan Qutb Uddin Mubarak Shah and divided the ladies of his *herem* among his supporters, people were filled up with indignation. On the decline of Khusrau Khan, Ghiyas Uddin Tugluq Shah (1320–1324 A.D.) and his son Sultan Muhammad bin Tughlaq Shah (1324–1351 A.D.) crossed the limits to show consideration and respect. Sultan Muhammad bin Tughluq had the widow of Qutbuddin Mubarak Shah remarried to an immigrant noble, the son of the *Qazi* of Cairo and on her account offered royal favours to him. The Sultan used to address her as his sister.[21]

Female Philanthrophists

The widow of Sultan Ghiyath Uddin Tughluq Shah and the mother of Sultan Muhammad bin Tughluq Shah (1325–1351 A.D.), entitled *Makhduma-i-Jahan* was a virtuous lady as a great philanthrophist. Ibn Battuta describes her as one of the most virtuous women and magnificent in charity. She had founded many hospitals and endowed them to supply free food to all travellers. The foreigners coming to India to seek fortune were first welcomed on her behalf as guests. They were entertained with tasty foods and then "invested with silk robes of honour embroidered in gold". Then they were gifted unsewn fabrics of silk, linen and cotton.[22]

Hindu-Muslim Matrimonial Relations

As far as the matrimonial relations between the Hindu and Muslim members of the ruling class are concerned, it seems to have been a well-established custom in Europe as well as in the Asian countries that the powerful lord or his deputies could demand the hand of their vassal's daughter for marriage with them or their sons. In Central Asia and Europe, the pagan Mongol rulers married Muslim and Christian daughters of their vassal chiefs, although the *nikah* of a Muslim girl with a non-Muslim was prohibited by the *Sharia* (Canon law). In India, the practice of the marriage with the vassal chief's daughter with the Sultan or his son might have begun since the reign of Sultan Ghiyath Uddin Balban. Prince Muhammad known in history as *Khan-i Shahib*, is said to have married the daughter of Rai Kalu in Punjab and then relations remained cordial.

On the munder of the Prince by the Mongol invaders on the battle-field in 1286, Rai Kalu payed a large sum to the Mongols to take back his dead body.[23] Sultan Qutb Uddin Mubarak Shah (Khalji), the son and successor of Sultan Ala Uddin Khalji is said to carry several daughters of chiefs. These girls accompanied the Sultan on his expeditions. They mounted on horses to the Suitan's left and right, rear and front, while the main troops moved keeping considerable distance. He halted wherever he was fascinated by the charm of meadow, sipped wine and enjoyed himself with his girls.[24] A chief could reject the request of a governor in this respect. To quote, Rana Mal Bhatti, the chief in the territorial unit of Abohar, included in the *iqta* of Dipalpur under the governorship of Ghazi Malik, refused to accept his proposal with regard to his daughter's marriage with *Sipahsalar* Rajab, his younger brother. Annoyed by refusal of Rana Mal Ghazi Malik to his *zamindari* and demanded the payment of annual revenue dues and harrassed the *Muqaddams* and *Chaudharies* when they could not clear the dues. The entire population in that territory had to suffer from the harsh measures adopted by the governor. Having heard of the suffering of people, the Rana's mother came to see his son weeping. The grand daughter asked her the reason of crying. When explained people's suffering, she said: "it should be taken as if one daughter was carried away by the Mongols as captive." As a matter of fact, the frequent Mongol invasions of the Punjab had affected the psychology of people and the two religious communities had come close to each other. Thereupon, her father changed his mind and she was married to Malik Rajab.[25] Similarly, a Muslim merchant, Khwaja Taqi in the Coromondel coast, also refused to marry his daughter to Khusrau Khan, the Commander-in-chief of the invading army from Delhi because the former was reluctant to accept the latter as his son-in-law. When Khusrau Khan seized his daughter, the father committed suicide.[26]

Further low-caste Hindus seem to have considered themselves fortunate if any Prince or Sultan fell in love with their daughter or sister and desired to marry her. The caste of the sister of Sahran, Kalal (liquor-brewer) by caste and may be explained. Saharan and his young brother were happy having heard about the love affair between their sister and Sultan Firoz Shahi. They married her to the Sultan and in return, got positions in the nobility. Later on, they met Shaikh Jalal U'ddin Bukhari, known *Makhdum Jahaniyan-i-Jahangasht* and adopted Islam under his influence. Saharan's sons, zafar Khan and Shams Khan Dandans founded the royal dynasties of Gujarat Sultanate and Naugaur Principality after the dissolution of the Delhi Sultanate in the beginning of the fifteenth century.[27]

Lenient Attitude Towards Wives

As regards strange male attitudes towards females the village women, the low-caste Hindus were not affected by the caste rules in their attitude towards their women; they accepted their women if they returned home even after staying with Muslims under unavoidable circumstance. The case of a woman from a village in the Kalehar region is a case in point. She was sold in the slave market of Badaon to Maulana Ala U'ddin Asuli, the teacher of Sheikh Nizam U'ddin Auliya. One day the Maulana found her crying and on being asked the reason thereof she told him that she missed her child. Moved by her grief, the Maulana inquired whether her husband would accept her if she was freed. She replied affirmatively. Next day, when it was still dark, the Maulana took her towards her village and turned back when he was requested by her not to go any further as her village was quite near and she could reach home safely.[28]

Conversion

Equally important are the cases of those village Hindu women who followed or refused to follow their men in adopting of a new faith. Some of the women have been committed to their religion and could make any sacrifice for its save. For example, a dacoit, later named Ali Maula, Shaikh Jalal U'ddin Tabrizi, an immigrant Sufi saint, during Iltutmish's reign and under his influence, embraced Islam. On-returning home he persuaded his wife to accompany him to Badaon and adopt Islam like him. She refused and got separated from him.[29] Unlike her, the woman in Ajodhan willingly converted to Islam alongwith her children having come to know as to how her husband bacame a *Mussalman* under the influence of the pious mother of Shaikh Farid Uddin Ganj-i-Shakar.[30]

Women's Interest in Religion, Piety and Education

According to Shaikh Nizam U'ddin Auliya,[31] there was dearth of such women to whom spiritually has a genuine concern. He spoke very highly of the religiousity of certain ladies, including his own mother and the mother of Shaikh Farid U'ddin Ganj-i Shakar[32] and is also said to have been deeply influenced by the piety of a lady of Indraprastha.[33] Similarly, his daughter, Bibi Sharifa, has been described as a pious woman. Her husband died in her early youth and she did not marry. She devoted herself to religion in such a way that her father remarked: "Had it been permitted to give the *Khilafatnama* (grant of diploma by a Sufi Saint, allowing his disciple to enrole *murids* in the *silsilah* or order) of the Sheikh and his sajjada (prayer carpet) to a woman, I would have given them to Bibi Sharifa." Further, he said: "if other women had been like her, they would have taken precedence over men."[34]

Education

As for the education of girls in *makatibs* (school) or *madrassas* (colleges) there seems to have been no provision for their education. *Purda* (veil) strictly observed by the women of elite class must have stopped the young girls to acquire higher education. Here the Muslim women of the seaport of Hinawr (situated on the western coast, south of Sandapur of modern Goa) were exceptions. The Muslims of Hinawr followed the shafai school of law and had separate schools for the female education. Ibn Battuta tells us that he found there thirteen schools for girls and twenty-three schools for boys, not witnessed anywhere in the entire Muslim world.

Music and Dance

Women had also acquired excellence in the arts of music and dance. Ziya U'ddin Barani's graphic narration of the pleasure parties arranged in the place of Sultan Jalal U'ddin Firuz Shah (Khalji) on

Fridays after the congregational prayer, shows that the singing and dancing girls, expert in their arts, enjoyed the patronage of the Sultan and the nobles. Barani further writes that Nusrat Khatoon, the daughter of the *Fuq'i* (the seller of drinker as well as cup-bearer) sang songs and due to her melodious voice, the birds came down from the air and the listeners lost their senses: their hearts palpitated and their spirit got stirred. Besides Nusrat Bibi and Mahar Afroz were matchless dancers, associated with the royal household possessing extraordinary beauty and charm. Well-adept in amorous playfulness and delicate etiquettes, they cast their spell in every direction they turned, looking languishly through half-shut eyes in coquetry. They danced to entertain the royal guests in the pleasure parties of Sultan Jalal Uddin Khalji and everyone happening to cast glance at their steps and see their amorous manners, desired to sacrifice men lives for them.[36] Ibn Battuta supplements Barani's account, when he narrates the decoration of Delhi when Sultan's returned alongwith his army from a remote territory, that the city is decorated with wooden pavilions, various stories high and covered with silk clothes. Every pavilion had singing and dancing girls. "wearing most beautiful dresses and ornaments." They addressed the Sultan and his followers with their performance.[37] Ibn Battuta also mentions Tarababad (pleasure spot), the colony of the musicians outside the walls of Siri along the bank of the *Hauz-i Khass* (the lake constructed by Sultan Ala Uddin Khalji).[38]

Slaves

In fact, female slaves were more in demand than the male slaves in all the civilized countries. Maid-slaves were required both for domestic service and cohabitation. In India they were evaporated from the different countries as far as eastern Europe in the west and China in the far east.[39] Though abominable, the slave trade had become much lucrative and therefore, the training and education of a slave in arts, crafts and popular sciences, irrespective of son or daughter, was considered a good investment. Barani states that the fairy-faced girls were trained in singing *gazals* (love songs) and the art of blandishment before their breasts fully developed: "Their coquetry could even turn away the recluse from the path of righteousness as well as restore the weary-hearted to life."[40]

Shihab U'ddin al-Umar, the fourteenth century Arab

encyclopaedist, was informed by travellers from India that a slave girl for household purpose could be had for eight *tankas* in Delhi. "Those who are fit both for domestic service and cohabitation would cost fifteen *tankas.* But in other cities (of India) they are still cheaper." He was also told that certain accomplished female slaves could cost even twenty thousand *tankas* due to the grace of their department and the refinement of manners:

> Many of them of this type know the *Quran* by heart, can write, recite verses, relate stories and play on *sitar.* They also make display of their skill in the games of chess and *chausar*. They take pride in these things. One of them says: I shall capture the heart of my master within three days; other would say: I shall be the queen of his heart within a day; The third retorts: I shall captivate his heart in an hour; while the fourth would say: What is to say about day and hour, I shall capture his heart in the twinkling of an eye... Though there are found in India the girls of every land, such as that of Turk, Qibchaq, Rum (Byzantium), etc., the preference is given to the attractive (saltish) Indians on account of their charm and other qualities which the words cannot describe.[41]

To conclude, the Indian society during the middle ages was male dominated and ladies suffer from male chauvinism. Hardly any women of talent could manoeuvre for position in the society without the support of strong men. Those became successful in manupulating the situations in their own interest or in that of their sons, depended on the male support. In short, she was always at receiving end. The survival of various types of classical dances owes as much to the female dancers of medieval times and as to their trainers. In the art of dance and singing *ghazal* man could never surpass her.

References

1. *Quran* 16, 97.
2. Minhaj-1 Siraj Juzjani, *Tabaqat-i-Nasiri,* Kabul, 1963, Vol. 1, pp. 454, 455.
3. *Ibid.*
4. Cf. *The Struggle for Empire,* ed. R.C. Majumdar, Bombay, second edition, 1966, p. 78.
5. *Tabaqat-i Nasiri, op. cit.* Vol. 1, p. 457.

6. Amir Khusrau, *Dual Rani Khizr Khan (Mathnavi),* Aligarh, 1917, p. 49.
7. Isami, *Futuh-us-Salatin,* ed., A.S. Usha, Madras, 1948, p. 134; Eng. tr. Agha Mahdi Husain, Aligarh, 1976, Vol. 2, pp. 253-54.
8. *Tabaqat-i Nasiri,* Vol. 1, 463.
9. According to Minhaj Juzjani, Nasir Mahmud and other princes seem to have been thrown in prison after the death of Iltutmish. As regards Nasir U'ddin Mahmud, he was born after his elder brother Nasir U'ddin Mahmud died in 1230 A.D. and, therefore, must have been brought up in prison till his release in 1244. When he was about fourteen years old. *Tabaqat-i Nasiri,* Vol. 1. p. 479.
10. *Tabaqat-i Nasiri,* Vol. I, pp. 488-89; also Iqtidar Hussain Siddiqui. Politics and Conditions in the Territories under the Occupation of Central Asian Rulers in North-Western India-13th and 14th Centuries. *Central Asiatic Journal, Wierbaden,* Vol. 27, no. 3-4 1983, p. 290, foot note, 5, for Prince Jalal U'ddin's alliance with the Mongol Emperor.
11. *Tabaqat-i Nasiri,* Vol. I, p. 489.
12. *Ibid.* Vol. I, p. 490.
13. *Ibid.,* Vol. I, p. 492-93.
14. *Ibid.,* Vol. I, p. 494.
15. Ziya Uddin Barani, Tarikhi-i-Firuz Shahi, Calcutta, 1862, p. 157, (hereafter cited as Borani); Isami, *op. cit.* p. 186.
16. *Barani,* p. 187.
17. *Ibid.,* pp. 245-46.
18. Barani, p. 246; Isam, pp. 247-48.
19. Amir Khusrau, *Tughluqnama,* p. 25.
20. Barani, pp. 373-74.
21. *The Travels of Ibn Battuta,* Vol. 3, p. 759.
22. Ibn Battuta, *The Travels of Ibn Battuta,* Eng. tr. H. Gibb, Cambridge, 1971, Vol. 3, p. 736.
23. Isami, pp. 180-181.
24. Isami, pp. 564-65; Barani, p. 392.
25. Shams Siraj Afif, *Tarikh-i Firuz Shahi,* p. 40.
26. Barani, pp. 398-99; Isami 369-70.
27. Sikandar bin Manjhu, *Mirat-i Sikandari,* Bombay, 1308H, p. 566. Shaikh Kabir Batini, *Afsanah-i Shahu,* Ms. British Library, London, Add. 24, 409, ff. 90b-91a, for the Kalal caste to which Zafar Khan belonged.
28. Mir Hasan, Sijzi, Fawaid. *ul Fuad* p. 165.
29. Hamid Qalandar, *Khair-ul Majalis,* Aligarh, 1959, p. 192; *Fawaid-ul Fuad,* p. 132.

30. *Fawaid-ul Fuad,* pp. 121-122.
31. *Travels of Ibn Battuta,* Vol. 3, pp. 613-14.
32. Isami, pp. 275-76.
33. *Fawaid,ul Faud,* p. 22.
34. Cf. K.A. Nizami, *The Life and Times of Shaikh Farid U'ddin Ganj-i-Shakar,* reprint, Delhi, 1987, p. 65.
35. Ibn Battuta, *Rehla,* Eng. tr. by Agha Mandi Husain, p. 179.
36. Barani, p. 199.
37. *Travels of Ibn Battuta,* Vol. 3, p. 668.
38. *Ibid.,* p. 625.
39. Shams Siraj Afif, *Tarikh-i-Firuz Shahi,* Calcutta, 1890, pp. 399-400, pp. harem of Khan-i Jahan Maqbool where the girls from different countries were collected. They are said to have been more than a thousand.
40. Barani, pp. 156-157.
41. Shihabuddin al-Umar, *Masalik-ul Absar fi Mamalik ul Amsar,* Eng. tr. *A Fourteenth Century Arab Account of India under Sultan Muhammadbin Tughluq,* Iqtidar H. Siddiqui, Aligarh, 1973, pp. 51-52.

9

The Mughal Women

Right of women to be sovereigns of kingdoms was familiar to the Persians and the Mongol as well as the Turkish royal women also did enjoy certain political privileges. Babar's family which had assimilated the traditions of Chingiz Khan and Temur, provided women tangible opportunities to participate in political affairs, but they were not conceded the right to sovereignty.[1]

Babar Nama is often regarded as one of the remarkable pieces of world literature and perhaps the best autobiography of medieval Indian history as it contains the literary beauty of poetry and the dignity of an empire builder. It owes its perennial interest to its extensively spreadout matter as well as the autobiographic presentation of a most arresting historical personality for its entire 'manner, style and decision'. A.S. Bevride considered Turki, in which Babar wrote as 'terse, word-tarifty, restrained and lucid'.[2] The remark applies also, to Babar's treatment of women in his work, rather than the idea of Babar having kept the women in *Purdah.*

Babar makes few and brief references about 'royal' women only and the role some of them played in shaping the course of his life and career. But they sound enough to indicate the overall impact and the rest is completed by Babar's daughter Gulbadan Begum.

There has been a growing emphasis on the social, economic, political and cultural life of women in general, of the Mughal period, as well as that on royal women like Gulbadan Begum, Nurjahan, Mumtaz Mahal, Jahanara and Zeb-un-Nissa.[3] The 'royal' women of Babar's era though technically on the prephere of Indian history, are no less relevent or notable. They may have failed to attract to Lane Poole's attention but they too provide in their own way a 'link between Central Asia and India' for not only playing an important role in moulding the man and the king—Babar, as the initiator of the Mughal rule in India, but also foreshadow their more written about royal counterparts of the later Mughal period.

Qut-luq-Nigar Khan and Aisan Daulat Begum

Many of the attributes of Babar, whether of the author, the lover of nature and poetry, self-restraint, discipline, his refined and aesthetic temperament, appear to have been nurtured in the fertile soil of his family tradition in general and that of women folk in particular. His maternal grand-mother Aisan-Daulat Begum and his mother Qut-lug-nigar Khan influenced him the most.[4] From them only Babar, as a child, learnt to respect the achievements of his prudent and illustrious maternal grand-father, Yunus Khan, who had descended from Chaghtai Khan, the second son of Chingiz Khan and whom Babar mentions in his Memoirs.[5] His mother, *Qut-lug-nigar,* was thus well born and a scholar's daughter, educated in Turki and Persian, apart from her other accomplishments.[6] According to Babar, "she was with me in most of my guerilla expeditions and throne less times."[7]

Aisan-Daulat Begum, too, contributed a lot to the making of Babar a disciplined and persevering man. A born namadic and sternly brought up,[8] she was virtually his counsellor through his early struggle to hold Farghana. In 1494, when Umar Shaikh Mirza died, Babar was less than 12 years of age and was confronted with two mighty armies within the borders of Farghana. Then the wise Aisan-Daulat, took charge of the crisis, and her 'prudent advise was responsible for much of his success.'[9] Babar appreciates the role of his mother and maternal grandmother in his strife to take Samarkand by the strength of Andijan thus, 'such letters, so anxious, so beseeching, coming from my mothers, that is from my own and hers... with what heart would a man not move'? Again, about latter, Babar says, "Few amongst women will have been my grandmother's equal for judgement and counsel. She was very farsighted and most affairs of mine were carried through under her advise".[10] Two paintings depict her as 'ordering the realm of her grandson Babar and as giving orders for the arrest of the conspirators'.[11] Babar's paternal grandmother Shah Sultan Begum, wife of Abu-said-Mirza, and mother of Umar Shaikh Mirza, must have influenced Babar quite differently from that of Aisan-Daulat Begum, as a town lady of high Turkish birth, used to the sophistication of a wealthy house of Samarkand, Babar has described her as a mediator during his campaign against Tambal in 1500 A.D. and also that the news of her death in Andijan reached Babar in 1501.[12]

Khan-Zada Begum

A multifarious role in the affairs of Babar was played by Khan-zada Begum, daughter of Umar Shaikh Mirza and Qut-liq-nigar Khanan, full sister of Babar and five years his senior.[13] Her life portrait reads like a record of life-long devotion to Babar; in the process she also served the cause of the Mughal empire in India in its in-fancy. In 1501 she married to Shabani when he captured samarkand from Babar. Gulbadan in *Humayun Nama* makes the marriage a condition of Shaibani's peace with Babar. Mirza Haider in *Tarikh-i-Rashishi* says that she was given in exchange for Babar's life and according to Khafi-Khan, as a ranson (batariq-i-faida).[14] Babar gives no details regarding marriage and merely says, "She fell into Shaibani's hands."[15] She was in Shaibani's power and could have been married without consent of Babar. In 1501 she was twenty three years old. She had almost certainly been married earlier possibly to Mahdi. Her marriage arrangements with Shaibani must have included divorce which the Muslim law requires persumably as himself of Timurid birth. Shaibani would treat a Timurid women respectfully even when she was virtually spoil of battle. To marry Khan-zada, he divorced her maternal aunt, Mihr-nigar Chaighati.[16] Khan-zada Begum was subsequently divorced by Shaibani because she was suspected of leaning to Babar's side when Shaibani's interests clashed with Babar's. Khan-zada was back to Babar in 1511 A.D. Regarding her efforts for peace and amity as well as her role as a mediator, Gulbadan Begum records Humayun's request to her as 'pray do me the honour of going to Qandhar and advising Mirza Hindal and Kamran to be friends among themselves... if mirza Kamran will agree to carry out what I have written to him, I will do what his heart desires'. Later Khanzada Begum is depicted as advising the two brothers "If you ask me, well as his majesty, *Firdaus-Makani* decided it and gave his throne to the Emperor Humayun, and as all of you have read the *Khutba* in his name till now, so now regard him as your superior and remain obedient to him."[17] Khan-zada Begum is described also as the loving custodian of baby Akbar, entrusted to her care by Askari at the age of about 2½ years and who she discovered 'Babar altogether'.[18]

Addressed by Mirza Haider as the one who 'honours the throne of chastity' and by Gulbadan Begum as her 'Dearest Lady', Khanzada Begum is mentioned in all the contemporary details with reference and is a dignified character in the turmoil of her day. After the death of Maham Begum, Khanzadam Begum was in 1532–33 A.D., elevated to the status of the prinapal lady of the palace and was confessed the title of Padshah Begum.[19]

Ayisha-Sultan Begum

Of the wives and concubines of Babar[20] Ayisha-Sultan Begum, Zainab Sultan Begum, Maham Begum and Bibi Mubarika draw attention to verying extent. Ayisha-Sultan Begum, third daughter of Sultan Ahmad Mirza and a first cousin of Babar is mentioned by Babar as his first wife-bethrothed in samarkand when he was five years old. Babar says that it first "he had no small affection for Ayisha and that it declined". Babar records the birth and death of his first born; within a period of 40 days and that Ayisha-Sultan Begum deserted him at the instigation of her elder sister Saliqa 'who was married to one of those kinsmen who tried to overthrow the boy king of Fanghana'.[21]

There were obviously other causes for her decision to desert him, which disclose a candid confession of Babar too. At the time of their marraiage, he was infatuated with a smart young boy, named Babari, 'In those days... I discovered in myself a strange emotional upsurge. A boy named Babari in the camp bazar fascinated me beyond words... under the stress of that youthful folly, my brain lost control over my actions.'[22] Under the circumstances, probably Ayisha Begum 'Proud' as she is mentioned, could not have taken the neglect.

Zainab Sultan Begum

When Kabul was captured, Babar was married to Zainab Sultan Begum, fifth daughter of Sultan Muhammad Mirza and first cousin of Babar. Babar writes, "I took her at my mother's insistence... she did not become very congenial."[23] According to some, Zainab was neither a good looking nor a good-tempered woman and in this political marriage thrust upon him by his mother, Zainab too proud of her parentage, failed to win Babar's affection. Babar does not even remember the year of her death.[24]

Maham Begum

Maham Begum played an active role in the political affairs of Babar as well as in the royal household. He married her in 1506 and she mentioned as the 'one who was to Babar, what Ayisha was to Muhammad'.[25] She is recorded by Abul Fazal to have 'belonged to a noble Khurasan family and to have been related to Sultan Hussain Mirza of Herat and a Shia.[26] Gulbadan invariably addresses her as 'My Lady' and confirms her qualities of extreme intelligence and good looks. She accompanied her husband to Badakshan and Transoxiana and stood by him through thick and thin.[27] She was the chief lady of the royal household. Her son Humayun's birth was celebrated with his assumption of the title *Padshah*.[28] Maham Begum was the chief queen and the only one, privileged to sit by the side of Babar on the throne of Delhi.[29] She had well defined rights over other inmates of Babar's *harem.* She herself took her own guardianship of, two of Dildar Begum's children, Hindal and Gulbadan in 1519 and 1525 respectively and Babar's affirmation of it, though she already passessed a son, Humayun.[30] She took a decisive part in foiling the ploy by Nizam-ul-Din Khalifa to have Mehdi Khwaja named her to Babar; but for her role in the entire episode, the history of Mughal empire in India would have been different. Maham received her cleverness of the conspiracy and bade Humayun to return from Badkhshan. She played an important role in promoting successfully the cause of Humayun.[31] She continued to be the *Padshah Begum* and participating in the affairs of the royal household, organisation of social functions and the maintenance of her husband's tomb, till her death in 1533 A.D.

Bibi Mubarika

In dealing with the Yusufzai tribe of the Afghans, Babar was assisted by his marriage to Bibi Mubarika. He says 'In order to conciliate the Yusufzai horde, I had asked for a daughter of my well wisher Malik Shah Mansur, at the time he came to see me as envoy from the Yusufzani Afghans.'[32] This marriage was the 'sign and seal of amity between him and her tribe'. She was one of the small and select party of ladies who were the first to join Babar in India alongwith Maham and Gulbadan begum in 1529 A.D.[33] Also it was she who performed the duty of bringing Babar's body from Agra to Kabul and it would be in harmony with Shershah's generous character if he safe-guarded her in her task.[34]

Thus whereas the Persianized Turks in India had already accepted female right to sovereignty, the tradition of chingiz and Timur which Babar inherited, also provided royal women certain rights and opportunities to participate in political matters. Yet the Mughals did not concede to women the right to sovereignty; as clearly indicated by the letter of Shah Begum of Badakhshan to Babar 'though I, being a women, cannot myself attain the sovereignty, yet my grandson Mirza Khan can hold it'. This claim was recognized by Babar fully.[35]

Yet the role of royal women studied above whether, in nurturing the future initiater of Mughal role in India in the rich Turk-Mongal heritage or as counselling the boy king of Farghana and seeing him though in the early crisis in his political career, or in saving him and forging peace whether with Shaibani or with Yusufzai's, in attempts to create amity amongst warring royal camps camps within the family, or in foiling the plot against Babar's children in matters of succession, can never be under-estimated. While Mubarik bibi took away as per his wish Babar's corpse to rest on the slopes of the Shah-i-Kabul hill, the royal women alongwith Babar, not only remain as much link between Central Asia and India, they also foreshadow the multifarious roles the royal ladies of the forthcoming era of Mughal period, were to play.

References

1. In Persia Puren Dukht and Arjumand Dukht, daughters of Khusuru Perviz of Sassahid Dynasty, ascended the throne in early seventh century and ruled successfully *Indian Historical Quarterly*. Vol. II 1940, p. 753 'Sultan Razia' by A.B.M. Habibullah, vide A.B.M. Habibullah's *The Foundation of Muslim Rule in India,* Central Book Depot, Revised edition, Allahabad 1976, p. 115. The rights of Turk-Mongal women included the widow's assumption of all the rights of her husband, including the leadership of the tribe as well as of becoming the Regents. They also accompanied the cavalcase on military expeditions, see Ralph Fox, *Genghis Khan,* John Lane, London, 1936, 44. and Mirza Haider Doghlat *Tarikh-i-Rashidi* tr. is *A History of the Mogals of Central Asia* by Denison Ross London, New Impression, 1972, p. 203.
2. Babar, *Babar-Nama* tr. by A.S. Beveridge as *Memoirs of Babar,* first published 1922. Reprinted by Oriental Books, Reprint

Corporation, New Delhi 1970, Preface by A.S. Beveridge, XXX, XXXI, lix S.M. Edwards. *Babar diarist and despot,* reprint, Heritage Publishers, New Delhi, 1977, Preface 5. K. Jena *Babar-Nama and Babar* Sundeep Prakashan, Delhi 1978, Introduction IX, X.

3. These works included Magan Lal's *The Diwan of Zeb-un-Nissa,* John Murray, London 1913, Sunita Devi's *The Beautiful Mughal Princess,* W. Thacker & Co. London 1918.
   Batenschon A., *The Life of a Mogal Princess, Jahanara Begum, Daughter of Shahjahan,* London, 1931.
   S. Lane-Poole's *Nurjahan and Jahangir,* Sushil Gupta India Ltd. Calcutta, 1950. P.N. Chopra's *Some Aspects of Society and Culture During the Mughal Age,* Agra, 1955, Rekha Mishra's Women in Mughal India. Munshiram Manoharlal, New Delhi, 1967. Renuka Nath's *Notable Mughal and Hindu Women in the 16th and 17th Centuries,* inter India Publications, New Delhi, 1988.
4. Babar, *Babar Nama* tr. A. Bevridge, p. 21.
5. Mirza Muhammad Haidar Doughlat, *Tarikh-i-Rashidi;* Tr. by E. Denison Ross as *A History of The Moghuls of Central Asia* Second edition New impression, London, 1972, pp. 155-156 mentions, as 'He excelled in penmanship, painting, singing and instrumental music... He was graced with good qualities and perfect manners, was unequalled in bravery and heroism, and excelled especialy in archery. He studied under sharaf-ud-Din Ali Yazdi, with whom he spent twelve years. In a word, no one of all his family can be compared to him'; also see Babar's *Babar Nama* trans. by A.S. Beveridge as *Memoirs of Babar* Oriental Books Reprint Corporation Reprint, Delhi, 1970, pp. 19–24.
6. *Ibid.* Preface by A.S. Bevridge, XXVIII.
7. *Ibid.* p. 21; She died about six months after the capture of Kabul.
8. *Ibid.* pp. 21-22.
9. Rushbrook Williams, *An Empire Builder of the Sixteenth Century,* London, 1918, p. 34.
10. *Babar Nama* pp. 43, 89.
11. Agra Codex, reprints also in Rushbrook Williams *'An Empire Builder of the 16th Century'.*
12. Babar narrates "On the following day, my father's mother, my grandmother, Shah Sultan Begum arrived from Andijan, thinking to beg off Jahangir Mirza, if he had been taken '*Babar Nama* p. 113, also see p. 149.
13. See Mirza Muhammad Haider's *Tarikh-i-Rashidi* tr. Denison Ross pp. 117, 155, Gulbadan Begum's Humayun Nama tr. by A.S. Beveridge as *The History of Humayun,* Idarah-i-Adabiyat-i Delhi, 1972, pp. 85, 175, 250–251. Eldest of her father's daughters.

She is recorded to thrice married, first, to Shaibani in 1501, secondly, to a man of inferior rank, Sayyid Hada, and thirdly to Mahdi Muhammad Khwaja. Her only child, her son by Shaibani, Khurram Shah died a young man. She died in 1545 A.D. and was laid in the burial place of Babar.

14. Khafi-Khan, I, 33 quoted by A.S. Bevridge, in Appendix A, p. 251.
15. Babar, *Babar Nama* tr. A.S. Beveridge, p. 147.
16. Gulbadan Begum, Hamayun Nama, tr. A.S. Bevridge p. 250.
17. *Ibid.* pp. 160-161, 250-251.
18. Gulbadan Begum narrates that "she (khanzada Begum) was very fond of him (baby Akbar) and used to kiss his hands and feet and say, 'They are the very hands and feet of my brother, the Emperor Babar' and he is like him altogether". p. 174.
19. Rekha Misra, *Women in Mughal India,* Munshiram Manoharlal Delhi, 1967, p. 19.
20. See translators. note on it in *Babar Nama*, pp. 711-712 which mentions apart from the four wives listed here, also Masuma Sultan is mentioned as the one married by Babar, for love, in 1507, she died the following year in childbed and her name was given to her daughter. Babar records I saw her when I went to Khurasen (1566 A.D. liked her and asked for her.' She was a sister of Babar's first wife Ayisha. See *Babar Nama* p. 36. Gul-rukh Begum who was married to Babar in 1508 A.D. and bore Kamram and Askari and Dildar Begum who was married in the same period as Gul-rukh and bore Gul-rukh, Gul-rang, Gul-Chihra, Hindal and Gulbadan. The two circassian slaves Gul-nar Aghacha and Nargul Aghacha gifted by Shah Tahmasp to Babar in 1527 A.D., also became recognized ladies of her royal household.
21. A.S. Bevridge, Introduction to *Babar Nama,* p. 36.
22. Babar, *Babar Nama* tr. A.S. Bevridge, p. 120 Muni Dal, *Babar Life and Times,* Vikas Publishing House, Delhi, 1977, p. 108-109.
23. Babar *Babar Nama,* p. 48 'Two or three years later she was struck by small pox and passed away'.
24. See E.M. Edwards, Babar diarist and despat Heritage Publishers reprint, New Delhi, 1977, p. 93.
25. A.S. Bevridge, Appendix A. to her translation of Gulbadan Begum *Humayun Nama,* p. 256.
26. Abul Fazal, *Akbar Nama* tr. by H. Bevridge, reprint by Rare Books, Delhi, 1972, Vol. I, pp. 257, 272, 285.
27. Gulbadan Begum, *Humayun Nama,* tr. A. S. Bevridge pp. 81, 111, 127, Babar, *Babar Nama* tr. A.S. Bevridge, p. 358.

28. See Gulbadan Begum, Humayun Nama tr. A.S. Bevridge, p. 90. 'That same year (i.e. 1508). His Majesty was pleased to order the Amirs and rest of the world to style him *Padshah* (Emperor). For before the birth of Emperor Humayun, he had been named and styled Mirza Babar... In the year of His Majesty Humayun's birth he styled himself *Padshah".*
    Before 1508, Babar's career had been a chequered one but by the beginning of 1508, Babar was the 'only Timurid who could pride himself on being chieftain of a considerable area. He had asserted himself against Muqim Arghan... with the birth of a son, he was not to be looked upon as a mere adventurer... the birth of a son ensured the continuity of his line and the principles of his govt. 'S.K. Banerjee, *Humayun Badshah,* Oxford University Press. 1938, pp. 1-2.
29. Abul Fazl, *Akbar Nama* trans. H. Bevridge, Vol. II, 272, S.K. Banerjee *Humayun Badshah*, p. 60.
30. Gulbadan Begum, *Humayun Nama* trans. A.S. Bevridge Intro. pp. 9-10.
31. Babar was annoyed at Humayun's desertion of Badkshan. Maham's role in restoring Humayun to grace is attributed to Maham considerably. See Gulbadan's *Humayun Nama* trans. A.S. Bevridge p. 104.
32. Babar, *Babar Nama* tr. A.S. Bevridge, p. 375.
33. An attractive account of Mubarika Bibi and her marriage is given in Hafiz Muhammad's *Tarikh-i-hafiz-i-rahmat-Khani* translated by H. Bevridge in full under the title 'An Afghan Legend' appended to A.S. Bevridge translation of Babar Nama XXXVI–XLI.
34. The body of Babar must have been taken before 1544 A.D., the year in which Humayun refers to Bibi Mubarika who had conveyed their father's body to Kabul, see Gulbadan Begum's *Humayun Nama* p. 138, and the translators note in *Babar Nama* pp. 709-710.
35. Mirza Haidar Doughlat, *Tarikh-i-Rishidi,* tr. as Denison Ross. *A History of the Moghals of Central Asia,* p. 203.

10

Outstanding Women

Whereas the earlier invaders of India merged with and became absorbed in the life of the sub-continent, incorporating their gods into the Hindu pantheon, the Muslims who came in the eleventh century A.D. were very much the rulers, whom the Hindus could not accept. The first comers, Turks and Persians, looked upon Indians "as an inferior race" while Indian Muslims who proved worthy were, at times, given positions of trust. Hindus as a class were generally made to feel that they were a subject race whose salvation lay in absolute obedience to the Muslims."[1]

Hinduism, tolerant as it always is credited to be, could not include Islam. Neither could the Muslims extinguish the Hindus. This must have angered the rulers, for their militancy had so far crushed the countries which they had conquered, and annihilated the original religions which existed in Egypt, Asia Minor and Syria. Zoroastrianism had also been crushed. And here were the Hindus unshakeable and adamant as far their faith was concerned. The Muslims did not so openly condemn Christianity or Judaism as these two religions were mentioned in the Book, which made their adherents Kithabias.[2]

But the cultures of the two countries did to a certain extent mingle, and such Islamic customs as Purdah enveloped Indian women with all its force. The first five hundred years of Muslim rule were particularly oppressive but changes for a better understanding between the people took place when Ibrahim Lodi was defeated at Panipat in 1525 by Babar, the founder of the Mughal Empire. Though the new rulers brought the laws of Chengiz Khan with them, and Mongol culture, they were far more civilised and less aggressive than their predecessors. The first three hundred years, however, were ones of dark despair for India, especially for its women, for the Muslims not only ruled and looted the land, desecrated the lovely temples and mocked at the Indian way of life; but it threatened the very sanctity of Hinduism.

The Muslims practised Polygamy, but the Prophet himself, though he married and indulged in many pleasures, had a deep respect for women. The position of women in the Muslim world, nevertheless, deteriorated. In the Caliphate at Baghdad, Arab sodomy was combined with Byzantium and Persian vices. Great orgies of sensual pleasures were the order of the day. This life of ease and luxury nevertheless made the men jealous of their women, whom they considered as their own precious possessions. "With such flamming vices running in their veins, men were insisting on the fidelity of their women; and what they could not get by love they decided to force by the cudget; the development of the Purdah, particularly its more undesirable features, was in no small measure due to this masculine effort to break the spirit of women."[3]

When purdah was first introduced in Arabia it is said that a niece of Ayesha, the Prophet's wife, refused to wear the veil. She said: "On me God has set the seal of beauty, and I rejoice when my beauty is seen and the mercy of God therein acknowledged. Never shall I cover my face for no flaw or fault finds a place in God's work."[4]

Such was not the good fortune of her sisters of the Islamic faith. Women were not allowed to show their faces in public and even to attend mosques. Any women who did not veil her face was taken to be a shameless hussy, and because she exposed herself to the public gaze, she was often molested. When such a form of purdah was introduced in India, naturally Indian women also could not appear in public and took to the veil, not covering themselves entirely with the Burkha but with the end of their *saris.* Hindu kings introduced the Muslim harem in their palaces, and even till a few decades ago, royal Kshatriya ladies strictly observed purdah. Ladies of high caste in the medieval period never went out into the streets except in palanquins and litters.

Apart from purdah, other evils seemed to have prevailed more extensively. New cultures and habits were introduced by the conquerors. There was an unheaval of economic, social and political life and for many years the people were unsettled, and afraid, for they seemed to have lost their old morale, which had existed before the decadence of Hindu India set in about the eighth century and left the country free for the Muslim conquest. Evils such as polygamy, sati, child-marriages and the prevention of widows from re-marrying considerably lowered the status of women.

Sati became much more widespread, even though the law made it optional whether a widow wished to burn herself or not. "A strong convention had risen among high caste Hindus that a widow unencumbered by pregnancy, infant-in-arms or old age should voluntarily announce her intention to become Suttee immediately on the death of her husband; in most cases, the decision so announced was genuine as the woman was in extreme distress. And once the decision was announced, it was irrevocable."[5]

Bernier and other Europeans relate harrassing and heroic experiences of Suttees, and also some incidents when priests and on-lookers forced a Suttee, whose courage failed her at the last minute, into the funeral pyre.

Women were not educated in the medieval period, and apart from the Bhakta poetesses, we know little of the educational system for girls. It must be remembered, however, that this may not entirely have been the fault of the rulers. As has been seen, at the end of the Hindu period, child marriages virtually stopped girls' education. The Muslim conquest was but the final push into further retrogression. The education allowed to girls and the sanction of nuns by the Buddhists now disappeared. Ashrams and monasteries and forest universities were uprooted. *Parivarajikas* or wandering nuns who had become a part of India and had free access to rich and poor homes were now no longer seen. After the sixteenth century, general change for the better seemed to have occurred, especially when Akbar became the Emperor, but five centuries of the darkest period of the story of women had not left the country with any of its former buoyancy. The occasional alliance between a Muslim prince and a Hindu lady helped to raise the standards of the latter, but they were still very afraid of their rulers. Education after the sixteenth century, however, did seem to be possible, and even the teaching of Sanskrit was allowed to women. They blossomed forth into classical Sanskrit poetry, and like the earlier Bhakti poetesses wrote mostly in praise of Krishna. For this reason they can be classed with the spate of religious women singers who started in the early part of medieval India and continued in a sense the religious songs of the Buddhist Bhikkhunis.

Glimpses of Intellectual and Religious Emancipation

In spite of the general decadence and the low status into which women had fallen in medieval India, there were glimpses, every now and then of women being honoured and encouraged in their intellectual careers. Many instances of individual worth proved to be landmarks in a dreary background of suppression and ignorance. There were great queens, writers and poetesses, and devout followers of God.

For centuries despite foreign invasions, a thirst for seeking the Truth had prevailed in the country. The Bhakti school was especially pronounced during the reign of the Muslims. There were also many secular writers, few of whom are mentioned below.

A poetess of outstanding merit of the Vijayanagara period was Oduva Tirumalamba who was, strangely enough, a reader of poetry to the ladies of the royal family. She was also an excellent musician, grammarian, and rhetorician, thus proving that learning was by no means denied to women. Apart from being a scholar and linguist, she was also very beautiful and king Achutaraya raised her to the status of the queen. A strange characteristic of hers was that she, a junior queen, actually eulogised the marriage of her rival, the principal queen, whom she seemed to have loved.

A Shudra woman, Honnamma also proved a great writer. She belonged to the Kannada group of writers probably of Mysore state. She was a queen's maid, and her patroness had her educated. Her teacher was so overcome by her prowess that he called her "the goddess of charming literature."[6] Honnamma, at the instance of her queen and king, wrote *Hadibadeya Dharma,* dealing with the duties of a chaste woman, and her verses are sung even today. Here we find a genealogy of the king of Mysore up to the seventeenth century.

In fact, in the South a free flow of art and literature flourished in the Vijayanagara period. Learning was patronised by the Rajas and other chiefs of States and Sanskrit, Telugu, Tamil and Kannada *Prabandhas Padas* and stage plays were encouraged. Kings and nobles entertained themselves by going to dramas and such folk plays as *Yakshagana.* Many glimpses of life in the middle ages are also discernible from the literature and poetry of the time. The fact that women, despite all the restrictions placed on them look so lively a part in art and poetry shows that medieval India was not entirely decadent and that Hindu India still possessed much energy and intellectual output.

King Kumara Kampana II brought the whole of the Tamil country under the Vijayanagara empire in the fourteenth century. His queen, Ganga Devi was educated and accompanied her husband during his campaigns. She was the author of a Sanskrit epic called *Madhura-Vijayam* in which she portrayed her husband as the hero. She was well-read in Sanskrit and praised the Sanskrit poets of Andhra Desh. Ganga Devi was herself a Telugu princess. She wrote in the *Vairabhi* style, and her diction is simple and charming. Often she adopted Kalidasa's manner of description but her scenes are transformed with her own inventive skill. Her nature poetry is very beautiful: "With eyes like full-blown lotuses, eager to behold her own countenance, verily did autumn draw out of her bodice of clouds the mirror of the sun."

Another poetess not of royal birth but a mere potters' daughter who lived in the Nellore district was one of the earliest and perhaps the greatest of Telugu writers of the fourteenth and fifteenth centuries. She wrote the Ramayana which was till quite recently prescribed as a school text-book.

In fact it is not possible to mention the many poetesses who flourished in the South and who helped to raise the standard of poetry in an age which almost reached the depths of despair. When these are added to the Bhakti school of writers. India was by no means sterile: but rich in poetry and art. Religion also played an important part.

Medieval poetry also encouraged Muslim writers of whom there were some women. The poetry is now more personal. A well-known Muslim poetess of the thirteenth century was Sultana Raziya Begum who was the daughter of Shams-ud-din

Altamish, one of the "Slave" Kings. She ruled with a strong hand for five years after her father's death. Here is one of her Persian verses:

I have only heard thy name and I love, I have
not seen thee, and yet I love thee as if I had
seen and known thee.

A good part of the best religious poetry of India, which forms a background for our Bhajans and Kirtans today, was written during the medieval period by the Bhakti School. The Bhaktas were devotees who followed the Bhakti marg or the Path of Love, one of the three ways to reach God. The other two ways were Jnana marg and Karma marg, wisdom and action. Bhakti means "affection" and devotion. It denotes the ecstasy in which followers of God worship a personal deity. Most of the Bhaktas worship Krishna and his life converges around Brindaban or Gokul in the North and Pandharpur in the west.

Among the songsters there were many women. Those who worshipped Vitthal or Vithoba, the deity of Pandharpur in Western India were Mukta Bai, Jana Bai and other Marathi Bhaktas. Vitthal is another name for Krishna. The Bhakti of these women is far quieter and more meditative than those of the Brindaban School. The Bhaktis are of a mystical kind and with their unsullied devotion merge themselves with God. They seek deliverance from birth and re-birth, like the Buddhists, but their God is positive and personal.

Mukta Bai's outpourings are quite as poignant as those of the previous Buddhist sisters.

Where never darkness comes my home I've made,
There my delightsome lodging ever find.
That perfect shelter could find our need,
Going and coming trouble us no more,
Beyond all vision and above all spheres,
He, our delight, our inmost soul indwells.
He, Mukta says, is our heart's only home ![7]

A bid for freedom, perhaps from the foreign rulers, made them seek shelter in God. The times which produced Vallabhacharya, Ramanand, Chaitanya, Namdev, Kabir and Nanak also produced Lalla, Mira Bai, Lal Deb and countless others during the unhappy time when clashes and wars were continuous. Lalla says:

Be his sins misfortune, be it guilt:
Be the guerdon ashes, be it flowers,
O Bhagwan, Thou blessest whom Thou wilt.
O Bhagwan, how wondrous are thy powers.

After the 15th century, a general change for the better seems to have occurred and the status of women began to rise. Education now became possible and even the teaching of Sanskrit was now allowed to women. Women even blossomed forth in classical Sanskrit poetry. Priyamvada lived in Faridpur district soon after A.D. 1600. Both her father and her husband were scholars, and the latter trained her and she is said to have helped both with their own literary work. A sample of her work shows her as a Bhakta, a lover of Lord Krishna. This God is said to have sported with the maidens of Gokul, Mathura and Brindaban, on the banks of the Ganges or the country called Braj. The love songs composed for Krishna from the famous Radha Krishna theme and many women poets flourished in the middle ages who expressed their fervent devotion to the God who attracted them with his divine flute. This medieval poetry is symbolic and also deeply religious and sensuous and erotic Krishna is often called "Kanha" or Govinda, Manmohan—mind-bewilderer, Girdhar mountain-holder and other names.

Priyamvada's poem to Krishna runs as follows:

Who sports upon the Jumna's leafy bank,
Who Kamsa slew, and other demon foes,
Longed for by all the cowherd folk of Braj,
Adored with love-filled laughs from lotus eyes
By shy sweet milkmaids in their youthful bloom,
His head with peacock feathers gaily crested.
His fair form bent in graceful triple curve
Braja's dark-hued Apollo with his flute,
Remover of the pains and burdens of the world,
Govinda, him I worship.[8]

Gangadevi was a princess of Vijayanagar in the 14th century, and the wife of Prince Kampa Raya, son of one of the founders of the Empire. She wrote the epic *Mathura Vijayam.* She seems to have a low estimate of women.[9]

Women were therefore educated if they so wished, in the medieval period of Indian history, as there is hardly any other age, except perhaps the modern, when women composed so much in all parts of India from Kashmir to the South and Maharashtra to Assam. A Malayalam author of the 15th century wrote *Chandrotsavam* in which a general idea is given of women's education and of the types of Sanskrit works they read. In fact, Sanskrit was read and written in all parts of India and constituted more or less the common intellectual language of the country.

Avvai or Avvaiar is included among classical writers and her verses have today become household proverbs. She is said to have been the daughter of Bhagvan and Adi the First. She was found in an inn near Trichinopoly and though never educated spoke with the tongue of angels. She spent her life in wandering hither and thither and begging; she was known as the "Singer who sings for a cup of porridge." Her verses mingle moral teaching with beautiful diction. These two daughters are all the more illustrious because they bore alone the flame of learning in a world which had lost its ancient splendour in an age of decadence.

Mira Bai

Of all the great Bhakti singers of the middle ages. Mira shines out in pure splendour. She sang in Vraja-bhasha mixed with Rajasthani. Her Lord was Shri Krishna (Girdhar Gopal) and her Bhajans resound in all parts of India even today. She is said to be the writer of *Raj Govind* and commentary on *Gita-Govinda* of Jayadeva.

History believes that Mira Bai was from Rajasthan, daughter of the Raja of Merta and the wife of Rana Kumbha of Marwar. She was well-known for her beauty and piety. From *Annals and Antiquities of Rajasthan* we learn that she may have first learnt her songs of Govinda from her husband or from some other source. "Her history is a romance and her excess of devotion at every shrine of the favourite deity, from Yamuna to Dwarka gave rise to many tales of scandal."[10] Later historians say that Mira could not have been the wife of Kumbha but of Prince Bhoj Raj. She was born in 1498 and died in 1546 at Dwarka (Kathiawar) where she had resided for many years.[11] The latter story is the more probable. Mitra stayed with her grand-parents in Merta. Rao Dudaji, her grandfather was not only a prince but a devotee of Vishnu, and Mira was religiously inclined from childhood. She also learnt music, and was familiar with skills need by all royal Rajasthani women. From earliest childhood she worshipped an idol of Krishna which she took with her after marriage and refused to acknowledge her husband's idol Kali. She married Bhoj Raj in 1516 and her husband the crown prince of Marwar died in 1521. She then lived the life of a widow, but also became interested in the politics of the times. Her religious fervour was objected to by her brother-in-law when he became ruler. Her devotion to Krishna and her patronage to mendicants and Sadhus was resented. She resisted her opponents and wrote:

I took to keeping hermits' company
Lost conventional modesty.
My mother-in-law says
I lost the family honour,
I have ceased to care
For people's opinion.[12]

She miraculously escaped many attempts made to kill her. She sang:

Oh king, I know you gave me poison
But I emerged
Just like gold burned in fire
Comes out bright as a dozen suns.

Again she wrote:

Mira sang ecstatically of Hari's virtue.
The King sent her a serpent basket
and placed it in Mira's hands
When, bathed and washed, she took a look
and found an image of God.[13]
Mira's Lord is her eternal saviour removing obstacles.
Drunk with the mood of pious songs
she vows herself to Girdhar.[14]

In the Mira Bhajan, "Govind is my life", Mira is steeped in love divine. The original words by the poetess are as follows:

"Govind is my life, the world tastes better to me
I love Rama and Rama alone; let my eyes see no other

In Mira's palace dwell Hari's saints.
Hari dwells far from intrigue with the saints.[15]

Some of the Mira Bhajans which Subhalakshmi and Omkaran Thakur and others sing are now heard in all parts of India, steeped in devotion to Hari. In *Kunjan Baba Chhadi* she pours out her devotion: *"If only I were a fish, I would touch your feet as you bathe in the stream, had I been a cuckoo I would chirp sweetly when you come to the forest grazing the cattle: If I were a pearl I would sparkle in your bosom as a gem in the necklace. But being not any of those, how am I to get you? Where am I to seek for you?"* Her famous song *Hari Tum Haro* was Mahatma Gandhi's favourite Bhajan. Here Mira relates the many mystic moments when Krishna came down to earth to comfort his devotees such as Draupadi, Prahlada and Gajendra. The refrain is, *"Oh Lord, take away pain from mankind."*

Mira symbolizes Krishna himself as the greatest of divine lovers, and he is represented as possessing countless wives and gopis. Vyasa in writing the *Mahabharata* has typified Krishna as satisfying the erotic longings of human beings, the sensual intoxicating feeling he induces is but a reflection of divine love as so many mystics of all religions have felt. For human symbolism can best express divine love for many.

Though Krishna is the perfect divine lover as so many Bhaktas aver, in the Gita, his great song, he soars to transcendental heights. Here all symbolic references of God being the divine lover in human form are absent. The adoration and selfless devotion to God surpassing all human sensations shines magnificently over all such more earthbound references as Krishna the beloved of the Gopis.

Mira's devotion was concentrated on Krishna the divine cowherd so loved by his milk-maids. From childhood she felt a passionate love for Girdhara (Krishna) and she abandoned her husband and kingdom to pour out her adorations to God. She called forth the Radha-Krishna story and popularised the theory of mutual personal love between Krishna and his devotee. At times she called her God Rama possibly because her Guru Raidas was a follower of Ramananda, who worshipped Rama. "The worship of Krishna, as he is said to have lived and sported at

Gokul, Mathura and Brindaban, on the banks of the Jumna (his countryside is called Braj) has produced a special type of poetry, filled with rich and fervent devotion, in some cases expressive of a very deep religious experience, in others sensuously beautiful and full of symbolism,but also highly erotic. The word Krishna is colloquially coupled with "Kanha".

Kanha have I bought; the price he asked I paid,
some cry, "Too great" while others jeer, "Twas small".
I paid in full, weighed to the utmost grain,
My love, my life, myself, my soul, my all.[16]

The *Bhaktamal* (or *Garland of Devotees*) compiled by Nabha Das in the 17th century has depicted the life of Mira. It says: "Forsaking the fear of people's opinion and breaking the ties of her family Mira Bai worshipped Girdhar. Like a cowgirl living in the age of Krishna, she revealed her love in the Dark Age (Kali Yug). Fearless and free, she sang the praise of Krishna.

There are many beautiful legends built around the iife of Mira Bai, the greatest poetess of Medieval India. There is a story that Vikramajit asked her to drown herself, and characteristically she tried to please her adversary and did throw herself into the water, but she did not sink. Then again to Rana Vikramajit's successor Udai Singh, tried to bring Mira back from Dwarka, and sent a Brahmin to fetch her. But Rajasthan was war-weary, and also Mira did not wish to abandon her life of devotion. The Brahmins tried to force her but she sought refuge in the temple Ranchhorji (Krishna) and in the morning she could not be found. Some say that she was absorbed into the body of Krishna, and others that she may have fled secretly and wandered about anonymously in different parts of India.

Mira Bai is said to have written about 400 Padas or song verses, and also to be the author of other poems. How were her work preserved considering that after the death of her husband and father-in-law she was persecuted by the Ranas? Kabir's works were collected by his disciples. But she had no disciples, though musicians were strongly attracted by her, and possibly kept her songs alive. Her poems are found in three languages. Hindi, Gujarati and Rajasthani, which shows that with the song-lovers of India kept her works alive. It is also said that Mira had a maid Lalita who followed her and wrote down her songs. But this manuscript was said to have been looted by a Muslim ruler. The works of Mira however are many. Her signature consisted in her mentioning her own name in her poems.

Religious Devotees

From the various poems and snatches of life histories which we can gather, a rough idea of life among the Bhaktis can more or less gathered. Despite the acute political disturbances of the Middle Ages, wars and continuous clashes between the conquered and the conquerors, and the intrigues of court and civilian life, the Bhaktis seemed to have been allowed a certain amount of freedom from the Muslim rulers. They were persecuted more by their own families, who objected to their neglect of home and family and complete devotion to God. Krishna's tenet to the Bhakti school was a clear call to those who wished to follow Him and leave the world alone:

"Have your mind on me, your devotion towards me, your sacrifice to me, worship me.To me you will come, I promise you, for you are dear to me."

Mira Bai and other Bhaktis kept company with ascetics and went on pilgrimages with them to sacred places connected with Krishna. They sang Kirtans, which often Mira composed and led these singers who followed her with cymbals and drums. Having arrived at the holy shrine, they worshipped the "lotus-like" feet of Girdhar.

Women then were allowed to withdraw from the world, though the ancient practice of becoming nuns seems to have been discontinued, when they were allowed to visit houses. The women poetesses sang of life in their secluded world which was completely indifferent to the troubles of the times. Detachment was their aim. For instance, Mukta Bai sang in Marathi:

Our destinities and those past deeds are ours
That called for payment, all
Are auspicious now. So set we forth
To seek that farther bank. Release
That which erst spring from the Essential Source,
Would merge itself within that Source again.[18]

The Bhakta school wiped out all caste and race prejudices. The *Bhaktamala,* a Vaishnava treatise relates a story of the reformation of a sweeper. One day, this man who belonged to the lowest of castes, went to steal from a royal treasury. While he was hidden in the bedroom of the king and queen, he heard the latter say: "are you not going to get your daughter married?" and the king replied that he would offer her to the first Yogi he would meet. The sweeper immediately aspired to become the rich son-in-law, and giving up his idea of robbing the royal treasure, he set under a tree and became a Yogi. In due course the king saw him and fulfilled his promise to the queen by offering his daughter to him. The Yogi was delighted and was treated in a royal fashion in the court. But he realised that if only the garments of a saint could make him so rich, how much more would he not gain, if he really abandoned the world and all its wealth and became a true devotee! He therefore left his throne, and became a true Bhakta. Thus was the sweeper saved.

Among the many obstacles which a Bhakti had to avoid was the voluptuous thoughts about women. He is admonished: "Listen not to talks about women, rich men, atheists and enemies."[19] The reverse was the rule for women. They had of course to relinquish the company of men and worship only God. Those who followed the Bhakti Marg had to abandon lust, anger, envy, greed and all worldly temptations. Thus they were inspired and many wrote and sang the most exquisite kirtans and padas. The best poetry of the Medieval age was written by Bhaktas. Poetesses wrote in Sanskrit, Hindi, Tamil, Telugu, Kannada, Malayalam, Gujarati, Kashmiri, Marathi and almost every other tongue in India. Most of the Bhaktas were devotees of Krishna, but Lal Deb was a Saivite and came from Kashmir.

Kabir had some women disciple, one of whom was the poetess Kshema or Kshemashri. Kamali, his daughter was also said to be his devotee.

The religious thinker Dadu (A.D. 1603-60) initiated his two daughters Nani Bai and Mata Bai, who remained devotees all their lives and never married. Charan Das the founder of the Charan Dasi sect of the eighteenth century had two devoted women disciples, Sahajo Bai and Daya Bai. Each wrote two religious books.

Gujarat produced many saint-poetesses, as in fact many other parts of India, some of whom I have already mentioned. Sachdevi, Chaitanya's mother was a self-effacing saint. She belonged to the Nadia district of Bengal and was married to a quiet pious Brahmin. Two of Sachi's sons Vishwambhara and Chaitanya became sannyasins, leaving their mother and childless young wives. But the mother obeyed the will of God and lived on in loneliness through many years. A cruel blow was dealt to her with the death of Chaitanya at the age of forty-eight when his mother was still alive. Chaitanya's first wife died of snake bite and he married Vishnupriya. She was left with her mother-in-law when her husband became a Sannyasin, and she had to care for Sachi. She never appeared before others in public, and when the younger disciples of Chaitanya came to the house, she appeared behind a curtain so that only her feet could be seen. She led an austere life, counting the name of God by putting aside grains of rice. When her chanting was over; she would boil the rice which had been counted. This was her only meal.

The lives of women, between austere saints and women kept strictly behind the veil, between valiant heroines and courageous queens and the number of women who committed Suttee and followed the ordeal set out for women, by Hindu priests, must have on the whole produced a true mixture of women who lived unworldly lives. They must have formed a grey back-ground of austerity, whether heroine, saint or poetess which fitted into a picture of an age replete with wars and intrigues which the women in one way or the other managed to escape. Certainly the heroines also, like the Bhaktis, though they lived in a secular and grayer world, were not afraid of surrendering their lives when it came to upholding the honour of their clan, husband or the unblemished virtue of women.

Women of Warrior Families

Never was there so great a spate of historic heroines as in the Middle Ages. Among them, Rajputs predominated. "Rajput" is not a term which denotes a social group. It "has no concern with race, meaning descent or relationship by blood. It merely denotes a tribe, clan, sect, or caste of warlike habits, the members of which claimed aristocratic rank, and were treated by the Brahmins as representing the Kshatriyas of the old books."[20] It was not only the men who were heroes and warriors, but the women also, who were even more valiant, perhaps more than their men, standing behind in solid support, preserving their honour and prestige against the Muslim invaders. The names of the Rajput heroines stand out in letters of gold in the annals of the history of India. Though the royal ladies were kept in purdha, their strength and courage was astounding. It is not possible to touch on the lives of all the heroines, but a brief selection may point a picture of the warlike days in which our ancestors lived, and of their trials and difficulties which they so bravely overcame.

Sanyogita was one of the heroic Rajput women whose courage and devotion to husband and family has become so famous. She was the daughter of Jayachandra, a ruler of Kannauj. She married Prithviraj whom she chose at a Swayamvara. But her happy married life came to an end when Mu'izuddhin Muhammad of Ghur marched against Prithviraj for the second time near Thanesar. Samyogita armed her lord and sent him to battle with the words: "To die is the destiny not only of man but of the gods: all desire to throw off the old garment; but to die well is to live for ever. Think not of self, but of immorality; let your sword divide your foe, and I will be your *ardhanga* hereafter." Prithviraj fought valiantly but was overcome and his wife mounted the funeral pyre of her lord and sacrificed herself with him.

Padmini of Chitor was of course the model Rajput heroine of the middle ages. She was the queen of Rana Ratan Singh of Mewar and very beautiful. Her story has been highlighted in history and in the Hindi classic *Padmavat* by Malik Muhammad Jayasi. It is believed that Ala'uddin Khilji was infatuated by Padmini and invaded Chitor in order to capture her; but there is no actual proof of this story. When the famous fort at Mewar as besieged by Ala'uddin, the Rajputs resisted bravely, but after eight months they were at last vanquished as the Muslim army from Delhi was far superior. Just before the surrender, Padmini and her Rajput women fell into the fire of *Jauhar* (self-immolation) so that they may not be polluted by the enemy. Col. Tod, the historian says: "The funeral pyre was lighted within the 'great subterranean retreat', in chambers impervious to the light of the day, and the defenders of Chitor beheld in procession the queens, their own wives and daughters, to the number of several thousands.The fair Padmini clored the throng, which was augmented by whatever of female beauty or youth could be tainted by Tartar lust. They were conveyed to the cavern and the opening closed upon them, leaving them to final security from dishonour in the devouring element." Thus, this heroic queen and her retinue went to their final rest.

The popular story is far more romantic. Ala'uddin of Delhi had heard of Padmini's beauty and fidelity. She was the wife of the Rana of Chitor. The Muslim besieged the fort where, after a gallant fight by the Rājputs, he conquered and entered the fort. Padmini then granted the conqueror a glimpse of herself in a mirror, as she could not be seen herself by an outsider being in purdha. Then Ala'uddin laid an ambush and seized Lakshamsi, Padmini's husband, saying he would be released only on Padmini's surrender. Padmini consented to yield and said she would take a retinue of women with her. She asked to be allowed to bid farewell to her lord, for an hour within the Muslim camp. But instead of women, Chitor's warriors were sent and a youth instead of Padmini. These rescued Lakshami. Alauddin returned to Delhi but his passion for Padmini had not died, and when he re-entered Chitor as conqueror Padmini and her women committed *Jauhar,* after which the Rana and his men fought to the death. When Ala'uddin entered the citadel he could not find Padmini but only her bones and ashes within the cave.

Tarabai was a Rajput woman of military might, fearless and strong. She was of sixteenth century, the daughter of Rao Surthan of Bednore, descended from the renowned Chalukya Kings. They migrated to Central India under pressure of the Muslims and took possession of Tonk Thoda. But the Muslims followed them here also and finally Tara Bai's father went to Bednore. By now, her ancient military blood which coursed in her veins inspired her to ride on horseback and smite her enemy with an arrow. Tara joined the cavalry troops of her father when they unsuccessfully tried to defend Tonk Thoda and the Rana Prince, Jaimall offered her his hand. Tara promised to marry him if he redeemed Thoda. Jaimall was however killed by her indignant father for so hastily wishing to possess Tara Bai. Now his brother, Prithwiraj wished to redeem Thoda. Tara consented to be his consort provided, like a true Rajput, he kept his pledge. Prithwiraj slew the Muslim usurper and an arrow was let loose by Tara Bai herself in the struggle. The invaders were now routed and Thoda was recovered for Tara's father. When Prithwiraj was later poisoned by one of his own relation, Tara committed Suttee. The ashes of the devoted warrior husband and wife repose at the Temple of Hama Devi on the road to Marwar.

Among the other Rajput heroines are Rani, Durgavati, a lovely woman, who defended her kingdom against the Mughals. Durgawati ruled her kingdom for her minor son, a brave and gallant warrior in defence of Gondwana against Asaf Khan. She wore armour and mounting her elephant, she herself led her troops and defeated the Mughals. The next day, her son Bir Narayan was wounded and her followers deserted her but with only 300 troops she fought until she herself was wounded. She begged her faithful officers to put an end to her life and died like a soldier.

Other Rajput heroines are Dhatri Panna, a nurse of Udai Singh and Kurma Devi, a princess and many more.

These valiant women set a record of bravery, patriotic devotion, pride of their clan and love of tradition, not to speak of devotion to their loved ones, which outshine even the fame of the mythological heroines of Indian literature.

Jijabai (1594-1674), the mother of Shivaji is a typical example of a heroine of the times. A true Hindu, she proved a worthy mother of a great national hero, dictatorial but pliable to her son's wishes. She was not a Rajput but a descendant of the Yadava kings of Devagiri, and her father was a powerful Sardar in the court of Ahmednagar of Nizam Shah. With her husband Shahji who eventually fell into the opposite camps of Jijabai's father, Jadhavrao she took her husband's side. She staunchly supported his cause and her fortitude and courage passed on to her son Shivaji who founded the Maratha empire. Her son was born at Shivneri where she stayed behind rather than go to her father's home after a war between father and husband. Seeing the plight in which her country suffered at the hands of the Mughals she prayed to Shivai, the guardian deity of Shivneri that she may be given a son who would conquer the enemy and found a Maratha kingdom free from Mughal tyranny. Shivaji was born and named after the goddess Shivai. Truly did this great warrior spring from a renowned mother who took up the building of his character and fired his imagination with good qualities. She willed him to be a great king who would be just and fair to his subjects and devoted all her energies in creating a staunch warrior. As his father's ideas seemed to clash with his, he stayed with his mother in Poona who taught him administration, for by now, she was managing her husband's *Jagir.*

Then Shivaji met and killed Afzalkhan at Fort Pratapgarh while his mother prayed for his safety. It was she who persuaded poet Ajnandas to compose a ballad in honour of her son. Once, while she played chess with her son and checkmated him, he asked her what her reward should be and she demanded Fort Kondana, near Poona, then ruled by the Mughals. The Fort was won.

In 1966 when Shivaji left for Agra, Jijabai became the regent of the small kingdom of Poona. Shivaji instructed his soldiers to honour women and follow a tolerant religious policy. Jijabai did not encourage the condemnation of Hindus when they were forcibly converted to Islam. This was not only a pernicious habit: but it depleted the ranks of the Hindu and she reconverted Bajaji Nimbalkar to Hinduism and gave her own grand-daughter, Shivaji's daughter in marriage to him. She lived until 80 and saw the power of Maharattas increase and the coronation of her son.

Remarkable women rulers and queens also feature in this rather gloomy and sad period of our history. They proved to be admirable administrators. Marco Polo, the explorer, mentions Rudramba, the Kakateya queen. She succeeded her father, King Ganapatideva and ruled her kingdom for over thirty years. He bestowed the name of Rudradeva Maharaja on his daughter and took great pains over her education and trained her in administration, as he had no sons and wished to keep the kingdom in his family. Rudramba ascended her father's throne but was not accepted as sovereign by all sections of the people. The nobles of Southern Andhra objected to a woman ruling them. As they had been previously conquered by Rudramba's father they felt they could now regain their independence. But the queen was able to suppress all the rebels and restore peace.

She reigned until A.D. 1295 in perfect security. She ruled justly and well and reconstructed her kingdom by giving better irrigation and promoting trade, industry and education and tolerant religion. Marco Polo was astounded at the manner in which the country flourished, especially in diamond mining. She died meditating under the guidance of Pashupata priests. Rudramba was one of many efficient queens and administrators.

Tarabai was a Maharatta heroine who resisted Aurangzeb. She married Rajaram, the son of Shivaji and was said to be more spirited than her husband. Due to her undaunted opposition after her husband's death, Aurangzeb was unable to establish a kingdom in the Deccan. She ordered the armies and so ruled the fortresses that the Moghuls could not enter.

Ahalyabai was the daughter-in-law of Malhararao Holkar and a great warrior. One day when they were in camps, a canon ball killed Khanduji, Ahalyabai's husband, and her father-in-law begged her not to commit Suttee. He said: "Khanduji is living, while Ahalya is dead. I shall take it that way, child. Don't be a Sati and follow your husband even in death. Please listen to me." Ahalya was only 20 when she became a widow. She decided to live on and be a solace to Malhararao. She was married, at the Peshwa's wish to Khanduji at the age of eight. He was not a very great character and he also did not treat his wife well. She, on the contrary, was dutiful and responsible and her father-in-law could trust her and often took her with him in his campaigns. Having decided not to commit Suttee she decided to look after her State and religion. Her son eventually followed his grandfather as ruler, but Ahalya was the virtual ruler and was much respected by the Peshwa because of her just administrative qualities. She also won some battles. She organised a regiment of women when her son died and sent word to Raghoba, the uncle of the ruling Peshwa: "It seems that you want to meet me in the field. I am prepared. I am but a woman, and it will not add to your glory even if I am defeated. But think of the consequences in case the reverse happens." Raghoba changed his mind and instead sent a message of condolence to her and no longer looked for a male heir.

Ahalya's life was not a happy one in husband or children. Her son went mad and her daughter committed Suttee on the funeral pyre of her husband. This final shock made Ahalya retire to a life of great austerity until she died in 1795. Sir John Malcolm writing about her says: "The success of Ahalya Baee in the internal administration of her domains was altogether wonderful . . . In the most sober view that can be taken of her character, she certainly appears, within her limited sphere, to have been one of the purest and most exemplary rulers that ever existed."[21]

Muslim Women

The splendour of Mughal architecture, especially the Taj will always recall the great character of Muslim women in India, and the power they wielded, with their virtue and devotion and beauty, over their husbands, whether they were mighty emperors or mere Muslim citizens of India. Though Muslim historians, due to the habit of keeping women in the background, have highlighted the deeds of men more than women, the gracious Mughal Queens and the activities of women, political, cultural and social, despite being kept in strict purdah, will always be remembered.

Muslims, despite believing that the women's place is in her home, did not actually relegate them to an inferior position, and benevolent peace-loving rulers like Akbar even tried to unite Hindus and Muslims and went to the extent of allowing their Princes to marry Hindu princesses. Jodha Bai was the Hindu wife of Akbar and he built her a separate palace in Fatehpur Sikri. It is a double storey edifice and the Emperor was so broad-minded that Hindu architecture and ornamental carvings are noticed in the palace.

Muslims are said to hold women in sacred trust in the *harim* or *hiram,* and they have to be protected from the common gaze of mankind, and they are also not permitted much publicity, though the mausoleums built in honour of their queens are eternal public monuments. But Muslims even went to the extent of not mentioning the names of women and reference was made to a woman as the daughter, wife or sister of a person and praise was given with such words as *ismat panah* the refuge of innocence or *iffat ma'ab* the asylum of chastity and so on. This reticence is followed in the opposite direction by Indian women, when they consider a husband's name as too sacred to be pronounced by them, and usually refer to them as "Oh" or "Ogo" or him or the father of a woman's son or daughter.

Despite the hush-hush attitude of Muslim men towards their women, many have stood out prominently as dynamic characters, especially those of Turkish or Mongol origin who were not Syeds, Lodis or Surs. They were monads and a pastoral people and enjoyed much more freedom than their Arab sisters. In fact, they were equals with men and were also skilled in warfare. Thus despite the practice of polygamy, women were not only respected but wielded a strong position at home and in their society. Polygamy being recognised as a known and ancient custom was also tolerated by women themselves, and co-wives often behaved as sisters. This custom is also true of Hindu wives, and there is a story of two queens of Tangore who decided simultaneously when their husband died to commit Suttee on his funeral pyre. They lay on either side of the corpse and held hands across the dead body of their lord and were burnt with him. They were both considered as saints who had reached Moksha after their immolation. It was never the custom of Muslim women to commit Suttee.

Among famous Muslim queens of India Raziya Sultana, the daughter of Iltutmish, a slave king actually occupied the throne of Delhi. Though the nobles and subjects of the king objected, Iltutmish nominated her as his queen and preferred her to his sons who were in his opinion, not suitable to become his successors. Raziya was educated, well-read in the Koran, and highly courageous for she had often accompanied her father in his campaigns. Firishta says: "The men of discernment could find no defect in her except that she was created in the form of a woman."[22]

Iltutmish died in A.D. 1236 and despite his wishes the Turkish subject set one of his sons on the throne. But he was too gentle and too fond of pleasures. The nobles then placed Raziya on the throne. She began to reign in the same year as her father's death and overcoming the trammels of purdah, she held open court in her palace. Some nobles still gave her trouble but she succeeded in routing the rebels and ruled in peace for a while. When she placed an Abyssinian slave, Yakut in a high office, the revolt against her was too strong. Raziya was taken prisoner and her brother was proclaimed Sultan of Delhi. Still, Raziya fought and married her captor and marched out to capture her throne. But she was defeated and was finally murdered together with her husband in 1240. Her three and a half years of rule were benign and a history writes: "Nobody could point out any mistake committed by her." She was buried in a mousoleum called Bulbuli Khana in Delhi.

Gulbadan Begum (Princess Rose Body)

Gulbadan Begum was talented daughter of Babur, a worthy sister of Humayun and the most honourable paternal aunt of Akbar. She immortalised her name by authoring 'Humayun Namah', a valuable record of events that took place in the reign of Humayun. She was born in 1523 A.D. to Dildar Begum.[23] In 1525 A.D. when Gulbadan was about two years old (shortly before her father left Kabul) she was adopted by Babur's most favourite wife, Maham Begum who brought up and educated her. Gulbadan herself tells us, 'I was two years old when Her Highness, my lady took me into her own house and cared for me'.[24] Before 1519 A.D. Maham Begum was deeply shocked by the death of four children, younger than Humayun, and, so, adopted Dildar's two children—Hindal (1525 A.D.) and Gulbadan (1525 A.D.). Thus latter's initial education started under the supervision of Maham Begum, the chief lady of Babur's household. 'She was supreme and had well defined rights over other inmates',[25] writes Gulbadan in 'Humayun Namah'. This is the second evidence of her age. In 1528 A.D. when Gulbadan was six years old, she came to Hindustan from Kabul alongwith Maham Begum and met Babur. She expressed her joy by writing, 'I got into my litter and went and paid my duty to my royal father. I fell at his feet; he asked me many questions, and took me for a time in his arms, and this insignificant (she herself) person felt such happiness that greater could not be imagined'.[26]

In December 1530 A.D. Babur died. "Black fell the day for children and kins folk and all. Each passed that ill-fated day in a hidden corner". When Gulbadan was ten years of age, Maham Begum died and the stamp of orphanhood was set anew, particularly on her, who felt lonely and helpless and in great afflicton. After one year Gulbadan returned to her own mother, Dildar's charge.[27]

When Gulbadan reached the age of puberty, she was married to a Chugtai Mughal, Khizr Khwaja khan.[28] She was a worthy lady loved by her brothers deeply. After the death of

Babur and Maham Begum, Humayun always expressed her kind affection and favour and, 'spoke with such boundless compassion that she did not know she was orphaned and headless.'[29] Another brother Kamran was curious to give her more respect than her mother to which she never agreed.[30] Hearing the dreadful news of Hindal's death on 20th November 1551 A.D., Gulbadan burst into tears and cried out-Aia daregha aia daregha aia daregha, Aftabam shud nahan dar zer-i-mabagh.[31] (O well-a day! O well-a day! O well-a day! My sun is sunk behind a cloud). Gulbadan mourned her loss long by saying, 'I do not know what pitiless oppressor slew that harmless youth, with his tyrant sword I would to Heaven that merciless sword had touched my heart and eyes, or Saadatyar, my son's, or Khizr Khwaja Khan's! Alas! a hundred regrets! a thousand times alas!"[32]

During the period of Akbar her life became peaceful. Her husband Khizr Khwaja Khan was appointed as the governor of Lahore. Being an educated lady she often used her leisure hours in literary pursuits, for which she had plenty of opportunities. Akbar was very respectful to her, and her tent was always pitched beside the former's tent.[33] This helped her to a great extent in knowing the consequences of political and administrative matters of the court. Gulbadan's suggestions on different matters were regarded so valuable by Akbar that he often consulted her in political matters.[34] He was so affectionate to her that when she started her pilgrimage on 15th October 1575 A.D. Akbar was reluctant to let her go and permitted her sadly.[35] Gulbadan was then eighty years old. On 7th, February 1603 A.D., her parting was heralded by a few days of fever; Hamidah Bano was with her upto the end. As she lay with close eyes, Hamidah Bano spoke to her by the long used lovely name, *Begum Jie* (dear lady) but got no response. Abul Fazl records, "As they had long used loving expressions to one another, she repeated the endearing expression. The other lady Gulbadan Begum, opened her eyes on the blessed face of Miriam Makani and died after uttering this verse.

> *'Man zar bhar-dam umrat bada arzani'*
> (I'm weak and dying, may you live long!)

Akbar loved her, and with respect he supported her bler for some steps on his own shouldeer.[36]

Gulbadan Begum, a woman of extraordinary talents, appeared to have possessed an excellent education. She was combined with great natural gifts accompanied by a rare variety of accomplishments. She was master of several languages,[37] but well versed in Persian and Turkish.[38] She was a lady of poetic temperament.[39] As was the trend of the day, she utilised her leisure in composing beautiful poems. But unfortunately her verses have not been preserved. Only two lines of her's, in which her thought of 'no love, no fruit of life', is found.

'Her pari ru-i-ke o ba aashiq-i-khud yar nist'
Tu Yaqeen maidan ke heich az umar bar khuddar nist".[40]

Her extraordinary literary talents were expressed in the form of *'Humayun Namah',* a book of great historical imporance. It was authored on the request of Akbar himself, in order to help the compilation of the *'Akbar Namah'.*[41] *'Humayun Namah'* has no literary pretensions, even though it is of great historical significance. Besides, the contemporary socio-political life and the cultural life of the Mughals found its best expression in it. The language of the book is simple. This book provided abundant research materials for scholars, and reading material for commoners to spend the time. Therefore, Gulbadan was undoubtedly the first literary gem of the Mughal age.[42]

She had a passion for the collection of valuable books, and possessed a personal library of containing important books from different parts of the country.[43]

Bega Begum

Humayun's wife of his youth, Bega Begum, well known as Haji Begum, was a learned lady. She, for the first time, came to India after Babur's death. Gulbadan Begum says that once, during an excursion Bega Begum, due to some misunderstanding, complained to Humayun that the quarters of her's alongwith Gul-barg's was not being visited by him for long... on being heard Humayun had instructed them to write letters[44] to him if it was so felt; and she wrote for the second time at this issue and got settled the matter. Thus she was quite conversant on the technique of writing and could divert the emperor's heart at her will. Bega Begum had profound knowledge of medicine and treatment also.[45] She accompanied Humayun in the battle of Chausa but unfortunately was captured by Sher Khan. Since Timur no queen was made a prisoner, except Humayun's wife Bega Begum. But afterwards she was sent back to Humayun under the security of Sher Khan's best General, Khwas Khan.[46] After 1545 A.D. she went to Kabul with the royal family and again in 1557 A.D. she returned to India to join Akbar.

Bega Begum was very interested in patronising education, and so when she built her husband's tomb near Delhi, she founded a 'Madrasa' near it.[47] Thus she had keen interest in education from the very beginning. Akbar is stated to have been much attached to her, and respected her like a second mother. This learned lady died in 1581 A.D. shortly before Gulbadan's return from Mecca.[48]

Hamidah Bano Begum

Hamidah Bano Begum was a beautiful and worthy daughter of Hindal's precepter, Mir Baba Dost.[49] She was a highly learned lady[50] and was conversant in the art of conversation. When Humayun after seeing her in a feast sent Subhan Qull to call the *Begum,* Hamida Bano, she replied, "To see kings once is lawful, a second time it is forbidden. I shall not come".[51] She had strong character too. Gulbadan described the story of her marriage with the emperor Humayun. She informs that when Humayun offered to marry her, she refused because she opposed anyone who occupied too elevated a social position compared to her own rank. When Gulbadan suddenly said, 'Oh yes, I shall marry someone; but he shall be a man whose collar my hand can touch, and not one whose skirt it does not reach"[52] it means that, she insisted on the equality of treatment. Later on, on being satisfied she consented to the marriage and became a wife of Humayun.

Hamidah Bano Begum was renowned for her sharp understanding, warm heart and elevated emotions. She was intelligent and had deep knowledge of Islamic doctrines. 'Massir-ul-Umarah' refers to an important happening when Akbar's tutor Mullah Abdun-Nabi tore off Akbar's saffron coloured dress in open court only because it contravened Islamic rules. Akbar became furious and complained to his mother, Hamidah Bano Begm. But she hacified, "This will be a cause of salvation to you on the last day. Till the day of Resurrection they will tell how a poor Mullah dealt with the king of the age and how the king of happy augury submitted."[53]

Thus, the mother of the great Mughal Emperor Akbar was as great in her own field as her son was. Hamidah Bano Begum who was designated Maryam Makani (ranking with the blessed virgin) died on 29th August 1604 A.D. and Akbar was the first to bear her on his shoulder.[54]

Maham Anagha

Maham Anagha, the wet nurse of Emperor Akbar, was a highly educated and distinguished lady. She was the wife of Nadim Koka, and mother of Baqi and Adham Koka. Maham Anagha, by her abundant understanding and straight loyalty, had much influence over Akbar. She was retained in charge of the *harem*[55] of Akbar till her death. She was very interested in the promotion of learning, patronised education with heart and soul, and spent her money and energy on it. To promote education, she founded a *'Madrasa'* at Delhi with a mosque attached to it, and gave it the name, *'Khair-ul-Manzil',*[56] now in ruins. When she died, Akbar out of regard for her long services expressed his respect by escorting the dead body for some distance, and sent it off to Delhi with all respect where a grand building was erected over the tomb[57] in her memory.

Salima Sultan Begum

Salima Sultan Begum was another educated lady of the Mughal age. She was the grand daughter of Babur and Salha Sultan Begum. Salima's mother, Gulrurkh,[58] married to Nuruddin Mohammad Chaqaniani, was also a highly literate lady who had a poetic vein and composed a number of verses. To quote her famous verse:

> *Heechgah aan shokh gul rukhsar be aghyar nist*
> *Rast bud ast aan ke dar alam gul be khar nist.*[59]

> The roles cheeked, active beloved, never live without others. It is true that in the world there is none a rose flower without thorns.

Salima Sultan Begum attended Hindal's marriages feast[60]. In December 1557 A.D. (Safar 15, 965 A.H.) she was married to the vigorous noble Bairam Khan-i-Khanan. But after three years, when he was murdered, she remarried Akbar. About this Jahangir himself writes in his memoirs, "H.M. Humayun, by way of kindness (to Bairam), had betrothed her who was his sister's daughter to Bairam Khan... after the said Khan had been killed, my revered father married her himself',[61] although she was a few years elder to him.

Salima Sultan Begum was adorned with all good characteristics. She was a highly cultured lady, possessed good taste in Persian literature and was a composer of Persian poems, under the nom de plume of Makhfi[62] i.e. (concealed). Her famous verse runs as follows:

Kakulat ra raan-z-masti rishta-i-jan gufta um
Mast budan Zeen sabad har fe parishan gufta um.[63]

(In my passion, I called thy lock the thread of life. I was wild and so uttered such an expression).

Her collection of poems, called *'Diwan'* is of very high status and still occupies an important place in Persian literature. She was very fond of reading books, and, being a wife, she utilised Akbar's library,[64] besides her own library,[65] where there were many books written by her. This accomplished lady of versatile temperament died issueless in the seventh year of Jahangir's reign on 2nd January, 1613 A.D. (10th Zilqada 1021 A.H.)[66] and was buried in the building in Mandakar Garden, laid out by herself.

Jahangir appreciates Salima Sultan Begum in his Memoirs, both for her inborn qualities and her acquirements. She had an image of charming and cultivated lady by pleading with Akbar for Salim's forgiveness when the latter revolted against his father Akbar.[67] Abul Fazl also appreciates her by saying, "Salima... was distinguished for good qualities, purity and nobility of disposition".[68]

Jaan Begum

Jaan Begum was the most beautiful and highly learned daughter of Akbar's courtier Abdur Rahim Khan-i-Khanan, son of Bairam Khan. She was married to prince Danyal towards the closing of 1598 A.D. (1006 A.H.)[69] and became a widow in 1605 A.D. (1013 AH). She was very generous and a great patron of learned scholars. She also respected saints and *Mashaikhs.*[70] She had proficiency in the Holy *Quran,* and wrote a commentary on it[71] and was rewarded with 50,000 (fifty thousand) Dinars by Akbar.[72] Thus she was an eminent and established scholar of the faith.

Jaan Begum was a poetess too and her following verse is quoted below:

Khair ta rah brah guzar kunem,
Khuish ra chashm intazar kunem.
Za rah amn O Salamat kase be O barasad
ghubbar to na shawad khak-i-pe baru narsad.[73]

Dai Lado

Dai Lado was the wet nurse of Emperor Jahangir. She was a great patron of learning. She founded a school at Lahore, presided over by a learned scholar, named Maulvee Asmatullah.[74] Following her death, the school, with the mosque attached to it, continued to be a centre of learning and existed till the downfall of Mughal sovereignty.

Nurjahan

Nurjahan, the esteemed wife of Emperor Jahangir, a highly talented lady, was the beautiful daughter of a Persian noble man, Mirza Ghiyasuddin Beg. Being reduced to dire straits, Ghiyas proceeded towards India. On his way to India his wife Asmat Begum gave birth to a girl at Qandhar and that girl was named Mihir-un-Nisa (the sun of women). When she grew up, her name really proved true. As the sun eclipses the stars, so her charmed qualities eclipsed her contemporary women. From the very childhood, great care was taken to make her master in all spheres.[75] Her learned and highly cultured parents taught her what they could.[76] Consequently, she gained proficiency in many branches of learning, such as music, dancing, painting, sewing, cooking, decoration, riding, hunting and all fine arts.

At the age of seventeen, she was married to the governor of Bengal, Ali Quli Istajlu (later on given the title of Sher Afgan) who was also a brave soldier. After four years of the death of her first husband, Emperor Jahangir married with her in 1611 and bestowed the title of Nur Mahal (light of the palace) and then 'Nurjahan'[77] (light of the world). Nurjahan was a highly educated lady with a mind singularly gifted and able. She was clever in political matter and equally gifted in literature too. By these unique abilities she blossomed like a lovely flower, and her brain unfolded with the beauty of her appearance and figure. She was a highly cultured lady, well-versed in Persian and Arabic literature.[78] She was also an exalted poetess of beautiful verses. She composed verses in Persian under the pen name of Makhfi[79] (concealed).

A few lines of her undying verses are furnished below:

Dil basurat na dahum naushuda seerat maloom,
banda-i-ishaam wa haftad wa do millat maloom,
Zahida haufi-qiamat mu dar dil-i-ma,
hauli-i-hijran guzra na dahum qiamat maloom.[80]

> I give not my heart to form (surat) if the disposition (seerat) be known. I am a slave of (divine) love and know 72 creeds. O ascetic! cast not the terrors of the judgement day into our heart, we have lived through the terrors of the separation and so can visualize the day of judgement.

Nurjahan also patronished various contemporary renowned poets.[81] She loved books greatly and collected a fine library of rich books.[82] This beautiful Persian lady, with a quick understanding and piercing intellect, the greatest woman of her age, died in a simple white robe of widow's dress on (29th Shawwal, 1023 A.H.) i.e., 1645 A.D. and was buried in a plain tomb near Jahangir's mausoleum.[83]

Mumtaz Mahal

The lady of the Taj, Arjumand Bano Begum, well known as Mumtaz Mahal, was the favourite wife of Shah Jahan. She was the daughter of Yamin-ud-daulah Asaf Khan and niece of Nurjahan. She was an accomplished lady with a graceful counterance. Singularly gifted and highly educated, she was trained in the arts of music and painting. She acquired proficiency in Persian and Arabic literature.[84] She also had a poetic vein and composed Persian poems.[85] Mumtaz, a lady of etiquettes with political genius and administrative skill, often assisted her husband in the tough task of administering the empire.[86]

Being a great patron of learning, she helped many scholars, poets and learned men. She was the mother of fourteen children and always careful about their proper education.[87] She was a generous and pious lady, and often passed her afternoon in charitable works alongwith her husband. This dear and clever consort of Shahjahan was the only lady, the world held, always accompanying him both in war and peace. She undertook her last journey, in childbed, in her 39th year, leaving behind seven alive children and a husband madly in love with her. On 7th July, 1631 A.D. she was buried temporarily in the garden of Zainabad.[88] Subsequently her body was removed and buried in the Taj, built in her honour, as desired by her.

Sati-un-Nisa

Sati-un-Nisa, a learned Persian lady, was the sister of a renowned poet, Talib Amuli, who received the title of Malikhush-Shearai (king of poets). She was the wife of poet Nasira, the brother of Hakim Rukna Kashi.[89] She belonged to a family of scholars and fortunately joined the service of Mumtaz Mahal.[90] As she was gifted with an eloquent tongue and a knowledge of etiquette and house keeping; she advanced beyond other servants, and reached the rank of Muhardar[91] (Seal Keeper). For her charming etiquettes, versatility, talents, higher education and profound literary taste, she was appointed instructress to princess Begum Sahib.[92] Sati-un-Nisa was learned in Persian and Arabic. She was not only a good reciter of the Holy *Quran,* but knew it by heart[93] *(Hafiza).* She possessed a political faculty and was renowned as 'the princess of poets'.[94] She acquired proficiency in Persian and could throughly follow Persian prose and poetry.[95] She was also the master of medicine and treatment, as she belonged to a family of physicians.[96] After the death of Mumtaz-uz-amani (Mumtaz Mahal) Shahjahan, who was a great admirer of her merits, made her Sadr-un-Nisa,[97] (female *Nazir* of the *harem*). Being childless, she, after Talib Amul's death, adopted his two daughters.[98] She died on 27th Zil Hijja, i.e., in 1056 A.H.[99] Shahjahan gave Rs. 10,000 for her funeral and burial expenses and ordered to keep her body in a temporary grave, for the time being. After a year it was transferred to Agra and re-buried at price of Rs. 30,000 in a tomb in the west of the sepulchre of the Mahad Aliya (Mumtaz Mahal) in the Jailankhana Chauk. A village yielding 3,000 Rupees per annum was allotted to meet the expenses incurred for the upkeep of the tomb.[100]

Jahan Ara Begum or Begum Sahib

Jahan Ara Begum, a most lovely, generous, open minded and charitable lady, was the eldest daughter of Emperor Shahjahan. She was born on 1st April 1614 A.D. (21st Safar 1023 A.H.)[101] and was very wise and interested in the pursuit of learning. For her education, Shahjahan appointed a highly educated body as her governess, Sati-un-Nisa. Under her supervision Jahan Ara was taught the Holy *Quran* and Persian, and soon she acquired proficiency[102] in them. She was genius in poetry[103] wonderful for its simplicity and humility, which runs thus.

Beghair sabza na poshad kase mazar mera,
ke qabr posh ghariban hamin geyah bas ast.

Let not any person cover my tomb with anything other than earth and grass, for they are best fitted for the graves of the poor.

This epitaph can still be seen on her grave near the tomb of Nizamuddin Auliya in Delhi. In the area of prose she immortalized her name by writing 'Munis-ul-Arwah',[104] a biography of the Saint Khwaja Muln-uddin Chishti, buried at Ajmer. She also authored Sahabiyah,[105] the life of Mulla Shah Badakhshi, her spiritual *pir.*

Jahan Ara Begum was also a patron of learning and encouraged various scholars and fixed allowances and stipends for them.[106] Mirza Mohammad Ali Jauhar, a famous poet, has written a 'Masnavi' praising Jahan Ara,[107] which radiated her personality. Jahan Ara awarded him five hundred rupees for his one verse which she liked fervently. It runs thus :

Bzat-e-sifat Kard yar ast
Ke Khud Pinhan wa faiz-ash ashkar ast.[108]

Here the poet compared her generosity to the bounty of God. Once, when she was burnt seriously, Haji Mohammad

Khan Quddusi wrote a 'Qasidah' related to the incidence. Jahan Ara had given him five thousand rupees for this one verse, which was as follows:

> *Ta Sarz ala Haz shama chini be adbi*[109]
> *Parwana za Ishque shama ra sokhta ast.*

She liked history[110] and loved songs very much.[111] She was witty and generous and elevated to the rank of the first lady of the realm, 'Padshah Begum'.[112] She had deep interest in constructive works, and built a *Madrasa* at Agra, attached to the Jami Masjid.[113] In Kashmir, Masjid Mulla Badakhshi[114] was constructed by her. This highly cultured lady died at the age of seventy,[115] having done a lot of praiseworthy work.

Zabinda Begum

Zabinda, an accomplished lady, was Shahjahan's fourth daughter. Like other contemporary princesses, she had poetical talents. She wrote many contemporary of poems mystical in nature.[116] The poems are of a very high order, and still very interesting for readers.

Hafiza Maryam

Hafiza Maryam, an educated lady, was the mother of a high ranking noble man, inayat-ullah Khah.[117] She was the wife of Mirza Shukrullah of Kashmir. She was a highly educated lady and knew the Holy *Quran* by heart, that's why she has been called Hafiza. She was also famous for the art of reciting the Holy *Quran* attractively. The flavour of her good characteristics reached Aurangzeb gradually, and being impressed by her, he appointed her the tutor of his daughter Zebun-Nisa.[118] "From her, Zebun-Nisa learnt to commit to memory the words of God and the practice of the accomplishments'.[119]

She undoubtedly had a good image for her piety, otherwise she would not have got a place in the palace of Aurangzeb, who was quite a religious man. Thus she had mastery over the *Quran* as well as *Ahadis* (tradition), which made her a suitable teacher for Zeb-un-Nisa.

Zeb-un-Nisa

Zeb-un-Nisa was the eldest daughter of Aurangzeb and Dil-ras Bano Begum. She saw the first light of the universe on

15th February, 1638 A.D. (1047 A.H.).[120] Zebun-Nisa (one of the loveliest ladies of the age) inherited a good intellect from her father, and from her very childhood she showed remarkable symptoms of literary pursuits. Aurangzeb himself guided her learning. She was also taught by a number of tutors. Her first tutor was Roshan-Ara Begum.[121] Very soon Aurangzeb appointed a highly gifted and trained governess, Hafiza Maryam, for her. According to the Muslim custom, Hafiza Maryam first taught her the Holy *Quran*.[122] Consequently Zeb-un-Nisa mastered the Holy *Quran* and recited it to her father when she was only seven years old. Aurangzeb was ecstatic at this and offered her thirty thousand gold *mohars*, as a reward for her diligence.[123] A feast was arranged, and all the public offices remained closed for two days.[124] Between the age of eight and twelve she studied Arabic and became proficient in it. Later on Shah Rustum Ghazi, [125] an eminent scholar, was appointed as her teacher. Aurangzeb's former teacher, Mulla Jiwan, also guided her for some time.[126] Under his instruction, Zeb-un-Nisa was taught a number of books, and became master of Persian and Arabic prose and poetry. In her twenty first year Aurangzeb appointed Mulla Sayyed Ashraf Mazandrani as her tutor. She acquired proficiency in theology and also cultivated a taste for poetry under him.[127] In the beginning she tried her hand at Arabic and wrote a *'Qasidah'* but later on she began composing verses in Persian and proved a renowned poetess. A picture of the princess Zeb-un-Nisa is available in the Central Museum of Lahore, which can be seen even now. She has been shown in beautiful black garments and seated on a marble floor, busy in writing. The Ganges has been shown flowing at her back. Zeb-un-Nisa composed her verses under the pen name of *'Makhfi'* (concealed) like Nurjahan and Salima Sultan Begum. But Diwan-i-Makhfi, a beautiful collection of verses, is wrongly believed to be written by Zeb-un-Nisa. It is a general opinion that the author of Diwan-i-Makhfi, was a Persian poet from Khurasan who came to India during the reign of Shahjahan.[128] As for Zeb-un-Nisa, she was undoubtedly herself a poetess and had a fine collection of her own verses, but unluckily her book of poetry drowned in a tank when it slipped from her servant Iradat Faham.[129] The treasure was thus lost and only the memory remains. A few verses of persian are stated to be hers.

Tr. When from my cheek I lift my veil
The roses turn with envy pale
And from their pierced hearts, rich with pain,
Send forth their trangrance like a wail,
Or if per chance one perfumed trees
Be lowered to the wind's caress
The honeyed hyacinths complain,
And I languish in a sweet distress,
And when I pause, still groves among
(such loveliness is mine)
a throng of nightingales awake and strain
Their souls into a quivering song.[130]

Zeb-un-Nisa was quite conversant in letter writing, and a collection of her letters known as *'Zeb-ul-Manshaat'*[131] was seen by the author of *'Tazki-rat-ul-Gharaio'* himself.[132] Aurangzeb praised the sweet literary style of her letters.[133] She was fond of the art of calligraphy and, with the help of expert calligraphists of the age, she acquired proficiency in it. She could write correctly *'nastaliq', 'naskh'* and *'shikastah.'*[134] Her entire brain was centred on studying the leading books of the age, and she achieved mastery in Mathematics, Astronomy, History and Law.[135]

Being fond of administrative laws, she was often consulted or judicial and criminal cases by officers of the imperial court, and her deep knowledge of different codes never let her refer to any book,[136] for confirmation.

Being a great patron of learning she encouraged several erudites poets, pious men, writers, scribes, artists, and calligraphists[137] and the like. A special department was founded by her for translation of classical books and writing original works. She spent Mullah Safluddin Ardbeli to Kashmir, where he translated 'Tafsir-i-Kabir', the commentary on the Holy *Quran,* from Arabic to Persian, written by Imam Fakhruddin Razi, and entitled it *'Zeb-ut-Tafasir',*[138] in the name of Zebs-un-Nisa. She enjoyed publishing the works of leading scholars, poets and authors and also rewarded them according to their merits.[139] She had a scriptorium and a big personal library. The author of *'Maasir-i-Alamgiri'* praises it much and says, 'that the like of it was never seen before'.

"Dar Sarkar Elaih Kitab khana gard
amda bud ke ba nazar-i-hech yake dar neyamda bashad"[140]

This library contained books on various disciplines, *viz.* History, Literature, Law and Religion (Islam); and she used to pens several hours everyday in their study and none could disturb her during the course of study.

Zeb-un-Nisa was keenly interested in *'Mushairah'* (poetical competition), and often arranged it in her palace, and she herself relaxed behind a screen.[141] She led a pious, long unmarried life and refused to marry any one, even though her father Aurangzeb was eager to marry her with Farrakh,[142] a handsome prince of Persia. He was not able to answer the questions put to him despite the fact that he was also a very good scholar of the age. Moreover, the choice might be with her father Aurangzeb, who might have wanted an ideal person, suiting his daughter's status and qualifications. It is but natural for a well-versed lady to have married a handsome man of her own rank and ability, if available. Certain princes and scholars were brought before her, but none was found suitable.

Bernier and Tavernier have, however, tried to prove that she did not marry throughout her life, because, she had fallen in love with someone disliked by Aurangzeb. But Persian and other sources do not confirm this. Had the story of her love been true, it would have been refined to by Khafi Khan or other writer. Moreover, Aurangzeb was so orthodox that he would have undoubtedly punished his daughter, Zeb-un-Nisa.

Zeb-un-Nisa led a pious life without marriage and died on 26th May, 1702 A.D. at the age of sixty four, and was buried in Delhi.[143] When this news reached Aurangzeb, he was deeply shocked and under his command a tomb for her was constructed,[144] but it has since been demolished for railway lines (construction).

"Dokhtar-i-Shaham wa lekin ru ba foqar awardaam.
Zeb-o-Zeenat bas hamin num nam-i-man Zeb-un-Nisa ast,[145] said she of herself.

Tr: I am the daughter of am emperor, yet I have set my face towards poverty. This is what adorns my beauty and my name is Zeb-un-Nisa (the adorned of women).

Zinat-un-Nisa

Zinat-un-Nisa, the second daughter of Aurangzeb, was also a highly cultured lady. She saw the light of the world in Oct. 1643 A.D.[146] She was the daughter of Dild-ras Bano Begum. From her very childhood, her learned father had taught her under his strict supervision. Consequently she acquired proficiency in Islamic doctrines.[147] She composed poems.[148] One of her poems in Persian runs thus:

Tr: "In my grave the grace of God is my only help. It is enough if the shadow of the colour of mercy covers my tomb".[149]

Besides, being leading scholar of the faith, she was famous for her generosity and charity. Like other princesses of the Mughal age, she also encouraged erudites and fixed scholarships for them.[150] She was styled *'Begum Sahiba',* after the accession of Bahadur Shah.[151] She died at the age of eighty (80) on 18th May 1721 A.D.[152]

She belonged to a group of learned scholars and possessed a poetical vision. Her name appears in various texts, where her virtues have been frequently reerred to.

Badr-un-Nisa

Badr-un-Nisa, the third daughter of Aurangzeb and Nawab Bai, was born on 17th November 1647 A.D.[153] She was less educated than her sisters.[154] Under the guidance of her father, she memorised the Holy *Quran*.[155] She was loved by Aurangzeb for her marvellous character, eti quettes and kind heartedness.

She had more inclination towards religion, which became deeper, when she memorised the Holy *Quran* and simultaneously when she attained the age of maturity. She was less inclined towards spheres of education other than religion, and was distinguished only because of this, her father loved her deeply. Badr-un-Nisa died in April 1670 A.D. in the 13th year of her father's rule.[156]

Bibi Waliya

Bibi Waliya, educationally a highly accomplished and pious lady,[157] was the daughter of Syed Shah Azizuddin Amjhari. She was married to Shah Makhdoom and became the mother of Shah Aitullah Jauhari, a renowned saint of his age.

Bibi Waliya had command over three languages *viz.* Urdu,

Persian and Arabic. She composed verses in Urdu and Persian and had great interest in mysticism. Above all, she is better known as a mystic rather than a poetess, and acquired, by dint of her labour, a prominent place among contemporary mystics, and is still remembered.

Two lines of her famous *Qasidah* (ode), composed in praise of Maulana Mohammad Waris Rasulnuma Banarsi, in Persian, runs thus:

Na danam ke roz mahshar che bashad
Ke jurm wa gunaham guzasht ast az had.

In addition, two verses in urdu are also available:

Kaun Sati tadbeer batawen
Un apne kan hamko bolawen
Hazrat ki deorhi jo pawan
Sheer jhuka ke ankh lagawen.[158]

Her compositions, have been preserved in some personal libraries, in Phulwari Sharif (Bihar), can be seen even now.

Bibi Walia, died in 1139 A.H. and was laid to rest in the dust of Bihar to which she belonged, and will be remembered for long.

Begum Jiu

Begum Jiu, the daughter of Prince Mohammad Akbar, and the wife of prince Khujistea Akhtar, was a highly educated lady. A lady tutor from Ajmer was appointed to instruct her in Islamic scriptures. Under her tution, Begum Jiu, not only recited the Holy *Quran* efficiently, but also committed it to memory.[159] She died of temperature on 1st July 1699 A.D. and was buried at Mangalvir (north Bijapur), in a tomb, built for Rs. 420.[160]

Sheikh Rangrezin

Sheikh Rangrezin belonged to the dyer class. She had extraordinary characteristics, possessed great poetic talent, and composed mostly romantic verses.[161] Her poems were in the Braj dialect of Hindi. A Brahmin heard about her and being impressed, he embraced Islam and married her.

Mehri Hervi

Mehri Hervi, the wife of Khawaja Hakim, was one of

Nurjahan's accomplices and a well-known poetess.[162] Sher Khan has preserved these lines of her poems.

Hai her nukta ke bar fir khird Mushkil bud
Azmudem baik qatrah mi hasil bud
Khwastam soz dil khulsh bagoem ba shamaa
Dasht to Khud bar zoban ancha mera dar dil bud
Dar Chaman subh dam az kirya o az zardi mun
Lalai-sokhta khun dar dil-o-pa dar kul bud.[163]

Tuni Atun

Tuni Atun, the wife of Mulla Baqa was a great poetess of her age.[164] Her husband was also a poet and sometimes held poetical contests between each other. Once when Mulla said these verses:

Yaran-i-sitam pirah zani kisht mera
Kaw ek shuda chuni az wa Pusht mera
Kar pusht ba su-i-o-darai khwab kunem
bedar kunad bazarab angusht mera

Tuni Atun wrote in answer the verses:

Ham Khwabki mast ruki kisht mera
rozi-banud az bajuz pusht mera
quwat-i-pokhtankah Patu and bardasht
behtar bud az pusht was musht mera.[165]

Shirin

Shirin was a dancing girl of Lucknow, being well-versed in poetry. She composed poems both in Urdu and Persian and one of her Persian verses is as follows:

Tr. 'Do not count me among good people'
I know what I am
Do not entertain good thoughts of me
I am a prisoner of my treacherous passion
and am full of song.
This is no lie
I know what am I.[166]

Besides these ladies, Shahjahan's daughter Roshan Ara, Aurangzeb's daughter Zubdatun-Nisa, Sahebji, the daughter of

Ali Mardan Khan, wife of Amir Khan Mir Miran were other educated Muslim women of the time. Besides, the mother of Hafiz Draz Peshawari during the time of Akbar, was a highly accomplished and pious lady.[167]

To conclude, the Muslim fair sex, was not completely absent in the field of literary pursuits. The ladies of the royalty and the nobility, and several middle class girls, possessed an inclination for learning and acquired education. But education for the poorer women was mostly limited to the study of the Holy *Quran.*

On the other hand, the education of the great mass of women living in rural areas, was quite unsatisfactory, as they had no time being too busy with their routine livelihood, and also for want of teachers. But the village women were not entirely uneducated. There were well-to-do people in rural areas too, who could afford the teaching of the *Quran* and its regulations to avoid ignorance of their religion.

Highly educated ladies, belonged to the royalty and nobility, their number being not very large, but they acquired great fame in the fields of Arts, Law, Theology, Maths and the live. Some of the ladies surpassed their male contemporaries in the matter of education. And therefore, they have often been consulted in political as well as administrative matters, which is a historical fact.

Despite the *'purdah'* system and absence of liberal facility in regard to education, their performance was appreciably high, despite numerous hindrances in the pursuits of learning. On the whole, the contribution of Muslim ladies towards education has been great.

References

1. *Indian Women through the Ages,* p. 241
2. *Indian Women through the Ages,* p. 241.
3. Khuda Bux, *Studies Indian and Islamic* quoted in *Indian Women through the Ages,* p. 249.
4. *Ibid.,* p. 249.
5. *Indian Women through the Ages,* p. 263.
6. *Great Women of India,* p. 335.
7. *Poems by Indian Women,* p. 47.
8. *Poems by Indian Women,* p. 59.

9. "Shady places where all evil blossoms; snares that trap, as a deer is trapped, minds blinded with passion; weapons wielded by the deceiving emissaries of Desire: how can the wise have confidence in women?" *Ibid.,* p. 71.
10. *Mira Bai* by Usha S. Nilsson, p. 11.
11. *Ibid.,* p. 11.
12. *Ibid.,* p. 3.
13. *Ibid.,* p. 14.
14. *Ibid.,* p. 14.
15. Rama is Hari and is often identified with Krishna.
16. *Poems by Indian Women,* p. 59.
17. *Mira Bai* by Usha S. Nilsson in 'Makers of Indian Literature' Series, p. 16.
18. *Poems by Indian Women,* p. 56.
19. *Narada Bhakti Sutra* 63. Quoted in *Bhaktiyoga,* pp. 40, 41.
20. *The Oxford History of India* by Vineent A. Smith, p. 172.
21. Quoted in *Great Women of India,* pp. 360, 361.
22. Quoted in *Great Women of India,* p. 381.
23. Gulbadan's *Humayun Namah,* Introduction by Mrs. Bev. pp. 1-2.
24. *Ibid.,* Persian, p. 30; also Tr. (Bev.), 116.
25. *Ibid.,* Introduction by Mrs. Bev., p. 9.
26. *Ibid.,* Pers. pp. 18-19; also Tr. (Bev.) p. 102.
27. Humayun Namah, Pers. p. 30; Tr. p. 117.
28. Gulbadan's *Humayun Namah* Pers. p. 98, Tr. (Bev.) p. 199; Shah Nawaz Khan, *Maasir-ul-Umara,* Vol. I, also Abul Fazl's *Akbar Namah,* Tr. Vol. I, p. 466; Fn. 2; also Vol. II, p. 50, Fn. 2, also Badaoni, *Muntakhab-ut-Twarikh,* Vol. II (Lowe) p. 7.
29. *Humayun Namah,* Pers. p. 26; also Tr. (Bev.) p. 111; *"Khwateen"* (Urdu) edited by Md. Aslam, Delhi, 1951, p. 187.
30. *Humayun Namah,* Pers. p. 98; also Tr. (Bev.) p. 199;
31. (Urdu) edited by Md. Aslam, Delhi, 1951, p. 187.
32. *Ibid.* Tr. pp. 198-199.
33. *Humayun Namah,* Introduction by Mrs. Bev. p. 67.
34. *Khwateen,* p. 188.
35. *Ibid.,* p. 189.
36. *Akbar Namah,* Vol. III, Tr. (Bev) p. 1226.
37. B. K. Sahay, *Education and Learning Under the Great Mughals,* p. 130.
38. *Humayun Namah,* Introduction by Mrs. Bev. p. 79; *Bazm Taimuria* ed. by Sayyed Shahabuddin Abdur Rahman, p. 436.
39. Ahmad Ali Hashimi, *Makhzan-ul-Gharaib,* Pers. Ms. B.O.P.L. p. 739.
40. Ali Hasan Khan bin Nawab Siddique Hasan Khan, *Subh-i-Gulshan* (Taz-kirah Pers.) p. 348.

41. Gulbadan's *Humayun Namah,* Introduction by Mrs. Bev. pp. 76 and 78; also N. N. Law, *Promotion of Learning,* p. 201; *Bazm Taimurla,* pp. 436-347; *Khwateen,* p. 190; *Maqalat-i-Shibli,* Vol. IV ed. by Sayyed Sulaiman Nadvi, Azam Garh, 3rd edn. 1956, p. 59.
42. S.M. Jaffar, *Education in Muslim India,* p. 193.
43. Gulbadan's *Humayun Namah,* Introduction by Mrs. Bev., p. 76; S.M. Jaffar, *Education in Muslim India,* p. 193; N. N. Law, *Promotion of learning,* p. 201; Dr. Keay, *Indian Education in Ancient and Later Times,* p. 80; also Shelat's *Akbar* Vol. II, (Pub. by Bhartiya Vidya Bhawan, Bombay, 1st edn. 1959) p. 341.
44. Gulbadan Begum, Humayun Namah, Pers. p. 38.
45. Abul Fazl, *Akbar Namah,* Vol. III, Tr. (Bev) pp. 107-108.
46. Gulbadan Begum *Humayun Namah,* Tr. (Bev.) Appendix A. p. 219.
47. S.K. Banerjee, *Humayun Badshah,* Vol. II, p. 317.
48. *Gulbadan Begum, op. cit.* p. 220.
49. *Humayun Namah, pers.* p. 52; also (*Tr.* p. 149.)
50. K.M. Ashraf, *Life and Conditions of the People of Hindustan,* p. 243; also Yusuf Hussain, *Glimpses of Medieval Indian Culture,* p. 92.
51. Gulbadan, *Humayun Namah,* Pers. Tr. p. 151.
52. *Ibid.*
53. Shah Nawaz Khan, *Maasir-ul-Umara,* Vol. I Tr. p. 42.
54. Abul Fazl, *Akbar Namah,* Vol. III, Tr. p. 1245.
55. Shah Nawaz Khan, *Maasir-ul-Umara,* Vol. I, Tr. p. 146; also Abul Fazl, *Akbar Namah,* Vol. II, Tr. (Bev) p. 86.
56. Abul Fazl, *Akbar Namah,* Vol. II, Tr. (Bev.) p. 313; also Badaoni, *Muntakhab-ul-Twarikh,* Vol. II, Tr. (Lowe) p. 62; Shelat, *Akbar,* Vol. II 1st edn. p. 341; also *Islamic Culture,* Vol. 30, 1956; also Carr Stephensen's *Archaeological and monumental remains of Delhi* (1876) p. 200; also *Bazm Talmuriah* (Urdu) p. 441, also S.K. Banerjee, *Humayun Badshah,* Vol. II, 324.
57. Shah Nawaz Khan, *Maasir-ul-Umara,* Vol. I, Tr. p. 148.
58. *Tuzk-i-Jahangiri,* Vol. I, Tr. (R and B) p. 232.
59. *Bazm Taimuriah* (Urdu) p. 439; also *Subh-i-Gulshan,* p. 348.
60. Gulbadan Begum, *Humayun Namah,* Pers. edited by Mrs. Beve. p. 32.
61. *Tuzk-i-Jahangiri,* Vol. I, Tr. (R and B) p. 232.
62. Shah Nawaz Khan, *Maasir-ul-Umara,* Vol. I, Tr. p. 371; also Abul Fazl, *Ain-i-Akbari* (Bloch) p. 322; also Mutamid Khan, *Iqbal Nama-i-Jahangiri* Tr. (Urdu) p. 73.
63. Shah Nawaz Khan, *Ibid.,* also Mutamid Khan, *Ibid.* also quoted in Maulvi Mohammad Hussain Azad's *Darbar-i-Akbari* (1921)

Lahore, p. 736; also Kausar Chandpuri's *Md. Bairam Khan Turkaman* (Urdu), p. 105.

64. Badaoni, *Muntakhab-ul-Twarikh,* Vol. II, Tr. (Lowe) p. 389.
65. *Bazm Taimuriah* (Urdu) p. 440.
66. *Makhzan-ul-Gharaib,* M.S.B. p. 739.
67. Tuzk-i-Jahangiri, Vol. I, Tr. (R and B) p. 232.
68. *Ibid.,* p. 233; also Gulbadan Begum, *Humayun Namah,* Tr. appendix-A, p. 279.
69. Abul Fazl, *Akbar Namah,* Vol. III, Tr. (Bev.) p. 1223.
70. *Ibid.,* Vol. II, Tr. (Bev), p. 98.
71. Abul Fazl, *Ain-i-Akbari,* Vol. I, (Bloch) p. 322.
72. *Bazm Talmuriah* (Urdu) p. 442.
73. *Ibid.*
74. A.M.A. Shustry, *Outlines of Islamic Culture, (Bangalore,* Pub. in 1950) p. 589; also Chopra, *Society and Culture during the Mughal age,* p. 124.
75. Quoted in *Bazm Taimurian,* ed. by Sayyed Subah-uddin (Urdu) p. 442.
76. L.M. Bhagi, *Medieval Indian Culture and Thought,* p. 353.
77. *Introducing India,* Pt. I Published by R.A.S.B. Calcutta, 1947, Art No. 9; p. 90; also Robert Counter, *Nurjahan and Jahangir* (1950); p. 11; also Allexander Dow, *The History of Hindustan,* Vol. III, p. 22.
78. Beni Prasad, *History of Jahangir,* p. 149; it refers that Nurjahan got intelligency in heredity as her father Mirza Ghiyas was a man of learning and culture, a charming letter writer and a brilliant conversationist; also *Introducing India* Part I, 1947, p. 90; *Bazm Taimuriah,* p. 443; also Sunity Devi, *The Beautiful Mughal Princesses,* p. 92.
79. Major David Price's Tr. *Memoirs of Emperor Jahangir,* (London, 1829) p. 27; *Iqbal Nama-i-Jahangiri* (Urdu) p. 62 Francis Gladwin, *The History of Jahangir* (1930) p. 51 also Beni Prasad, History of Jahangir, p. 150.
80. *Tuzuk-i-Jahangiri,* Vol. I, Tr. (R and B) p. 319; also *Iqbal Nama-i-Jahangiri* (Urdu), p. 63; also *della Valle,* Vol. I, pp. 53-54; Peter Mundy Vol. II, pp. 205-206, Bernier Tr. (Urdu), p. 38.
81. *Chahar Gulshan,* Ms, By Chittraman Kayath, Azad Library, Aligarh University, F16a; also S.M. Jaffar, Education in Muslim India, p. 194 also Beni Prasad, *Few Aspects of Education and Literature under the Great Mughals* (I.H.R.C., Vol. V, 1923, p. 48; also Beni Prasad, *History of Jahangir,* p. 158; Robert Counter, *Nurjahan and Jahangir,* p. 84. *Khawateen* edited by Md. Aslam (Urdu) p. 199; Moulana Sadique, *Tarikh-i-Hind* (Urdu) p. 542, also *Edwar and Garett, Mughal rule in India,* p. 160; N.N. Law, *Promotion of*

learning, p. 202; *The nineteenth century,* 1899, p. 756 (Article by Justice Amir Ali).

82. Khafi Khan, *Muntakhab-ul-Lubab,* Vol. I, Tr. p. 270-271; also Shahnawaz Khan's *Maasir-ul-Umrah,* Tr. Vol. II, Part II, p. 1079. Makhfi was also the nomde plume of other Mughal royal ladies such as Salima Sultan Begum and Zebun Nisa who composed poems. For her talent of composing poem, refer to Sher Khan's *Maraatul-Kheyal,* Pers. p. 128.
83. Shahnawaz Khan, *Massir-ul-Umara,* Tr. Vol. II, part II, p. 1079; also Khafi Khan, *Muntakhab-ul-Lubab,* Vol. I Tr. p. 270; also *Marat-ul-kheyal,* Pers. p. 532; also *Bazm Talmuria* (Urdu), p. 445.
84. *Bazm Talmuriah* (Urdu) p. 445.
85. Lahori, *Badshah Namah,* Vol. II, p. 475; also Shah Nawaz Khan, *Maasir-ul-Umara,* Vol. II, Part II. p. 1079.
86. *Tuzk-i-Jahangiri* Tr. Vol. I, p. 224; also Mutamid Khan, *Iqbal Nama-i-Jahangiri,* Tr. (Urdu), p. 72; also *Padshah Namah,* Vol. I, p. 388.
87. D. C. Sen, *"Virhat Banga",* Vol. II, pub. by Cal. Univ. (B. S. 1342) 1st ed. p. 823; also Edward and Garrett, *Mughal rule in India,* p. 160.
88. *Bazm Talmuriah* (Urdu), p. 447; also S. M. Jaffar, *Education in Muslim India,* p. 195; also Beni Prasad, *A few Aspects of Education and Literature Under the Great Mughals* (IHRC, Vol. V. 1923).
89. I. N. Choudhary, Mumtaz Mahal', *Journal of Islamic Culture,* Hyderabad, Vol. XI, 1937, p. 373; also G. Yazdani, 'Jahan Ara' *Journal of the Punjab Historical Society,* Vol. III, 1912, p. 153.
90. J. N. Choudhary, *Ibid.* p. 374.
91. Shah Nawaz Khan, *Maasir-ul-Umara,* Vol. I, Tr. p. 294.
92. Lahori, *Badshah Namah,* Vol. II, p. 629 also Shah Nawaz Khan, *Maasir-ul-Umara,* Vol. I, Tr. p. 260.
93. *Ibid.*
94. *Shah Nawaz Khan, Massir-ul-Umara,* Vol. I, Tr. pp. 260-261; also *Bazm Talmuriah* (Urdu), p. 448; *Jahan Ara Begum,* by Ziauddin Ahmad Yazdani, p. 4.
95. *Lahori Badshah Namah,* Vol. II, p. 629, Shah Nawaz Khan, *Maasir-ul-Umara,* Vol. I, tr. p. 261; also *Akhma-i-Alamgiri* 151-173; also *Bazm Taimuriah,* p. 443.
96. *Bazm Taimuriah* (Urdu) edited by Sayyed Sahabuddin, p. 448.
97. S.M. Jaffar, *Education in Muslim India,* p. 197; also Sarkar, *Studies in Mughal India* (Cal. 1919), p. 22.
98. Lahori, *Badshah Namah,* Vol. II, p. 629.
99. *Ibid.* also Shah Nawaz Khan, *Maasir-ul-Umara,* Vol. I, Tr. p. 261.

100. Lahori, *Badshah Namah,* Vol. II, p. 629; *Maasir-ul-Umara* Vol. I, Tr. p. 261.
101. Lahori, *Ibid., Maasir-ul-Umarah,* Vol. I, Tr. p. 261.
102. Lahori, *Badshah Namah,* Vol. II, p. 629.
103. *Ibid.,* also *Maasir-ul-Umara* Vol. I Tr. p. 261.
104. Ziyauddin Ahmad Yazdani, *Jahan Ara Begum* (Delhi, 1921) p. 3; also Mutamid Khan, *Iqbal Nama-i-Jahangiri,* Tr. (Urdu) p. 78.
105. Lahori, *Badshah Namah,* Vol. II, p. 629.
106. *Bazm Trimurlah* (Urdu) ed. by Sayyed Sahabuddin, pp. 448-452.
107. Jahan Ara Begum by Ziauddin Ahmad Barni, B. A., p. 28; *Introducing India,* Pt. I (R.A.S.B Cal. 1947) p. 102; also Sir Sayyed Ahmad Khan, *Asar-us-Sunadeed,* Kutba No. 44, p. 32; also Hearn's *Seven Cities of Delhi,* p. 116; also N. Chatterjee *The Architectural Glories of Delhi,* p. 89.
108. Manucci, *Storia,* Vol. IV, Tr. p. 423, also Vol. I Tr. p. 217; also *Introducing India* Pt. I, 1947, p. 102; also *Bazm Taimuriah* (Urdu) p. 448.
109. Refer to Sufi's *Al-Minhaj,* p. 81.
110. *Khwateen,* Edited by Md. Aslam, p. 239; also N. N. Law, *Promotion of Learning,* p. 203; also S.M. Jaffar, *Education in Muslim India,* p. 196.
111. Mohammad Wali, *Mid-hat-ul-Su'Ara.* Fol. 123, M.S. Daftar-i-Diwani wa Mulki Library, Hyderabad, also refer to *Islamic Culture,* Vol. XXXIV, 1960, Hyderabad, p. 119; also *Khwateen op. cit.* also *Bazm Taimuriah* (Urdu) p. 452.
112. Quoted in *Bazm Taimuriah* (Urdu) ed. by Sayyed Sabahuddin, p. 452.
113. *Khwateen,* edited by *Md. Aslam* (Urdu) p. 239.
114. S.M. Jaffar, *Education in Muslim India,* p. 195.
115. Manucci, *Storia Do Mogor,* Vol. I, Tr. pp. 218-219.
116. *Ibid.* Vol. II, Tr. p. 127.
117. *Introducing India,* Pt. I, Calcutta 1947, p. 101; also Islamic Culture Vol. 30, 1956, p. 117; also Husuf Hussain, *Glimpses of Medieval Indian Culture,* p. 86.
118. *Introducing India,* Pt. I, Cal. 1947, p. 102; also *Khwateen,* edited by Md. Aslam (Urdu) p. 246.
119. Sir Sayyed Ahmad Khan, Asar-us-Sanadid, pp. 290-432, Kutba No. 44. It gives date 1093 A.H. (1681 A.D.) while *Manucci's Storia,* Vol. I, p. 217. refers 1662 A.D.
120. S.M. Jaffar, *Education in Muslim India,* p. 196.
121. Shah Nawaz Khan, *Maasir-ul-Umara,* Vol. I, Tr. p. 681.
122. *Ibid.,* also Sarkar, *Studies in Mughal India,* (Cal. 1919) p. 79.
123. Shah Nawaz Khan, *Maasir-ul-Umara.* Vol. I, Tr. p. 681.
124. Ishwar Das Nagar, *Futuhat-i-Alamgir,* translated and edited

by Tasneem Ahmad, 1st pub. 1978, p. 162, fn. 30. It refers that the Text M.A. is wrong by one year to Dil-ras-Bano Begum.

125. Md. Aslam, Khwateen, p. 256.
126. *Bazm Talmuriah,* p. 455; *Maqalat-i-Shibli,* Vol. V, edited by Moulana S. Sulaiman Nadvi, Dar-ul-Mossannefeen, No. 48, second edition 1955, p. 100.
127. *Maasir-i-Alagir,* Tr. by J.N. Sarkar, 1947, p. 322; *Diwan-i-Zeb-un-Nisa* ed. by Magan Lal 1913, p. 8; *Khwateen,* p. 250, Sunity Devi. *The beautiful Mughal Princess,* p. 55; *Hist. of India,* by Illiot and Dowson, Vol. VII, p. 196; Sarkar, *Studies in Mughal India* (Cal. 1919) p. 79.
128. *Diwan-i-Zeb-un-Nisa,* ed. by Magan Lal, p. 9.
129. *Md. Aslam Khwateen,* p. 256.
130. *Bazm Talmuriah,* p. 456; *Maqalat-i-Shibli,* Vol. V, pp. 101-102; *Journals of Bihar and Orissa Research Society,* Patna, Vol. XIII, 1927; Art No. 4. p. 42; *Bihar and Orissa District Gazetteers Monghyer* by L.S.S.O. Malley I.C.S. 1926, pp. 241-242; also *Makhzanul Gharaib* Pers. Ms. O.P.L.p. 312.
131. *Journal of Bihar and Orissa Research Society,* Patna, Vol. XIII, 1827, Art. No. 4. pp. 42-53; Khan Saheb, a Maqtadir also favours it in the O.P.L. Persian Catalogue, Vol. III, pp. 250-251, also *Bazm Taimuriah* (Urdu), p. 460.
132. *Maqalat-i-Shibli,* Vol. V (Urdu) pp. 104-106.
133. *Poems by Indian Women,* edited by M. Macnicol. (Cal. 1923) p. 77.
134. *'Zeb-un-Nisa and Diwan-i-Makhfi',* by H.S. Ahmad, *Journal of Bihar and Orissa Research Society,* Vol. XIII (1927) p. 42; also *Maqaiat-i-Shibli,* Vol. Vth, p. 105.
135. *Mukhzen-ul-Gharaib,* p. 312.
136. Mir Mah, *Muraqqsi-Mir Mah.* F. 1175, Ms No. 795 Daftari-Diwani-wa Mulki Library, Hyderabad.
137. *Maasir-i-Alamgiri,* Tr by J.N. Sarkar, p. 322; also *Sarkar Studies in Aurangzeb's reign* (Cal. 1933) p. 130; also *Maqalat-i-Shibli* Vol. V, p. 104; also Khwatun (Urdu) p. 256; also *Great Women of India* edited by Swami Madhavananda and R.C. Manjumdar, Pub. by Combhira Nanoa Advada Ashram, (Almora, 1953) 1st edition p. 388.
138. *Diwan-i-Zebun-Nisa,* edited by Magan Lal, p. 8.
139. Sunity Devi, *The Beautiful Mughal Princess,* pp. 57-58; also Moulana Sadique, *Tarikh-i-Hind* (Urdu) p. 670.
140. *Mansir-i-Alamgiri,* Tr. J.N. Sarkar, p. 322; *History of India,* Vol. VII, p. 196; Sunity Devi, *The Beautiful Mughal Princess,* p. 59; N. N. Law, *Promotion of Learning,* p. 204; Aslam Khwatoon, p. 257.

141. *Maasir-i-Alamgiri,* Tr. p. 322; *Maqalat-i-Shibli,* Vol. V, p. 105, *Bazm Talmuriah,* p. 456, *Aslam's Khwatoon,* p. 258, S.M. Jaffar, *Education in Muslim India,* p. 197; Yusuf Hussain *Glimpses Medieval Indian Culture,* p. 93; *The Beautiful Mughal Princesses,* p. 59; *History of India,* by Ellict and Downson, Vol. VII, p. 196; Yusuf Hussain, *Educational system in Medieval India, Islamic Culture,* Vol. XXX 1950, p. 121, *Journal of Bihar and Orissa Research Society Patna,* Vol. XIII 1927, Art. No. 4, pp. 42-43; Sarkar, Studies in Mughal India, p. 79, also *Studies in Aurangzeb's reign,* pp. 130-31.
142. *Diwan-i-Zeb-un-Nisa,* ed. by Magan Lal, p. 13; also *Islamic Culture,* Vol. XXXIV, 1950, p. 119; one of her tutor Mulla Mohammad wrote many Casidah in her praise (Bakhtawar Khan) *Mirat-ul-Alam* fol. 607-608 M.S. No. 1051, Daftar-i-Diwani-wa-Mulki Library Hyderabad, Neamat Khan Asli, a renowned poet of that time was rewarded. *Maqalati-Shibli,* Vol. V, pp. 107-108.
143. *Maasir-i-Alamgiri,* Pers. Text, p. 539; also Sarkar's Tr. p. 322.
144. Moulana Sidique, *Tarikh-i-Hind* (Urdu) Lucknow 1359 A.H. p. 671.
145. *Ibid.* pp. 674-675.
146. *Ibid.* pp. 674-675.
147. *Maqalat-i-Shibli* (Urdu) Vol. V, p. 103; also Md. Aslam, *Khwateen* (Urdu) p. 284.
148. Mustaid Khan Soori, *Maasir-i-Alamgiri, Persian Text, Bib. Ind.* (Cal. 1871) p. 468.
149. Quoted in *Khwateen* ed. by Md. Aslam, p. 259; also Maulana Sadique. *Tariq-i-Hind,* p. 675; *also poems by Indian Women* edited by Margarett Macnicol (Cal. 1923) p. 78.
150. Mohammad Mustaid Khan Saqi, *Maasir-i-Alamgiri,* Tr. (Sarkar) p. 323; also Elliot and Dowson, *History of India,* Vol. VII, p. 197.
151. *Maasir-i-Alamgiri,* Tr. (Sarkar), p. 323; also *Bazm Taimuriah* (Urdu) p. 464.
152. *Subh-i-Gulshan,* Pers. p. 12; also *Bazm Taimuriah* (Urdu) p. 464.
153. *Poems of Indian Women, ed.* by Margarett Macnicol, p. 79.
154. Sarkar's Tr. *Maasir-i-Alamgiri,* p. 323 also Elliot and Downson, *History of India,* Vol. VII, p. 197.
155. Shah Nawaz Khan, *Maasir-ul-Umara,* Tr. Vol. II, Part. p. 231.
156. *Ibid.,* Fn. 3.
157. *Maasir-i-Alamgiri,* Tr. (Sarkar), p. 323; also Elliot and Downson History of India, Vol. VII. p. 197.
158. N.N. Law. *Promotion of Learning,* p. 204.
159. *Maasir-i-Alamgiri,* Tr. (Sarkar), p. 323; also *Bazm Taimuriah* p. 464; also Elliot and Downson, *Hist.* Downson, Vol. VII, p.

197; also N.N. Law, *Promotion of Learning,* p. 204.

160. *Maasir-i-Alamgiri,* Tr. (Sarkar), p. 323; also Elliot and Downson, Vol. VII, p. 197.
161. R.R. Diwakar, *Bihar through the Ages,* p. 543; also Akhtar Orenvi, *Bihar Men Urdu Zoban wa Adab ka Irtaqa,* from 1204 to 1857 A.D. (Urdu) March 1957, Patna, pp. 222-223; also Mohd. Moinudd in Dardai, *Sufia-i-Bihar Aur Urdu,* Academy of Educational Research All Pakistan Educational Conference (Karachi, 1972) p. 53.
162. Quoted in *Bihar Men Urdu Zoban Wa Adab Ka Irtaqa,* pp. 222-223; also *Sufia-i-Bihar Aur Urdu,* p. 53.
163. Ishwar Das Nagar, *Futuhat-i-Alamgiri,* Tr. and edt. by Tasneem Ahmad, p. 282.
164. Saqi Mustaid Khan, *Massir-i-Alamgiri,* Bib. Ind. (Cal. 1871) pp. 372-393.
165. Jyoti Prasad Mishra, *Stree Kavi Kaumudi,* Pub. by Gandhi Hindi Pustak Bhandar Prayag (1913) 1st edn. pp. 21, 31, 44, 75, 76 also *Poems by Indian Women* ed. by Magaret Macnicol p. 30.
166. *Bazm Taimurlah.* p. 446.
167. Tazkirst-ul-Shayerat, Pers. p. 534.

Bibliography

Feasts and Holidays of Hindu and Mohammadan, Sehishti Zewar, Vol. VI.

'Jodha Bai' by the daughter of Nasiruddin Haider, ed. Md. Aslam. Khwateen, (Urdu).

'Zeb-un-Nisa and Diwan-i-Makhfi', by H.S. Ahmad, *Journal of Bihar and Orissa Research Society,* Vol. XIII (1927) also *Maqaiat-i-Shibli,* Vol. Vth.

A.M.A. Shustry, *Outlines of Islamic Culture, (Bangalore,* Pub. in 1950).

A.S. Bevridge, Appendix A. to her translation of Gulbadan Begum *Humayun Nama.*

Abul Fazal, *Akbar Nama* tr. by H. Bevridge, reprint by Rare Books, Delhi, 1972, Vol. I.

Abul Fazl, *Ain-i-Akbari* Tr. (Blochmann) 1965, second edition.

Abul Hamid Lahori *Badshah Namah,* Vol. II, refers to the naming of Dara's daughter, Pak Nahad Banu Begum; also Gulbadan, *Humayun Namah* Pers. edited by (Bev.).

Achutananda Das, *Haribams,* pub. by Radha Raman Pustakalaya, Cuttack, fourth canto.

Amir Khusrau, *Dual Rani Khizr Khan (Mathnavi),* Aligarh, 1917.

Aurangzeb took omens from the writings of Hafiz, *Storia,* Vol. II. Tr.

Aurangzeb's youngest son Kam Baksh's marriage reception was held in the palace of *Zeb-un-Nisa. Maasir-i-Alamgiri,* also *Maqalat-i-Shibli* ed. by Sayyed Sulaiman Nadvi, Vol. II, (1955), p. 102.

Babur Namah, Eng. Tr. by Mrs. Beveridge (London, 1921). Vol. I.

Badaoni refers to a lady who filed for separation (Khula) from her husband on the ground of his absence from her, *Muntakhabaul-Twarikh,* Vol. III, Tr. p. 147.

Beni Prasad, *History of Jahangir*; it refers that Nurjahan got intelligency in heredity as her father Mirza Ghiyas was a man of learning and culture, a charming letter writer and a brilliant conversationist; also *Introducing India* Part I, 1947; *Bazm Taimuriah*; also Sunity Devi, *The Beautiful Mughal Princesses.*

Bernier, Travels in the Mughal Empire, translated by A Constable, 1963, second Edition.

Bhojpuri Gram Geet by K.D. Upadhyaya; *Rajasthani Lok Geet* by S. Pareek; *Kannauji Lok Geet* by S. Anil.

Bikram Jit Hasrat, *Dara Shukoh, Life and Works,* First Published (Allahabad, 1953).

Book of Durate Barbosa by Mansel Longworth Dames, Vol. I, *Indian Costume* by Ghurye. Buhar Collection, N.L. Calcutta.

Cf. K.A. Nizami, *The Life and Times of Shaikh Farid U'ddin Ganj-i-Shakar,* reprint, Delhi, 1987.

Cf. *The Struggle for Empire,* ed. R.C. Majumdar, Bombay, second edition, 1966.

Chahar Gulshan, Ms, By Chittraman Kayath, Azad Library, Aligarh University.

D.C. Sen, *"Virhat Banga",* Vol. II, pub. by Cal. Univ. (B. S. 1342) 1st ed. also Edward and Garrett, *Mughal rule in India.*

E.D. Ross, *Feasts and Holidays,* also Women in Indian Folklore edited with an introduction by Sri Sankar Sen Gupta, Indian Publication, Calcutta-1.

Elliot & Dowson, Vol. III, p. 300, *Tarikh-i-Farishta,* Pers. Vol. I.

For Jahan Ara's birthday celebration see Muntakhab-ul-Lubab (Urdu) Vol. II.

For Prince's education in this age refer to *Bezm-i-Taimuria* Vol. I (First edn. 1973).

For reference of Jhula or Hindola see *Ghanannd Granthavall,* ed. by Vishav Prasad Mishra. Doha, 382, also Doha 516; Doha 517; Doha 688; Doha 1024.

For *salami* Hindal was presented a number of gifts by his wife's guardians after *Nikah* and at the time of marriage feast.

Mahbubullah Mujib, *Moghul Tahzeeb* (Urdu), Allahabad.

Francis Gladwin, *History of Jahangir,* ed. by K.V.R. Aiyangar (Madras, 1930).

Frederick Augustus, *The Emperor Akbar,* Vol. I, Tr. and edited by A.S. Beveridge (1973).

Ghulam Hussain Salim, *Riyaz-us-Salatin, a History of Bengal.* Tr. by Abdus Salam, (1975, reprint).

Hawkins, *Voyages during the reigns of Henry VIII, Queen* Elizabeth and James I.

Hindustan ke Hukumrano ke Tammadduni Jalwe (Urdu) ed. by Sayyed Sahabuddin.

Hindustan Ke Mussalman Hukumrano Ke Ahad Ke Tammadduni Jalwe; ed. by Sahabuddin Abdul Rahman (Urdu), Azamgarh, 1963.

Humayun was nineteen years older than Hamidah Banu Begum, S.K. Banerjee, *Humayun Badshah,* (Oxford 1938).

I.N. Choudhary, Mumtaz Mahal', *Journal of Islamic Culture,* Hyderabad, Vol. XI, 1937, p. 373; also G. Yazdani, 'Jahan Ara' *Journal of the Punjab Historical Society,* Vol. III, 1912.

Ibn Battuta, *The Travels of Ibn Battuta,* Eng. tr. H. Gibb, Cambridge, 1971, Vol. 3.

In 1672 Murad's daughter Aisha Banu was married to Mohammad Salih. a noble belonging to a Persian family, *Massir-i-Alamgiri,* Tr. (J.N. Sarkar) (Cal., 1947); also M. Athar Ali, *The Mughal Nobility under Aurangzeb,* 1966, p. 143.

Indian Travels (ed. Sen); also for the references of early marriages among Muslims; refer Colliver Rice, *Persian Women and their ways* (London, 1923); also S.M. Jaffar, *Some Cultural Aspects of Muslim Rule in India* (Peshawar, 1939).

Introducing India, Pt. I Pub. R.A.S.B. 1947 Art No. 9; also Powell Price, *History of Jahangir* (1955).

Iqbal Nama, (Urdu) refers that Jahanara garden was made on the side of Shahr-ara-garden.

Isami, *Futuh-us-Salatin,* ed., A.S. Usha, Madras, 1948, p. 134; Eng. tr. Agha Mahdi Husain, Aligarh, 1976, Vol. 2.

Ishwar Das Nagar, *Futuhat-i-Alamgir,* translated and edited by Tasneem Ahmad, 1st pub. 1978.

Johan Fryer, *A New Account of East India and Persia in Eight Letters* (London), p. 94.

John Albert De Mandelslo, *The Travels of East Indies,* (London, 1669 second edition), Vol. I, p. 42.

John Fryer, *A New Account of East India and Persia,* (London 1909) *MDCXC VIII.*

John Marshal in India (1668-72), ed. by Sri Ahmad Khan, Oxford, 1927.

Journal of Bihar and Orissa Research Society, Patna, Vol. XIII, 1827, Art. No. 4.

Journal of Indian Hist. Vol. XLIV Part I April 1966; serial no. 130.

Jyoti Prasad Mishra, *Stree Kavi Kaumudi,* Pub. by Gandhi Hindi Pustak Bhandar Prayag (1913) 1st edn.

K.M. Ashraf, "Life and conditions of the people of Hindustan" Journal Asiatic Society of Bengal, Art. No. 4.

K.R. Qanungo, *Dara Shukoh* (Calcutta), Vol. I; in Sapahr Shukoh's birth Shah Jahan gave two lakh rupees for birth celebration, Lahori, *Badshah Namah,* Vol. II, Persian Text.

Kashmir from Shahmir to Shahjahan by Dr. R.K. Parmu (Thesis).

Kaumudi for girls kite flying refer to painting No. 537, I.A.E. lent by the Central Asian Antiquities Museum. (Treasury wala collection).

Kaumudi, *Observations,* Vol. I, p. 306 for huqqah also refer to *Diwani-i-Faizi,* M.S. No. 367.

Khafi-Khan, I, 33 quoted by A.S. Bevridge, in Appendix A.

Khamsa-i-sarfi, Pers. Ms.; also Brij Narayan Translation on *A Duch Chronicle of Moghul India*; also Jauhar, *Tazkiratul-Waqlat* translated by Charles Stewart (Calcutta 1904), also Wahab Asharafi, *Kutub Mushtari are uska Tanqidi Jayeza,* 1977; also Saksena, *History of Shahjahan.*

Khuda Bux, *Studies Indian and Islamic* quoted in *Indian Women through the Ages.*

Khulasah Tarih Salar Masud Ghazi.

Khwaja Nizamuddin Ahmad, Tabqat-i-Akbari, Vol. II, Tr.

Khwateen, Edited by Md. Aslam; also N.N. Law, *Promotion of Learning*; also S.M. Jaffar, *Education in Muslim India.*

Kok Shashtra Granth is said to have been written by her. See Sinha, p. 252.

M.L. Bhagi, *Medieval Indian Culture and Thought* (Pub. in 1965); also *An Advanced History of India* by Majumdar, Raychaudhuri and Dutta, Part II (1951).

Maadan-ul-Maani; also Pt. I *Cal. Review* Dec. 1940; also R. Diwakar Bihar *Through the Ages.*

Maasir-i-Alagir, Tr. by J.N. Sarkar, 1947; *Diwan-i-Zeb-un-Nisa* ed. by Magan Lal 1913; Sunity Devi. *The beautiful Mughal Princess*; *Hist. of India,* by Illiot and Dowson, Vol. VII; Sarkar, *Studies in Mughal India* (Cal. 1919).

Maasirul Umarah, Vol. I Tr. (Bev), also H.G. Keene History of Hindustan (c) 1972.

Maasirul-Umara, *Akhir Chaharshamba,* Vol. I, Tr.; also *Qanun-i-Islam*.

Ma-hammad-bin-Saleh, Almaimuah, *Al-Nikah wa Al-Telaque* Arabic MS.

Major David Price's Tr. *Memoirs of Emperor Jahangir,* (London, 1829); *Iqbal Nama-i-Jahangiri* (Urdu) p. 62 Francis Gladwin, *The History of Jahangir* (1930) also Beni Prasad, History of Jahangir.

Makhdum Maneri, *Maadan-ul-Maani,* Pers. Text Pub. by Shah Md. Muqqabbil Hussain, Sherul Akhbar (Razbeyapur 1884 A.D.). also Pt. I as quoted in *Calcutta Review,* Dec. 1940.

Makhzan-ul-Gharaib, M.S.B.

Malik Md. Jaisi refers this game played by Padmavati with Ratan Sen, vide *Padmavat* Tr. by Agrawala.

Mansir-i-Alamgiri, Tr. J.N. Sarkar, p. 322; *History of India,* Vol. VII.

Maulvi Mohammad Hussain Azad, *Darbar-i-Akbari* (Lahore, 1921).

Md. Aslam, *Khwateen,* (Delhi, 1951). A reference may also be made to Aiyshah Siddiqa's child marriage in Badaoni's *Muntakh-ul-Twarikh,* Vol., II, Tr. (Lowe).

Md. Umar, Hindustani Tahzeeb Ka Mussalmano Par Asar (Urdu); also Mrs. Meer Hassan Ali, Observations.

Memoirs of Jahangir by Major David Price; also *Tarikh-i-Hind* by Sadique.

Memoirs of Zahiruddin Mohammad Babur, Emperor of Hindustan Tr. by Laden and William Erskine, Vol. II; also *Akbar Nama,* Vol. III, Tr.; also *Tarikh-i-Farishta* Vol. I.

Minhaj-1 Siraj Juzjani, *Tabaqat-i-Nasiri,* Kabul, 1963, Vol. 1.

Mir Hassan, *Masnavi Mir Hasan* (Urdu), Pub. by Pustak Bhandar, Patna.

Mir Mah, *Muraqqsi-Mir Mah.* F. 1175, Ms No. 795 Daftari-Diwani-wa Mulki Library, Hyderabad.

Mira Bai by Usha S. Nilsson in 'Makers of Indian Literature' Series.

Mirza Haidar Doughlat, *Tarikh-i-Rishidi,* tr. as Denison Ross. *A History of the Moghals of Central Asia.*

Mirza Mohammad Hassan Qateel, *Haft Tamashah,* Pers. Text Nawal Kishore, 1875.

Mishkat Book IV. Chapt. XI also Ajoul ilm Mansabat ibn Hajar. Al-Nikah (Risala) Arabic MS No. 3229 Khuda Buksh O.P.L. Patna, p. 23; Meer Hasan Ali, *Observations*.

Mishkat, Book XVIII, Chapt. IV; also *Muslim, Bokhari,* Tr. by Mirza Heyat, in Urdu.

Mishkat, Vol. III; also Sayyed Sulaiman Nadvi, *Sirat-un-Nabi* (Urdu) Vol. IV.

Mohammad bin Saleh, Ajmajmuah, *Al-Nikah wa Al-Telaque* MS. (Arabic).

Mohammad Mustaid Khan Saqi, *Maasir-i-Alamgiri,* Tr. (Sarkar); also Elliot and Dowson, *History of India,* Vol. VII.

Mohammad Wali, *Mid-hat-ul-Su'Ara.* Fol. 123, M.S. Daftar-i-Diwani wa Mulki Library, Hyderabad, also refer to *Islamic Culture,* Vol. XXXIV, 1960, Hyderabad.

Monserrate refers Nine Days Fast; for fasting also see Fryer, p. 109; Pelsaert.

Mrs. Meer Hasan Ali, *Observations on the Musalmans of India.*

Mrs. Meer Hassan Ali, *Observations on Mussalmans of India,* Indian reprint 1973, p. 9; see also Herklot's *Qanun-i-Islam* p. 37.

Muslim Bokharil, Tr. (Urdu), Vol. III, Book, 21, Kitab-un-Nikah.

Mustaid Khan Soori, *Maasir-i-Alamgiri, Persian Text, Bib. Ind.* (Cal. 1871).

Padmavat of Jayasi; *Sursagar,* Part I; *Raskhan Granthavali*; *Bihari Satsai*, Doha 121, Doha 127 (blue *Sari*), *Doha* 131, Doha 132 (white *Sari*), *Mati Ram Satsai.*

Poems by Indian Women, edited by M. Macnicol.

Prof. Khalique Ahmad Nizami, *Tarikhi Maqalat* (Urdu), Nadwatul Mussennefeen (Delhi, 1966, First edn.).

R.P. Tripathi, *Rise and Fall of the Mughal Empire,* 3rd edn. 1963, Allahabad.

R.R. Diwakar, *Bihar through the Ages,* 1st Pub. in Jan. 1959.

Rai Chatraman, Chahar Gulshan, MS. 39a. It refers to celebration on the bank of river Yamuna, also E.D. Ross, *Feasts and Holidays of Hindu and Mohammadans.*

Rekha Misra, *Women in Mughal India,* Munshiram Manoharlal Delhi, 1967.

Robert Orme, Historical Fragments of the Mughal Empire, ed. with an introduction by J.P. Guha (second re-print 1978, Delhi).

Rushbrook Williams, *An Empire Builder of the Sixteenth Century,* London, 1918.

S. Lane-Poole's *Nurjahan and Jahangir,* Sushil Gupta India Ltd. Calcutta, 1950.

S.C. Mishra, Muslim Communities in Gujarat, pub. by Asia Publishing House (1964).

Saksena, History of Shah Jahan of Delhi, (Allahabad 1938).

Sarfi, *Maslak-ul-Akhyar,* Foll 87-B-illa, M.S.

Sayyed Iqbal Ahmad, *Tarikh-i-Jaunpur,* Shiraz-ul-Hind Publishing House, Jaunpur (1963) 1st Edn.

Mirza Muhammad Haider's *Tarikh-i-Rashidi* tr. Denison Ross.

Senal Al Ghaznavi, Hadiqat-ul-Haqiqat, Pers. MS. Khuda Bakhsh, O.P.L. Patna.

Shah Abdur Razzaque Banswi, *Malfuzat-i-Razaqi* (Pers). ed. by Nawab Mohammad Khan Shah Jahan Puri, (Lucknow 1313 A.H.).

Shihabuddin al-Umar, *Masalik-ul Absar fi Mamalik ul Amsar,* Eng. tr. *A Fourteenth Century Arab Account of India under Sultan Muhammadbin Tughluq,* Iqtidar H. Siddiqui, Aligarh, 1973.

Sikandar bin Manjhu, *Mirat-i Sikandari,* Bombay, 1308H. Shaikh Kabir Batini, *Afsanah-i Shahu,* Ms. British Library, London, Add. 24, 409, ff. 90b-91a, for the Kalal caste to which Zafar Khan belonged.

Sir Thomas Roe, *The Embassy of Sir Thomas Roe to the Court of the Moghal.*

Stavcrinus, *Voyage to East Indies* (London, 1798), Tr. by Samuel Hill.

Sursagar, Dashamskandh; also Dr. Hargulal, *Sursagar Men Lok Jiwan,* Hindi Sahitya Sansar.

Tarikh-i-Magadh, edited by Maulvi Fasihuddin Baikhi, (Urdu), *Anjuman Taraqqi,* Urdu (Hindi), Delhi, 1st edn. 1944.

The Army of the Indian Mughals, its Organisation and Administration by William Irvine, (New Delhi, 1962), p. 200.

The Educational System in Medieval India by Yusuf Husain (Islamic Culture Vol. XXX, 1956); *Glimpses of Medieval Indian Culture* by Yusuf Husain.

U.P. Records Office, Allahabad, Accession Register of the U.P. Records Inquiry Committee Records. Nos. 1215 and 1216, as quoted in *Agrarian System in Mughal India,* by Dr. Irfan Habib.

W.Hawkins, *Voyages during the Reign of Henry VII, Queen Elizabeth and James I,* edited by C.R. Morkham, London, printed for Hakluyt Society, MDCCC LXXXIII.

Zarur-ul-Muslemin (Urdu), edited by Md. Tahir Ali, (Bombay); see also *Behishti Zewar,* Tr. (English) by Md. Masroor Khan (Delhi 1979, second edition) Part VII; also Maulana Sayyad Abul Hasan Ali, *Hindustani Musalman Ek Nazr Men* (Urdu) (Lucknow, 1974 second edition).

Index